Travesti

Sex, Gender, and
Culture among
Brazilian
Transgendered
Prostitutes

Don Kulick

The University of Chicago Press
Chicago and London

The University of Chicago Press, Chicago 60637
The University of Chicago Press, Ltd., London
© 1998 by The University of Chicago
All rights reserved. Published 1998
Printed in the United States of America
16 15 14 13 12 11 10 09 08 07   6 7 8 9 10

ISBN-13: 978-0-226-46099-4 (cloth)
ISBN-13: 978-0-226-46100-7 (paper)
ISBN-10: 0-226-46099-1 (cloth)
ISBN-10: 0-226-46100-9 (paper)

Library of Congress Cataloging-in-Publication Data

Kulick, Don.
    Travesti : sex, gender, and culture among Brazilian
  transgendered prostitutes / Don Kulick.
       p.   cm. — (Worlds of desire)
    Includes bibliographical references (p. 00) and index.
    ISBN 0-226-46099-1. — ISBN 0-226-46100-9 (pbk.)
       1. Transvestites—Brazil—Salvador.   2. Male prostitutes—
  Brazil—Salvador.   3. Transvestism—Case studies.   I. Title.
  II. Series.
  HQ77.2 B7K85   1998
  306.77—dc21   95-15319
                                                           CIP

⊗ The paper used in this publication meets the minimum
requirements of the American National Standard for Information
Sciences—Permanence of Paper for Printed Library Materials,
ANSI Z39.48-1992.

Travesti

Worlds of Desire
The Chicago Series on Sexuality, Gender, and Culture
A Series Edited by Gilbert Herdt

Este livro é para você Keila,
com agradecimento, com carinho,
e acima de tudo,
com admiração.

Contents

Acknowledgments

Research support for the fieldwork on which this book is based was generously provided by the Swedish Council for Research in the Humanities and Social Sciences (HSFR) and the Wenner-Gren Foundation for Anthropological Research.

I am extremely grateful to the following people, who have done me the tremendous favor of taking the time to read through an earlier version of the entire manuscript of this book: Inês Alfano, Anne Allison, Roger Andersen, Barbara Browning, Marcelo Fiorini, Sarah Franklin, Marjorie Harness Goodwin, Peter Gow, Cecilia McCallum, Stephen O. Murray, Christine Nuttall, Joceval Santana, Bambi Schieffelin, Michael Silverstein, Christina Toren, and Margaret Willson. The many comments, corrections, criticisms, and suggestions I received from these readers have been invaluable.

I acknowledge with great thanks the massive support and encouragement that Doug Mitchell at the University of Chicago Press has given me, from the moment he received the original manuscript. I also thank Matt Howard at the Press for support and help, and Nancy Trotic for superb copyediting.

My boyfriend, Jonas Schild Tillberg, rarely reads anything that I write, but he deserves mention anyway, because he is *meu coração*, without whom none of this would be much fun. Discussions and correspondence with Annick Prieur about her work among transgendered individuals in Mexico City continue to inspire me and help me refine my own arguments. Two other people in Scandinavia also need to be acknowledged: Kent Hallberg and Anita Johansson from the Swedish Association for Sex Education (RFSU). Kent and Anita not only provided me, free of charge, with approximately ten thousand condoms that I distributed to travestis throughout the time I was in Salvador—they also took care to see to it that the majority of those condoms were the ones I told them travestis loved, black condoms, and fruit-flavored ones.

In Brazil, I owe a large debt of thanks to Luiz Mott, who took the time to orient me in Salvador's *ambiente homossexual* and who kindly allowed me access to the overstuffed boxes of newspaper clippings that the Grupo Gay da Bahia (GGB) has been amassing since the early 1980s. Nilton Dias was the GGB coordinator who worked most closely with travestis when I first arrived in Salvador, and he was the one who provided the crucial introduction to Keila Simpsom and several of the other travestis who came to be my closest associates. That Keila and the others responded so graciously to me and my research is a direct reflection of the high esteem in which they hold Nilton. All of the other coordinators at the GGB, especially Marcelo Cerqueira, Jane Pantel, and Zora Yonara, have also always been friendly and helpful.

Joceval Santana provided me with extensive support and practical help when I first arrived in Salvador and needed all the help I could get simply to find my way around the city. I also thank Joceval for helping me to understand a great deal about the homosexual scene in Salvador, and in Brazil more generally. Throughout my stay in Salvador, the hospitality and generosity of Cecilia McCallum and her husband, Edilson Teixeira, were considerable. Their home always provided me with a welcoming environment whenever I felt that I needed a short break from fieldwork. In addition, the "academic" lunches that Cecilia and I had at least once a month in air-conditioned restaurants afforded me steady access to Cecilia's extensive anthropological knowledge about Brazil and Salvador, and an enjoyable refreshment of anthropological discourse and gossip.

Inês Alfano has also provided important input into this study. Inês performed the enormously laborious work of transcribing the majority of the interviews that I conducted with travestis. Extended conversations with her about the transcriptions have given me insights about gender and about the wider resonances of travesti actions and thoughts that I otherwise might have missed. Talks with Inês's sister, psychologist Marta Alfano, have also helped to deepen and nuance my understanding of travesti lives.

Yet another person who deserves special mention is Margaret Willson. Margaret and I have a history of research and friendship that began in Papua New Guinea over a decade ago, and that continues to be an important source of inspiration and strength. A tourist visit to Margaret's anthropological fieldsite was the impetus to my own work in Salvador. Our respective periods of fieldwork in the city overlapped only a few times, but whenever Margaret was in Salvador, her presence generated, as always, a kind of haven into which I could retreat in order to relax, drink too much, and think aloud about the kinds of things I found myself learning about travesti lives. Because Margaret is an anthropologist who knows Salvador well, she, like Cecilia McCallum, has been especially important when I have wanted to determine whether a particular idea sounded reasonable or whether it indicated that I had missed the point and simply misunderstood everything.

The people without whom this study could never have been completed are, of course, the travestis with whom I lived and worked in Salvador. I thank all travestis who permitted me to formally interview them: Adriana, Angélica, Babalu, Banana, Carlinhos, *a finada* Cintia, Elisabeth, Lia Hollywood, *a finada* Luciana, Mabel, Magdala, Martinha, Pastinha, and *a finada* Tina. I also thank Edilson, who was the only travesti boyfriend I came to know well, and who allowed me to interview him under difficult personal circumstances. In addition, I wish to single out Adriana, Banana, Chica, *a finada* Cintia, Pastinha, Roberta, Rosana, *a finada* Tina, and Val as providing me not only with information, gossip, and insights, but also with true affection and friendship.

Finally, I thank the single most important person behind this book, the one without whom it truly could never have been written—namely, my travesti coworker, teacher, and friend Keila Simpsom. In none of the places I have lived have I ever met a person who could analyze the contexts and conditions of her own life with the precision that Keila does and still stay sane. Keila took me under her ample wing, taught me Portuguese, integrated me into travesti networks, and helped me to see and understand the dimensions of travesti life that I develop in this book. It is impossible for me to adequately express my gratitude to her. What I offer Keila is this book, in the hope that she will enjoy seeing in its pages fragments of the story of her own life, and of the lives of her friends and colleagues in Salvador. I also hope that Keila will see in this work the firm imprint of her own insights, and that she will perceive that despite the fact that I may have been a slow and often exasperatingly thick student, I did, in the end, come to understand a thing or two.

Note on the Transcriptions

The following conventions are used in the transcripts presented throughout this book:

[overlapping (i.e., simultaneous) talk

/   interruption (between speakers this indicates that the speaker is
interrupted by the following speaker; within utterances it indicates self-interruption)

. . .   indicates either a short pause (when occurring within utterances) or a lengthened sound (when occurring at the end of
turns)

[ ]   author's explanatory comments, contextual notes, and nonverbal
actions

( )   material that was not audible on the tape

.
.
.   material that has been omitted from the transcript.

Introduction

As I walked past Banana's room on my way from the communal toilet at the back end of the house, I paused for a moment because it seemed to me that there was an unusual amount of smoke coming from her room. I poked my head in the open door to see what the smoke was, and the first thing I saw was Banana—a transgendered prostitute, or *travesti*, in her mid-thirties—standing naked in front of a little mirror dangling from a nail on the wall. Banana had just come back from her late-afternoon shower, and she was rubbing Neutrox conditioning fluid into her still-wet hair. "Venha, Don," she called to me when she saw me look in. "Venha sentar aqui." She motioned to the thin mattress on the floor against one of the walls.

Happy to have an excuse not to go back into the room I had just come from, where I had been sitting for over an hour with other travestis watching an insufferably boring *novela* (soap opera) on television, I entered Banana's tiny room and headed for the mattress. As I passed behind Banana, I realized that the smoke I had wondered about was wafting up from two small cones of incense sitting on the only shelf in the room. "Chama freguês" (Summon customers), Banana informed me without my asking, was the name of the incense. It smelled nice.

My presence in Banana's room immediately prompted the mandatory gesture of hospitality given by any travesti to a guest—she reached to turn on her little six-inch black-and-white television. My protest that I really didn't want to watch television elicited a predictable snort of disbelief from Banana, and with a flick of her wrist, the room was filled with the melodramatic shouts and cries and swollen crescendos of the same tawdry *novela* that I thought I had just managed to escape. Defeated, I sat down on the mattress, rested my back against the wall, and did my best to ignore the television. Instead, I watched Banana get ready. It was only four o'clock in the afternoon, but Banana was preparing for her evening of work.

The preparations were meticulous. Most attention was paid to the hair, which reached down to below her shoulders and which she had recently dyed black, having tired of her natural mouse-brown color. The black dye made her hair seem thicker, and it drew attention away from her somewhat receding hairline. It was definitely an improvement. But there was still something unsatisfactory about it, Banana seemed to feel. No matter how she parted it and swung it, the hair never seemed to quite satisfy her. She swung it to the right, still wet and dripping with conditioning fluid, only to return to the mirror two minutes later to part it on the left and swing it over in that direction. No, that wouldn't do, either. Over to the right again. Then to the left. I quickly lost track of how many times the hair was reparted, reswung, rearranged.

Eventually, as one of the protagonists of the *novela* was pressed behind a potted palm overhearing some traumatizing piece of news about her husband, Banana's hair was done, or at least acceptable for the moment, and she lit another cigarette. Still gazing intently into her mirror, she picked up a tweezers and rapidly plucked out a few stray hairs on her upper lip and chin. Satisfied, she now applied a light foundation to her face. She then started searching the room for a razor blade, which she needed to sharpen her eyebrow pencil. The places she looked for the razor blade made me wish I hadn't entered her room barefoot, and when she started searching in and underneath the pillow on her mattress, I quickly canceled the thoughts I had been having of perhaps using the pillow to cushion my back against the wall.

After a brief moment of despair, during which Banana voiced her suspicion that another travesti must have stolen her razor blade from her room ("Tá vendo como são as bichas daqui?" You see how these *bichas* are here?), she found the blade under an onion on the shelf, next to her deodorant.

Eyebrow pencil sharpened, Banana proceeded to draw on her thick, trademark Peking Opera–style eyebrows, which disappeared out into the hair at the sides of her head, and which were emphasized by the red eye shadow that she applied underneath. No other travesti I knew in Salvador made herself up quite so idiosyncratically, and when I once asked Banana why she did so, she replied that it *chama atenção*, it attracted attention. Much of Banana's prostitution these days was conducted inside a nearby pornographic cinema, and she explained that the dramatic makeup helped to single her out from all the other travestis who roamed the aisles of the cinema asking men if they wanted to "cum" (*gozar*).

Face on, hair still dripping and rearranged yet again, Banana lit another cigarette, took a swig of the coffee she was drinking out of an old plastic margarine container, and went over to the far corner of her room in search of a pair of panties. She started digging through the mound of crumpled clothes thrown in a pile on a chair, and then she began laughing and throwing them up over her shoulder into the air. "Panties, panties, *Ave Maria*, not one clean pair of panties, I can't believe it," she hooted. The "Roupinol" (i.e., Rohypnol—a barbiturate that when taken together with alcohol or coffee can become a stimulant) tablet she told me she had taken earlier was clearly kicking in.

Banana finally extracted a pair of lacy black panties from somewhere in the pile of clothes, and she put them on in the characteristic travesti manner of stepping into them and pulling them up to the knees, then squatting with legs apart to hold the panties up. In this position, Banana reached one hand around her back and up between her legs and caught hold of her penis and scrotum. Drawing them backwards, she pressed them flat and held them down against her perineum as she stood upright and pulled up the panties with her other hand. Tugging at her panties from the front and her penis from behind, she shifted her weight back and forth from leg to leg until the panties were on and her penis was firmly and comfortably in place against her perineum. The procedure was complete when Banana smoothed down the panties with both hands, making sure that they presented a tight, flat front. Looking up, Banana noticed that I was peering past the television to watch her. She patted the front of her panties once more. "Minha buceta," my cunt, she smiled.

Buceta in place, Banana now walked over to her own version of the small altar that many travestis maintain in their room. In most cases, the altar contains a small statue or painting of a Catholic religious figure, such as Jesus or the Virgin Mary, and/or a similar figure of a candomblé saint, such as Iemanjá, goddess of the oceans, or Iansã, the deity of winds and tempests. In addition to these images, on the altar will be a lit candle and perhaps a glass of water, a small plate of food, and/or a leaf of a plant—all this to bring luck, money, and customers and to keep away the Olho Grosso (the Evil Eye—literally, the Coarse Eye, or the Big Eye). Unlike most other travestis, however, Banana feels herself to be waging a continual battle against the Eye, and she is convinced that other travestis are always trying to drive her to ruin with the help of *macumba* (black magic) and general bad vibes. Hence, much of Banana's time (and a not inconsiderable amount of her money) is spent on countermeasures designed to deflect the Eye and keep its power from impairing her ability to work and attract clients. Chief among these countermeasures is the enlistment of the aid of a wide array of saints and candomblé deities. So whereas most travesti altars are sparse, Banana's is crowded: ceramic figurines of São Jorge killing his dragon, São José leaning on his shepherd's staff, Nossa Senhora de Fátima holding a large wooden crucifix, the sea goddess Iemanjá (two of them), the Virgin of Conceição looking piously up to heaven, the child saints Cosme and Damião—all these jostle for space on the little altar, together with burning votive candles, herbs, small plates of food, and offerings of deodor-

Banana and her altar

ants and soaps and shampoo (these are for Iemanjá, who is, Banana tells me, a *mulher muito vaidosa*—a very vain woman). When it comes to protection against the Big Eye, Banana makes sure that all her bases are covered.

From somewhere near the front of this altar, Banana reached up and took down a wad of newspaper filled with what looked like a pale green powder. She returned to the mirror, dipped her finger into the powder, and gazed into the mirror as she crossed herself on her chest, forehead, and back. She sprinkled some of the powder on her head as well. I asked Banana what the powder was for, and she replied, as I expected she would, with her habitual gesture of pulling down the lower lid of one eye and gazing at me meaningfully for a second: the Olho Grosso.

Thus protected, Banana walked over to her little shelf and took a small squeeze bottle of deodorant, which, working upwards, she sprayed out onto her crotch, anus, stomach, chest, underarms, neck, back, and hair. She then placed her hands above the smoke coming from one of the incense triangles and gathered some of it into her hands. This she directed towards her crotch, stomach, and face. She also lifted up the tiny, somewhat soiled black and green Lycra dress she was planning on wearing and let the smoke from the incense enter that as well. This evening, Banana was clearly taking no chances that customers would pass her by

Lighting another cigarette and taking another gulp of coffee ("to strengthen the effect of the Roupinol," she told me as an aside), Banana now squeezed into her dress. It seemed to me that the effect of the "Roupinol" must already have been pretty strong, because despite a couple of tries, Banana kept getting tangled up in the complex braids of shoulder straps that she had to sort out in order to be able to wear the dress. Finally, after two more attempts, with a cigarette and coffee break in between, the dress was on, and it was smoothed out around her hips and pulled up to near her crotch to her satisfaction. Now all that remained was moisturizing creme on arms and legs, dabs of perfume on crotch, nipples, neck, and hair and under nostrils ("I want people to smell me coming and going," she once told me), and another rearrangement of hair. At last, after an extended final posing session in front of the mirror, during which front, back, face, and hair were scrutinized and finally approved, shoes were found somewhere in the pile of clothes, a small pair of sharp nail scissors was slid, with a wink to me, into the front of her panties, and a tiny blue change purse was inserted into the front of her dress.

Banana was ready to go.

🏵 🏵 🏵

Banana is one of the nearly two hundred travestis who live and work in Salvador, Brazil's third-largest city with a population of over two million people. Like Banana, the overwhelming majority of these travestis live in extremely humble conditions, in tiny three-by-four-meter rooms, and they support themselves primarily by prostituting themselves on the streets of the city. The word *travesti* derives from the verb *transvestir*, or cross-dress. Travestis, however, do not only cross-dress. What is most characteristic about travestis in Salvador, and throughout Brazil, is that they adopt female names, clothing styles, hairstyles, cosmetic practices, and linguistic pronouns, and they ingest large amounts of female hormones and pay other travestis to inject up to twenty liters of industrial silicone directly into their bodies in order to acquire feminine bodily features such as breasts, wide hips, large thighs, and, most importantly, expansive buttocks. Despite all these changes, however, many of which are irreversible, travestis do not self-identify as women. That is, despite the fact that they live their lives in female clothing, call one another by female names, and endure tremendous pain in order to acquire female bodily forms, travestis do not wish to remove their penis, and they do not consider themselves to *be* women. They are not transsexuals. They are instead, they say, homosexuals—males who ardently desire men, and who fashion and perfect themselves as an object of desire for those men.

This specific combination of female physical attributes and male homosexual subjectivity makes travestis almost unique in the world. Although there are many other cultures in which individuals cross, in various ways and through various means, gender lines, travestis seem to be among the few who irrevocably alter their body to approximate that of the opposite sex without claiming the subjectivity of that sex.[1] Far from laying claim to a female subjectivity, travestis in Salvador are virtually unanimous in their incomprehension of any male who does so: there is a consensus among travestis that any biological male who claims to be a woman is psychologically unbalanced and in need of help.

Travestis appear to exist throughout Latin America, but in no other country are they as numerous and well known as in Brazil, where they occupy a strikingly visible place in both social space and the cultural imaginary. All Brazilian cities of any size contain travestis, and in the large cities of Rio de Janeiro and São Paulo, travestis number in the thousands. Travestis are most exuberantly visible during Brazil's famous annual Carnival, and any depiction or analysis of Carnival will inevitably include at least a passing reference to them, because their gender inversions are often invoked as embodiments of the Carnival spirit.

But even in more mundane contexts and discourses, travestis figure prominently. A popular Saturday afternoon television show, for example, includes a spot in which female impersonators, some of whom are clearly travestis, get judged on how beautiful they are and on how well they mime the lyrics to songs sung by female vocalists. Another weekly television show regularly features Valéria, a well-known travesti. *Tieta*, one of the most popular television *novelas* in recent years, featured a special guest appearance by Rogéria, another famous travesti. And most telling of all of the special place reserved for travestis in the Brazilian popular imagination is the fact that the individual widely acclaimed to be the most beautiful woman in Brazil in the mid-1980s was—a travesti. That travesti, Roberta Close, became a household name throughout the country. She regularly appeared on national television, starred in a play in Rio, posed nude (with strategically crossed legs) in *Playboy* magazine, was continually interviewed and portrayed in virtually every magazine in the country, and had at least three songs written about her by well-known composers. Although her popularity declined when, at the end of the 1980s, she left Brazil to have a sex-change operation and live in

Europe, Roberta Close remains extremely well known. As recently as 1995, she appeared in a nationwide advertisement for Duloren lingerie, in which a photograph of her passport, bearing her male name, was juxtaposed with a photograph of her looking sexy and chic in a black lace undergarment. The caption read, "Você não imagina do que uma Duloren é capaz"—you can't imagine what a Duloren can do.[2]

Because travestis like Roberta Close figure so prominently in the Brazilian cultural imaginary, there are scores of comments and essays about them. Indeed, travestis are frequently invoked by social commentators as symbols of Brazil itself. "These days in Brazil, everything seems like something that it isn't. Everything is relative. Even [the definition of] a woman," noted the former congresswoman Sandra Cavalcanti, in reference to Roberta Close. The poet Affonso Romano de Sant'Anna also sees Brazil when he gazes at travestis: "Biologically, travestis are men; psychologically, they are women," he says (inaccurately). "This is just like the regime under which we live: apparently it is an irreversible democracy, but, suddenly, it's like a regretful dictatorship (um arbítrio arrependido). In Congress, representatives can vote exactly as they please . . . as long as it's what the government wants." Some people, like the journalist Tarso de Castro, see Brazil's fascination with travestis as indicative of a national "crisis of virility." Others, such as the film director Walter Hugo Khoury, think that the fact that a travesti like Roberta Close could be publicly acclaimed as "the new passion of the Brazilian man" (a nova paixão do brasileiro) indicates that "Brazilians are an open-minded people, without prejudices."[3]

Comments such as these have everything to do with the idea of travestis and nothing at all to do with the real lives of actual travestis. Regrettably, the fact that a handful of travestis manage to achieve wealth, admiration, and, in the case of Roberta Close, an almost iconic cultural status means very little in practice for the vast majority of travestis. Those travestis, the ones that most Brazilians only glimpse occasionally standing along highways or on dimly lit street corners at night, or on the crime pages of their local newspaper, are one of the most marginalized, feared, and despised groups in Brazilian society. In most cities, including Salvador, travestis are so discriminated against that many of them avoid venturing out onto the street during the day. They are regularly the victims of violent police brutality and random assassinations. Most of them come from very poor backgrounds and many remain poor throughout their lives, living a hand-to-mouth existence and dying before the age of fifty from violence, drug abuse, health problems caused by the silicone they inject into their bodies, or, increasingly, AIDS.

This book is about those travestis. It is an account of their day-to-day lives—of how they live, how they talk, how they act, and how they think about their lives. It is far from the first or only account of travestis. On the contrary, the Brazilian fascination with travestis ensures that stories and articles about them appear regularly on television and in newspapers and magazines throughout the country.[4] With very few exceptions, however, all of that material is utter rubbish. At best, journalistic reports about travestis are superficial and inaccurate; at worst, they are sensationalistic lies.

Fortunately, in addition to journalistic reports, there are also two ethnographic studies of travestis written by Brazilian academics (Silva 1993 and Oliveira 1994).[5] These monographs have been groundbreaking in Brazil for their attempts to understand, rather than simply sensationalize or condemn, travesti lives. The authors of both works came to know a number of travestis over an extended period, and their compassionate writing constitutes a major break with the kinds of treatment that travestis generally receive from the mass media. Despite their importance, however, these works suffer from the fact that neither researcher actually lived with travestis; their contact with travestis was for the most part restricted to visiting them on the streets at night and once in a while in their rooms. This means that both Silva and Oliveira mainly heard about and witnessed the gaudy side of travesti existence—the prostitution, the body modifications, the self-mutilation that travestis occasionally practice when they are apprehended by police. And both books focus primarily on these more spectacular practices. In doing so, they (certainly unwittingly) contribute to the idea, continually reinforced by journalistic accounts, that travestis are somehow very different from most people—they are exotic, strange, bizarre, and scary. At worst they are to be feared, at best they are to be pitied. Neuza Maria de Oliveira, for example, begins her monograph on travestis with a text that is not so much a dedication as it is a message of condolence: "I dedicate this study to the 'monas' [the travestis] of the Yellow House [a house where many of her informants lived], who, for diverse reasons, transform their bodies into an 'ambulatory metamorphosis' in search of the idealic image of a woman who doesn't exist. To this day they are paying for that."

Throughout this book, I too will have a lot to say about the lurid dimensions of travesti lives that so disturbed Oliveira. I devote a great deal of space to hormone ingestion, silicone injections, early sexual experiences, prostitution, robberies committed by travestis, and the kinds of discourse that are used to explain and justify all those practices. But what I hope to do here that has not been done before is to contextualize those spectacular practices in much more mundane ones. By focusing on the day-to-day lives of travestis, by looking closely at how travestis think about their lives, and by attempting to explain the underlying logic that travestis draw on in order to make sense of their lives, I hope to show how the prostitution and the body modifications and the rest of it are not in fact the sad delusions of confused individuals. On the contrary, my argument is that these practices are all eminently reasonable (or, at least, eminently comprehensible) in the context of the social and cultural world in which travestis grow up and live their lives.

Whenever travestis make an appearance in analyses of Brazilian society, they often feature, as I have already mentioned, in the context of inversion—travestis, it is said, invert the roles of male and female through their practices of grafting female attributes onto a male physiognomy. This gendered inversion is usually tied to other instances of inversion, such as men dressing up in female clothes during Carnival, the male homosexual component in the Afro-Brazilian religion candomblé, and the androgynous personae of several of Brazil's most famous singers and songwriters. The conclusion is often that Brazilian society continually undermines and transcends its dour Roman Catholic patriarchal inheritance with displays and tolerance of behavior and persons that directly challenge that inheritance (Da Matta 1997b, 1991b, 1984; Kottak 1990; Parker 1991).

While there is certainly something to be said for this conclusion, and while it is clear that travestis could productively be analyzed as instances of a larger phenomenon of inversion, the argument that I will pursue in this book is a different one. In my view, a focus on inversion is a ruse—it is part of an elaborate myth that Brazilians enjoy telling one another about themselves, in an attempt to convince themselves and others that they are more liberated, tolerant, and hip than they really are. It is a smokescreen that effectively diverts our attention away from the ways in which travestis are *concentrations* of general ideas, representations, and practices of male and female. Thus, rather than simply inverting them, turning them upside down in classic Carnivalesque fashion, the argument here is that travestis elaborate the particular configurations of sexuality, gender, and sex that undergird and give meaning to Brazilian notions of "man" and "woman." They crystallize them. They perfect them, to use a word that travestis themselves use when talking about their bodily practices.

To say that travestis perfect the gendered messages that exist in Brazilian society is very different from saying that they invert them. The notion of inversion has a long and sordid history in psychological thought, and it is still used to classify someone as disturbed and in need of medical intervention. Furthermore, used as a way to describe and analyze a social phenomenon, inversion need not be particularly threatening, particularly in a culture that prides itself on its ability to ludically invert its own stereotypes and moral preoccupations. This non-threatening nature of the idea of inversion in Brazil is one of the reasons I suspect that the notion has such currency in Brazilian understandings of travestis. The problem, however, is that travestis *are* threatening. The Brazilian mass media uniformly portray them as dangerous *marginais*—"marginals," criminals. Throughout my stay in Brazil, I was repeatedly warned by people I met not to associate with travestis, not to trust them, not to let them near my belongings, not to believe anything they told me, and generally to stay away from them (how I was to conduct a study of them if I followed this advice was never really resolved by any of these well-wishers). Seeing travestis simply as "inverts" fails to adequately convey and account for the deep sense of fear and disgust that they evoke in many Brazilians. It also fails to explain the electric sense of allurement that they generate wherever they appear.

Throughout this book, I will be less interested in how travestis invert ideas, representations, and practices of male and female and more concerned with how they clarify and distill them—how they draw them to a logical conclusion, how they purify them to the extent that it becomes possible to see in them central elements in cultural configurations of sexuality, sex, and gender. In pursuing this kind of argument, I am drawing on two interrelated types of scholarly work. The first is the work of ethnomethodologically grounded scholars who have argued that transgenderism constitutes a privileged vantage point from which it is possible to observe how sex and gender are conceived and enacted in everyday life. Prefiguring contemporary theoretical concerns by at least a decade, ethnomethodologists have always insisted that sex and gender are not ontological states. They are, instead, "contingent, practical accomplishment[s]" (Garfinkel 1967:181; see also Kessler and McKenna 1985:163). And because transgendered individuals "have to work at establishing their credentials as men or women in a relatively self-conscious way, whereas the rest of us are under the illusion that we are just doing what comes naturally, they bring to the surface many of the tacit understandings that guide the creation and maintenance of gender differences in ongoing social life" (Shapiro 1991:252–53). This view has an important corollary, one that is argued by both ethnomethodologists and some feminists (e.g., Raymond 1979)—namely, that transgenderism does not occur in a "natural" or arbitrary form. Instead, it arises in specific social contexts and assumes specific social forms—forms that reflect the structures that structure them.

The second, related body of work that informs the arguments I develop here is recent feminist and historical writing that argues that the concept of biological sex is itself a gendered notion, dependent on culturally generated notions of difference for its meaning and its ability to seem "natural" (Butler 1990, 1993; Hausman 1995; Laqueur 1990; de Lauretis 1987). The insight that anything we say about sex must always already be implicated in and interpreted through understandings of gender has pushed theoretical discussions decisively away from the idea that gender is the cultural reading of biological sex. In doing so, it has highlighted the possibility of analyzing gender as sets of understandings and categorizations that need not be restricted to the biologically based categories of "man" and "woman." The relevance of this theoretical move for an analysis of travestis is that it encourages us to explore travestis' gendered practices without assuming that we already know anything about what "men" and "women" are (or whether those categories even exist as such) and without assuming, hence, that we already know what the intended referent or goal or end point of the travesti project is. Focusing on gender as understandings, processes, subjectivities, and practices that are not necessarily generated from or tied to reproductive organs compels us away from any view of travesti practices that sees them simply as inversion, or as deviance, or as the futile (and tragic, misguided, offensive, or whatever) efforts of men to be women. If we suspend all assumptions that gender is grounded in biological sex and focus intently on the lives, loves, and work of travestis—on the multiple ways in which travestis fashion themselves as gendered persons—it becomes possible to ask the question that this book poses, namely: what do travesti practices tell us about the ways in which gender is imagined and configured in Brazilian society?

Conducting Fieldwork among Travestis

The arguments developed in this book are based on twelve months of fieldwork in Salvador among the travestis about whom I write. For eight of those twelve months, I lived with travestis, renting a small room in a house where thirteen travestis lived, on a street in central Salvador on which about thirty-five travestis lived.[6] I associated with travestis pretty much continually during those eight months, eating breakfasts of sweetened coffee and buttered rolls with them when they woke up about midday, chatting with them as they sat on doorsteps plucking whiskers from their chins in the late afternoon sun, crowding onto mattresses with them as they lay pressed together smoking cigar-sized joints and watching late-night action movies on television. Every night, from about 8 P.M. until 1 or 2 A.M., I walked the streets where they worked, visiting them at their various points of prostitution. Even when I stopped living with the travestis to rent an apartment and sit writing the first draft of this book, I visited them frequently, often spending at least five or six hours a day in their company. What had started out as fieldwork had gradually developed into friendship. Although at first I had felt compelled to spend all my time with travestis because I was studying them, the relationships that I developed with several travestis in the house in which I lived became so close that by the time I left Salvador in early 1997, I found myself visiting travestis when I wanted to relax and *forget* work.

I first became aware of the existence of travestis during a three-week holiday trip to Salvador in mid-1993, where I flew to visit my colleague Margaret Willson. She had discovered the city several years previously and was already conducting anthropological fieldwork there. At the time I visited Margaret, I was more interested in Salvador's beaches than in the city's ethnographic offerings. But one evening when I was riding back to Margaret's apartment on a bus from the center of the city, I noticed a number of scantily dressed figures clustered around several street corners, talking and laughing and clearly looking out for customers to pick them up for sex. Although all those figures were dressed in female clothing, many of them seemed to lack breasts, and their voices, when they shouted things like *bicha* (pronounced BEE-sha) and *viado* (both words mean "effeminate homosexual," or simply "fag") at one another, were definitely not women's.[7] Although I had no plans to do fieldwork in Brazil, the minimally clad figures on the corners intrigued me. I contacted the local gay activist organization, the Grupo Gay da Bahia, and spoke with its president, the anthropologist Luiz Mott. He passed on to me a master's thesis on travestis (as I now learned they were called) by Maria Neuza de Oliveira, a sociologist who had conducted fieldwork among travestis in the early 1980s. Based on that thesis and on the conversations I had with Professor Mott and others about travestis, I began to understand that travestis did not conform to standard northern Euro-American sexual typologies—travestis were neither transvestites nor transsexuals. So what were they? I wondered. How did they see themselves? No one seemed to really know. In the end, I decided I would return to Salvador and try to find out.

Fieldwork among the travestis was not easy. The travestis with whom I worked live in one of the poorest and most dangerous parts of town. What is worse, Salvador is a city where the majority of the population is dark-skinned, and where a blond head like my own is still unusual enough to elicit double takes from passers-by. This meant that I could never hope to blend in and become an inconspicuous presence. Like most travestis, though for rather different reasons, I always stood out.

This conspicuousness was a continual source of anxiety for me, especially when I was walking alone to and from the various points of travesti prostitution late at night. The streets along with travestis work in the center of the city are rapidly abandoned after sunset, and several of them become lined with homeless people who bed down on cardboard boxes for the night. Gangs of street children roam the area, sniffing glue and looking for people to rob. Although I only had one thoroughly unpleasant encounter during the entire time I was there (early on in my stay, a ten-year-old child wearing an oversized T-shirt emblazoned with the normally benign but in that context leeringly ominous words *Só Jesus Salva* [Only Jesus Saves] threatened to shoot me if I didn't give him some money), I walked the streets of Salvador at night in a never-ending state of tense alertness, relaxing only when I was actually in the company of travestis—whom I knew street children and anyone else looking to rob someone would never dare confront, especially not when they stood chatting together in groups.

Even more distressing and bothersome than my foreignness, however, was the fact that my Portuguese, at the beginning of my fieldwork, was far from accomplished. Because I was able to return to Salvador quite quickly after I had made a decision to make the city a site for fieldwork, I had not had time to learn much of the language, and I began fieldwork among travestis knowing almost nothing. Although I had been in a similar situation several years previously, when I conducted fieldwork in Papua New Guinea (Kulick 1992), I had forgotten the enormous stress that linguistic incompetence generates. My inability to express myself or understand much of what anybody was saying was a source of torturous frustration, and I spent the first few months of my stay agonizing daily (not to say hourly) over how much more quickly and efficiently a fluent Portuguese speaker would be able to do the study I had set out to do.

In the end, though, after a great deal of thought about my foreignness and my initial linguistic incompetence, I came to the conclusion that both those handicaps proved to be advantages that greatly facilitated the kind of contact with travestis that I eventually developed. Because I was a light-haired foreigner from Sweden, a country whose exact location on the globe was a mystery to most people, I had a certain cachet of exoticness that appealed to many travestis. Several travestis enjoyed occasionally taking me to the bakery or the supermarket with them, so they could link their arm in mine and allow passersby to think that I was their gringo— their wealthy, non-Brazilian boyfriend.

But more significant than my status as a blond bauble, I think, was the fact that as a foreigner, travestis found it difficult to insert me into their existing understandings of how people think about them. Travestis know very well that all Brazilians are weaned on derogatory stereotypes about travestis, and they know that even gay men throughout the country tend to dislike and deprecate them. Because they experience discrimination and harassment on an almost daily basis, travestis assume that any stranger they encounter will have prejudices against them, even if that stranger is civil to them. The case of a foreigner, however, is different. A firmly established truth that circulates among travestis is that Europeans are more liberal and cultivated than Brazilians, and travestis who have been to Italy are all agreed that Italian men treat travestis with much more respect and kindness than any Brazilian man ever would. This all means that a person from Europe, like myself, is not assumed to bear the same kind of instinctive prejudices that travestis expect from Brazilians. And truly, I had no prejudices against travestis. Since I knew next to nothing about travestis when I began getting to know them, I was frankly ignorant of most of the stereotypes. I entered their rooms and greeted them on the streets at night feeling neither fearful, disdainful, or revolted, which is, I now know, how many Brazilians feel towards them. From the very first, I liked travestis. Even though I missed a lot of it in the beginning, I enjoyed their raunchy humor, and I admired the fact that they could take so much abuse from policemen and passersby in cars and on foot, and still remain defiant and concerned that their lipstick not be smudged. Although some of the violent acts they committed to rob clients disturbed me, I saw those acts contextualized in a society that itself is brutally violent to its lower classes, and I never allowed myself the smug first-world, finger-wagging conceit of condemning or challenging a travesti who laughingly recounted how she had robbed a terrified *maricona* (soft faggot) earlier that evening.

My genuine affection towards the travestis with whom I worked was compounded, in a complementary way, by the fact that I was able to say or understand very little for the first two months of my stay among them. Although my smiling, nodding, uncomprehending presence on their doorstep and in their rooms was undoubtedly stressful for them during the first month or so (it was certainly stressful for me), my initial linguistic incompetence made it possible for me to pass through an extended period of relatively wordless incorporation into their day-to-day lives. Travestis who attempted to focus on or entertain me when I was in their company realized quickly that I had no idea what they were saying, and so, bored, they turned their attention to one another. By the time I was able to understand and contribute to conversations and gossip, I was already firmly established as a fixed, agreeable, noncondemnatory, and nonthreatening presence in their lives.

Beyond my foreignness and my initial linguistic inability, there is one further feature of my personal biography that I believe greatly facilitated the kinds of relationships that I eventually developed with the travestis. That is the fact that I am gay. Before I began my fieldwork in Salvador, I spoke to the only two people I knew of who had conducted ethnographic work among transgendered individuals in Latin America—Annick Prieur, a Norwegian sociologist who had written her doctoral thesis on young transgendered prostitutes in Mexico City (later published as Prieur 1994a), and Neuza Maria de Oliveira, the Brazilian sociologist whose master's thesis on travestis in Salvador was what first alerted me to the peculiarities of travesti gendered identities. To my great distress, both these women expressed doubts that I, as a man, would ever be able to gain access to and acceptance by travestis. "Travestis won't relate well to a man," I remember Neuza de Oliveira telling me. "They like to talk about things like lipstick and hair and men."[8] But, I protested meekly, so do I.

As it turned out, the issue of my sexual orientation was one of the first questions that came up in my conversations with travestis. After names were exchanged, either I or the person who had introduced me was asked if I was a *viado*—a fag. Upon receiving an affirmative answer, travestis often nodded and relaxed noticeably. My status as a self-acknowledged viado implied to the travestis that I was, in effect, one of the girls, and that I probably was not interested in them as sexual partners. My behavior quickly confirmed that I was not, and after such preliminaries were out of the way, travestis realized that they could continue conversing about the topics—boyfriends, clients, big penises, hormones, and silicone—that most occupy their time, without having to worry that I might find such topics uninteresting or offensive.

I speculate that my status as a foreign, noncondemnatory, clearly identified gay researcher allowed me to become integrated in the lives of travestis in a way that permitted me access to dimensions of their lives that have not been described in previous works. Anyone familiar with the two Brazilian studies of travestis will note strong differences between the ethnographic data analyzed in this book and the data presented in those works.[9] The Brazilian monographs have virtually nothing to say about several of the topics, such as travestis' relationships with their boyfriends, that I have found absolutely crucial for an understanding of travestis—both as individuals and as a sociocultural phenomenon. I interpret the absence of this kind of material in the Brazilian studies as due partly to the kind of contact these two scholars had with travestis (I have already noted that neither lived with them on a day-to-day basis, as I did) and partly to their own identities: Neuza de Oliveira, of course, is a woman, and Hélio Silva reports (1993:150–54) that he presented himself to travestis as a potential client—a role that clearly must have had profound consequences for the types of relationships he developed with individual travestis. While my point is not to spitefully turn the tables on the women who warned me that travestis would never accept me, and propose that in fact only gay men can really do fieldwork among travestis (that would be meaningless, considering the value of the studies published by Prieur, Oliveira, and Silva), I do suggest that as an openly gay man, someone perceived to be a viado like them, I was positioned by travestis in a way that may have facilitated access to discussions and confidences that might not have been granted as easily to women (and certainly not to potential clients).

One final dimension of my fieldwork among travestis deserves mention here. From the very first days of my residence among travestis, I tape-recorded their speech extensively, using a pocket-sized Sony TCS-580V stereo cassette recorder. By the end of my stay, I had recorded and transcribed over fifty hours of speech, including twenty hours of spontaneous interactions and sixteen interviews lasting between ninety minutes and eleven hours (fifteen of those interviews are with travestis between the ages of eleven and fifty-eight; one is with the *marido*, or boyfriend, of a travesti). I justified my recording to the travestis by explaining, honestly, that I needed to tape-record and transcribe their conversations if I was ever going to understand a word they were saying. They graciously accepted this, and they quickly grew used to the sight of me sitting in the doorway of the house or lying on someone's mattress clutching my little tape recorder. Most of the time, I recorded openly in this way, and the travestis all knew exactly what I was doing. When I walked the streets at night, however, I was forced to conceal my tape recorder either in the pocket of my shirt or in the waistband of my shorts, so as to minimize the risk of theft. Although travestis sometimes spotted the red light on the tape recorder and asked me if I was taping, the fact that I was recording an interaction often went unremarked. I did not generally announce that I was recording on the street at night, because I knew that to arrive in the midst of a group of laughing and joking travestis and announce "OK, everybody, I'm tape-recording" would have ruinously altered the dynamics of the interaction. I realize that the ethics of tape-recording in this manner are questionable. My own conclusion is that the practice is not unduly unethical, partly because my identity as a researcher who was gathering material for a book about travestis was well known to all travestis, and everybody knew that I recorded compulsively; partly because I have changed the name, or

Transcribing tapes with Keila Simpsom

obtained permission to use the name, of any travesti whom I quote discussing illegal or incriminating activities; and partly because I believe that the material I collected in this manner is no more inherently intrusive (and it certainly constitutes significantly more reliable data) than the more usual ethnographic practice of attempting to reconstruct conversations from memory.[10]

As will quickly become clear in the text that follows, the interviews I conducted and the recordings I made of spontaneously occurring conversations between travestis constitute the backbone of this study. In structuring my analysis of travesti bodily practices, affective relations, and subjectivity around conversational examples of what travestis say to one another and to me, I am building on the fundamental ethnomethodological insight that unless we can show how agents invoke and orient towards a co-constructed reality, we can never be certain that the patterns, identities, and structures we analyze are anything other than our own outsider models. The ethnographic puzzle, as I see it, is to attend to contextually situated interactions and attempt to make explicit the unexpressed logic that undergirds those interactions—the logic that makes it possible for people to act in certain taken-for-granted ways and say things to others and expect understanding. My goal in this book is to attempt this kind of analysis for travestis, by focusing on their bodily and social practices and on the words they use to talk about their lives. Rather than speak for travestis, I try here, as far as is possible, to let travestis speak for themselves. So while the interpretations in this book are all mine, many of the words, in what follows, belong to them.

One   The Context of
                         Travesti Life

The shortest route to São Francisco Street from the square where the bus lets you off at the end of the line is down a steep, narrow alley through which cars cannot pass because the potholes are too big. The gutters of this alley are filled with orange peels, cigarette butts, tiny plastic *cafezinho* cups, banana skins, corncobs, popsicle sticks, and empty plastic bags that residents and passersby have tossed away. The corners are piled high with mushy, foul-smelling trash that has been disgorged from the houses in the area. I was never able to discover the name of this street. I looked on maps, it wasn't named; I asked residents, nobody seemed to know. Although people lived on it, the street seemed more of a thoroughfare, a passageway, a gateway to something, than a street in its own right.

On a wall at the very beginning of this apparently nameless gateway, somebody had long ago spray-painted, in spindly black letters, the words "Isso não é verdade"—This is not real. Maybe the author of those words meant them as a protest, or a wry commentary on Brazil—an indigenous, folk echo of Charles de Gaulle's famous comment about Brazil: "This is not a serious country." Maybe "Isso não é verdade" was the chorus of a samba tune that was popular at the time the words were written, and the writer was dancing as he painted them. I don't know. I just know that every time I picked my way down that street and saw "This is not real," I read the words as a kind of road sign—an announcement that one was about to enter another kind of realm, a place where appearances might be deceiving and where what was real and what was not was very much a question of one's desires, frame of mind, and point of view.

At the end of this alley is São Francisco Street. About a kilometer long, São Francisco stretches from a hill topped by a gold-encrusted baroque church bearing the same name as the street down to a heavily trafficked road that connects the "upper" part of Salvador to its "lower"

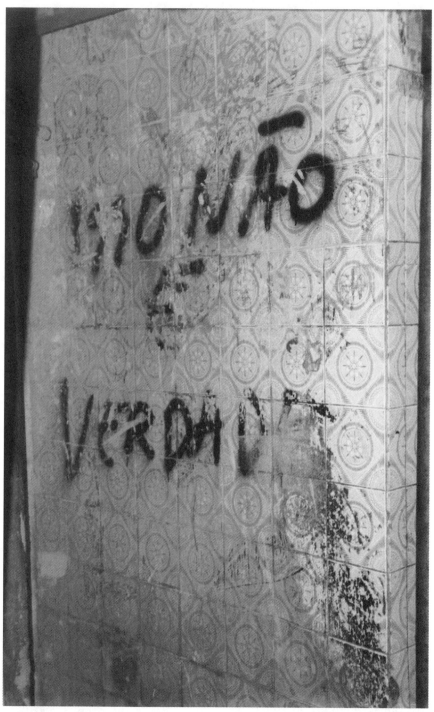

"This is not real"

part. The street is located at the edge of the part of the city known as
Pelourinho, or the Historic Center. This area was established in the six-
teenth century and reached its full social and architectural splendor at
the end of the 1700s. By the latter half of the nineteenth century, however, the balance of money and power in the city had shifted from the
old landed gentry (many of whom went bankrupt with the collapse of
the Brazilian sugar market in the middle of the century) to a new class of
urban bourgeoisie, who began constructing spacious mansions on the
periphery of the city. This started a trend, and the wealthy began moving out of Pelourinho to establish themselves in exclusive new neigh-
borhoods south of the city. They sold or leased out their old houses to
others, who divided them up into tiny cubicles and squeezed in as many
people as they could. The elegance of the city center began to face, and
the area entered a long period of neglect and decay. By the 1920s,
Pelourinho had become a predominantly poor neighborhood, and by
the 1930s it was publicly viewed as a dangerous part of town inhabited
largely by prostitutes and criminals. A popular saying of the time was "In
Maciel [a particularly disreputable part of Pelourinho], the only ones
with money are the thieves" (*No Maciel quem tem dinheiro é ladrão*). A 1969
population survey concluded that 57.8 percent of the women of Maciel
worked as prostitutes (Bacelar 1982:52–69; Oliveira 1994:103–5;
Cerqueira 1994:36; Espinheira 1971).

Since the late 1970s, but especially since the beginning of the 1990s,
the city and state governments have been "renovating" Pelourinho, re-
building its crumbling facades and reconstructing the ruined interiors of
the former elite mansions in order to attract tourists and members of the
Brazilian middle class. Rumors of the renovation, which had been in the
air since the late 1960s, eventually sent property prices in the area sky-
rocketing by 300 percent. Property owners responded to these inflated
prices and the promise of fat indemnification checks for residents either
by evicting their tenants and selling their decaying houses or by packing
even more tenants into the already crowded houses and taking a cut of
the checks they received (and then selling the houses at an enormous
profit). The government gave tenants the choice of relocation far outside
the city center or indemnification checks, where averaged twenty minimum salaries—the equivalent of almost two years' wages for many
people. Most residents opted for the money. In this process of renovating the city center, which continues today, thousands of people were dis-
located and forced to move elsewhere. Some of them used their money
they had received from the government to buy small houses that they
could afford, far outside the center of the city or in the interior of the
state. But many more simply spent the money and then moved a few

blocks to consolidate themselves in the fringe areas around Pelourinho that were not under renovation (Bacelar 1982; Cerqueira 1994; IPAC 1995; interview with Lúcia Sepúlveda of IPAC [Institute of the Artistic and Cultural Heritage of Bahia], 9 January 1997).

The area around São Francisco Street is one of these areas. It is today like what the worst parts of Pelourinho must have been like in the mid-1960s, inhabited by individuals and families who are extremely poor and/or extremely criminal. The poverty is most evident in the living conditions of the area. The streets are potholed and littered, happy rats the size of Labrador puppies abound, cockroaches are everywhere. The house facades, clearly once magnificent, and painted in cool pastel colors, are all fading and molding and crumbling. Large ferns sprout from cracked walls. Roofs are slowly sliding off their center beams. Inside, the houses have been gutted and divided up into windowless little cubicles, the largest of which are about three by five meters. These are separated from one another by thin plywood walls that reach, if one is very lucky, almost up to the ceiling. There is electricity and running water in all houses, procured by illegally tapping into electric cables and water mains, but both electricity and water fail regularly. And at most, there is one sink, toilet, and showerhead on each floor of the house, shared by everyone who lives on that floor.

Many of the houses have three inhabited floors, and people living on the top two can peer through the cracks in their floor to look down into the rooms of those who live directly beneath them. These cracks in the floor became something of a personal horror for me in my own room on São Francisco Street—the old man living above me was the owner of an incontinent dog, whose urinary problem trickled, shall we say, into my consciousness (and onto my papers and my mattress) at least once a day. And the family living below me would sometimes, without any warning, put down an odd kind of roach repellent in their room that didn't ever seem to actually kill any cockroaches—it merely prodded them into motion, compelling them to heave their fat bodies up through the cracks into my room. On one particularly memorable occasion, my travesti coworker Keila Simpsom and I were forced to end our transcription session and flee the room after we realized that the twenty-six four-inch roaches we had squashed in between interlinear glosses were only the vanguard of an invasion that we were powerless to stem.

The criminality of the area around São Francisco Street is evident by the things that the residents do to earn a living. Although a large number of people throughout the area presumably engage in noncriminal means of earning money, such as selling popsicles or cigarettes or coffee on the street, giving pedicures, or washing other people's clothes, it seemed to me that virtually everybody I met or heard spoken about around São Francisco Street supported themselves largely through doing something illegal. The area is known throughout Salvador as a place where drugs exist in abundance, and many of the people I knew sold marijuana, cocaine, Rohypnol, and, beginning in 1996, crack. Every day, at least four or five women or young men would approach travestis sitting on their doorstep, reach into a bag, pull out a skirt, a big cheese, a pair of shoes, a pair of jeans, a bottle of whiskey, some silky lingerie, a wristwatch, a piece of jewelry, a bottle of hair conditioner, or some other item that they had stolen from a store or a person, and ask the travestis if anyone was interested in buying it. Several people in the area specialized in stealing checkbooks and writing bad checks. These men and women would buy groceries worth four hundred reais (about four hundred U.S. dollars), pay with a stolen check, then sell the food to others for half that amount, thereby earning an easy two hundred reais for themselves and saving whoever purchased the food from them an equivalent amount of money. On one corner of the street, there is a never-ending gathering of tough-looking, shirtless young men, always on the lookout for the stray tourist or middle-class Brazilian who might have gotten lost on their way to a chic bar in the spruced-up Historic Center, and always ready to procure drugs for whoever might come by asking for them. The criminality of the area is so high that the residents, I noticed, always turned first to the crime pages of a newspaper, in order to see if anybody they knew was featured there. And the crime rate is so well known that several taxi drivers flatly refused to drive me home at night when I told them where I lived.

In early 1995, there were two houses on São Francisco Street that had only travestis living in them and two other houses, one of which I moved into, that had mostly travestis on one floor but families and others on the remaining floors. All in all, there were about thirty-five travestis living on São Francisco Street at any one time, which made it the highest concentration of travestis in the city.

The house in which I lived was divided up into eleven rooms on the top floor, eleven on the middle floor—where I had my room—and twenty-one truly minuscule cubicles on the basement floor. The top floor was occupied mostly by the landlady's friends and family members; the middle floor contained seven travestis, a man in his thirties who sold coffee and cigarettes on the street, and two old pensioners, both of whom rented a tiny, airless box. The basement floor of the house was derisively called the *favela de cocô*—the slum of shit—by travestis. The majority of people living here were young couples or single mothers with small children, but a number of travestis also lived on this floor in rooms not much larger than broom closets. At the back of the house was a muddy yard that adjoined the "favela." It contained the only open spigot on that floor, and it was always in use by children bathing, or by women or travestis washing clothes or preparing food. To one side of the yard lay an enormous pile of garbage flung by people from the top two floors and by residents of the favela themselves. This pile not only emitted a continual smell of fermenting rot; it also attracted scores of rats, who poured into the yard as soon as night fell, driving all the residents into their rooms and forcing them to keep their doors closed tight.

Despite the relative squalor of the living conditions, rents in that house and others in the area around São Francisco Street are high. In 1996, the tiny rooms that travestis live in were renting for between thirty-five and fifty-five reais a week, while the minimum monthly salary was only 112 reais, that is, twenty-eight reais a week (the rooms rented by families in the *favela de cocô* were cheaper, at fifteen to twenty-five reais a week). Since the Historic Center of Salvador became inhabited predominantly by poor people, criminals, and prostitutes, it has been known as an area in which tenants are ruthlessly exploited—paying the highest rents in the city per square meter of space, in houses that have been left to deteriorate and eventually collapse (Bacelar 1982:104; Oliveira 1994:105; Espinheira 1971; FPACBA 1969). Landlords in the area around São Francisco Street keep this exploitative tradition alive by continuing to charge whatever they want for rooms (and travestis are usually charged more than others, because landlords know that they generally earn more than many others). They raise the rent without notice whenever they feel like it, and they make no effort at all to patch leaky roofs or fumigate vermin-infested walls. If tenants complain, they are told to move out. Landlords know that they can continue squeezing travestis and many of the others who live in the area because most of those people stand almost no chance of ever being accepted as tenants in other parts of the city center. In addition, landlords can continue exploiting their tenants because they do not mind the prostitution that travestis practice in their rooms, and they have no objections to the wide range of drug deals and other illegal activities that go on inside other rooms in their houses. On the contrary, a not insignificant number of the landlords are themselves accomplished drug dealers, and they recruit their tenants to sell drugs on the street for them.

I moved into the house on São Francisco Street at the invitation of Keila Simpson, the travesti who during the course of my fieldwork became my teacher, coworker, and best friend. Keila is a big-boned travesti in her early thirties who made me think of a Maori warrior when I first saw her. She has the large, round, almost Polynesian face and skin color

Pastinha in the room in which she lives and works. The room is only slightly larger than the mattress on which she is sitting.

characteristic of people in her native state of Maranhão, in northern Brazil. She was also, at that first meeting, wearing a garment that looked to me like a muumuu; this undoubtedly cemented the South Sea associations in my mind. And although Keila has since cut her black hair short and bleached it blonde, at the time I met her she was letting her hair grow out in a fan that reached outwards and upwards from her head. Her big hair made her look even more expansive than she really is, and my impression of her size was further augmented by her booming, no-nonsense voice that I first heard ordering travestis to line up to receive the condoms that she was about to distribute to them. She intimidated me utterly.

I had been brought to meet Keila by Nilton Dias, a program coordinator at the Grupo Gay da Bahia (GGB), one of Brazil's oldest gay activist groups and the only gay organization in Salvador. For about a year previous to my initial visit to Salvador, in mid-1993, GGB had been distributing free condoms to travestis once a week. This distribution took place in front of the house in which Keila lived because Keila, who had worked briefly with GGB in 1990 and subsequently with another non-governmental organization that distributed free condoms to travestis, had agreed to fill out a questionnaire that the president of GGB, Luiz Mott, had designed to be asked of each travesti who came to receive free condoms.[1]

Travestis and AIDS

The free condoms were, of course, one response to the AIDS epidemic that has decimated Brazil's travesti population since the early 1980s. Since the disease was first diagnosed in Brazil in 1982 and 1983, the country has consistently ranked among the leaders in number of cases reported to the World Health Organization. As of December 1996, Brazil had registered 94,997 cases of AIDS since the epidemic's outbreak. Even though this number is high, it is universally regarded as severely underrepresentative, and the Brazilian Ministry of Health estimated that a more realistic figure is about 130,000. What is worse, estimates of the number of people currently infected with HIV in Brazil range from 338,000 to one million (*Folha de São Paulo*, 21 December 1996). Salvador, which as of August 1996 had reported 1,295 cases of AIDS since the epidemic was first diagnosed, ranks ninth among Brazilian cities in number of registered cases (*Boletim Epidemiológico*, weeks 23–35, 1996). This relatively low number, however, says much more about the local population's access to health care than about the true incidence of AIDS among the city's residents.

As prostitutes who often assume the insertee role in sex with their clients, travestis are particularly hard hit by AIDS.[2] It is impossible even to guess, however, at how many have died of it. Statistics on AIDS in Brazil do not report on travestis—they are subsumed under the categories "men" and "homosexual transmission." And asking travestis to estimate the number of their friends and colleagues who have died of the disease is pointless. Whenever journalists approach them on the street at night and ask them about AIDS (this is one of the few topics journalists are interested in knowing anything about from travestis), individual travestis will rapidly come up with a number, usually a large one. But in conversations with one another, those same travestis will later be quick to point out that travestis die of many things, and AIDS—which is most commonly only referred to euphemistically as *a menina*, "the girl," or *a tia*, "the aunt"—is only one of them. And besides, they ask, how does anyone know that a particular travesti's death was caused by AIDS? The

overwhelming majority of travestis, like the majority of Brazil's population, have no access to adequate health care, and travestis—again, like
most other Brazilians—spend their lives self diagnosing their infirmities
and curing them by using pharmaceutical products recommended by
friends or by pharmacists, who dispense a wide array of powerful drugs
over the counter with no medical prescriptions. In a context like this,
AIDS is more a matter of opinion than of medical test results. (This same
line of reasoning is used by travestis whenever people suggest to them
that injecting silicone into their bodies might result in health problems.
Travestis know that many people consider silicone injections to be dangerous. But they dismiss those concerns and ask rhetorically how anyone
can be absolutely certain that the death of a particular travesti was
caused by silicone.)

Some travestis have had HIV tests, and some have tested positive. But
there is a widespread belief that HIV tests are unreliable, and that one
may test positive one time and negative the next. So one never really
knows if one is HIV positive or not. Also, there is a firm idea in the milieu in which travestis live that HIV infects people in varying quantities,
and that if one acquires only "a little" of it (um pouco do virus), one's health
will not be significantly compromised. And in addition to these difficul-
ties that, according to travestis, prevent anyone from ever knowing if an
individual really has AIDS or has died of AIDS-related causes, there is
also the fact that being HIV positive or having AIDS carries a strong
stigma among travestis. A common, and strong, term of abuse among
travestis (and among Brazilians generally) is aidética, which means "AIDS
carrier." This word is hurled as a kind of accusation in arguments, and a
travesti will frequently use it in talking about some other travesti whom
she for some reason intensely dislikes (usually because she has lost a boyfriend to the object of vituperation).

The fact that it is still considered disgraceful and embarrassing to be
infected with HIV means that travestis' diagnoses of AIDS in others must
be heard more as a statement about their feelings towards those others
than as an accurate representation of medical fact. Travestis will be quick
to claim that those they dislike have AIDS, but at the same time they will
be extremely hesitant to attribute the actual sicknesses and deaths of travestis they like to the disease. During the time I spent in Salvador, at
least nine travestis I knew died of what seemed to my untrained eye to
be health failures related to AIDS. In almost all of these cases, travestis
who were close to the deceased consistently denied that the cause of
death had anything to do with AIDS. Instead, they invoked everything
from tuberculosis to unspecified lung problems (problemas pulmonários) to

Lining up for condoms on São Francisco Street

an equally nebulous "stomach infection" (*infecção no estômago*) to a "swollen heart" (*coração inchado*) to a "lack of will to go on living" (*ela não tinha vontade de viver mais*).

In the foreseeable future, travestis will probably continue to be extremely hard hit by AIDS. All of them know by now that condoms are essential in preventing the transmission of HIV. All travestis also seem to use condoms much of the time while working, and they usually insist that their clients also use them (some travestis will not even perform fellatio on a client if he is not wearing a condom, and a few travestis say that they routinely put two, or in some cases even three, condoms on clients before allowing penetration). Condoms sometimes burst, however, or remain inside the travesti's rectum when the client's penis is withdrawn, thereby facilitating transmission of the virus. But perhaps more serious than these occasional accidents is the fact that most travestis do not always insist on condoms. There still seem to be many clients who are willing to pay a travesti more if he does not have to wear a condom while penetrating her, and if the price is right and the travesti needs the money desperately enough, she may comply. Some travestis also routinely permit coitus interruptus without a condom. And if the person with whom the travesti is having sex is what travestis call a *vício*—that is, if he is an attractive male with whom she is having sex for free—then condoms will often not enter the picture at all.

The most significant vector of HIV transmission among travestis is probably neither their clients nor their *vícios*, however, but their boyfriends. I have only ever heard one travesti claim to always use condoms during sex with her boyfriend (not coincidentally, that travesti is Keila, who, through her work with GGB and various nongovernmental organization, is the travesti in Salvador who is most engaged in HIV-prevention efforts). *All* other travestis openly dismiss the thought of ever asking their boyfriend to put on a condom, even though the boyfriends are often highly promiscuous, even though they regularly penetrate their travesti girlfriends, and even though many travestis change boyfriends very frequently. For better *and* for worse, travestis have come to equate condoms with work. And this means that whenever they feel they are not working, condoms can be dispensed with.[3]

Travestis and Violence

If it is difficult to know when the death of a travesti is caused by AIDS, it is not hard to know when her death is caused by violence. Brazil is a violent society. Not only is it a society saturated in what the anthropologist Nancy Scheper-Hughes (1992) has called "the violence of everyday life"—the routinized suffering and humiliation that a large majority of Brazil's population must endure at the hands of a social and political system that is corrupt, corrosive, and harshly class and race biased—it is also a society in which more than seven thousand street children were murdered by exterminators between 1987 and 1991 (*Jornal do Brasil*, 6 December 1991, cited in Simpson 1993:132) and in which stray bullets fired by police and drug syndicates kill dozens of innocent bystanders a year (*Istoé*, 13 November 1996:40–41).[4] In Salvador, hardly a day goes by without one or even two armed bank robberies, or without a car or city bus running over someone trying to cross the road and then speeding off without stopping. Each month the city sees at least two brutal lynchings of people who have committed, or are suspected of having committed, a crime. A nationwide study published in late 1996 concluded that 70 percent of all deaths among males between the ages of 15 and 29 are caused by violence (reported in *A Tarde*, 24 October 1996). Violence is an integral dimension of life in most places and for most people throughout Brazil.

But almost nowhere is this violence more ubiquitous than in the day-

to-day existence of travestis.[5] Violence is an ever-present backdrop
against which all travestis live their lives. Even though they all habitually
dress in female clothing and wear female hairstyles, cosmetics, and accessories, the majority of travestis do not easily pass as women, especially when they are seen in the harsh light of day. Instead, they seem to
give an incongruent impression that compels people seeing them on the
street to stare or comment. A travesti walking down a city street during
the day will thus tend to attract attention. This attention is not only condemnatory—on the contrary, whenever I went out in the company of
any travesti during the day, I was always struck by how she attracted a
steady stream of openly lustful looks from men of all ages, even though
she did nothing more seductive than buy some rolls at the bakery or
pause at a shop window to look at some sandals. But even as some males
are openly desirous of travestis who pass them on the street, others are
openly hostile, and a travesti must be prepared to confront abusive remarks from men and women or physical violence from males. Travestis
find themselves obliged to continually reassert their rights to occupy
urban space, and they live their lives aware that they may, at any moment,
suddenly become the target of verbal harassment and/or physical violence from anyone who feels provoked by their presence in that space.

The danger is greatest at night. In order to attract clients, travestis
stand on street corners and along highways, thereby exposing themselves to public scrutiny in ways they are otherwise usually careful to
avoid. This exposure makes them vulnerable to harassment by policemen and passersby in cars and buses. Much of this harassment takes the
form of verbal abuse, but gangs of young men sometimes severely bash
travestis, and people speeding by in cars often throw objects such as
rocks and bottles at them. Sometimes they even shoot them. Usually the
perpetrators of these crimes are never apprehended, and even if they are,
the sentences they receive are light. In one infamous case, a military policeman in Rio de Janeiro was convicted by a court of military justice of
having killed a travesti, shooting her once in the face and twice in the
back. This same policeman was also under investigation for the deaths of
five other travestis, who in addition to all being shot in the face were
found with their genitals cut off. When the policeman's case was appealed and retried in the High Court of Military Justice, however, his
sentence was reduced from twelve years to six, because, the decision
read, "the activity in which the victim was engaged was a high-risk activity, extremely dangerous; thus the fact that he was taken by surprise
cannot be used in his favor (*não lhe socorrendo assim, o fator surpresa*)" (*Folha
de São Paulo*, 9 October 1994). Travestis working as street prostitutes, in

other words, are asking for it, and no one should expect courts to unduly penalize a man just because he shoots travestis in the face.

As this case indicates, policemen are a major source of violence against travestis—in Salvador, without a doubt the most common source. There are three types of police in Brazil: federal police (*polícia federal*), civil police (*polícia civil*), and, presumably a remnant of the country's long history of authoritarian rule, military police (*polícia militar*). These different types of police are further divided into special branches, such as the highway police (*polícia rodoviária*), operating as a branch of the federal police; the feared Batalhão do Choque (Combat Battalion) of the military police; and the Delegacia de Jogos e Costumes (DJC), a kind of vice squad within the civil police that was disbanded, travestis told me, by President Fernando Collor de Mello in the early 1990s ("the only good thing he ever did," quipped the travesti who first told me this, recalling that Collor de Mello was impeached in 1992 on charges of massive corruption and extortion).[6]

Both the civil and military police patrol the streets in Salvador and all other large cities. Military police are the more numerous. They are also more visible, because they are uniformed, whereas civil police are not. Both types of policemen have the same powers to make arrests, and both are equally likely to harass travestis. However, travestis in Salvador are unanimous in claiming that it is the military police who are most violent and most likely to abuse them, coerce them into performing sex against their will, rob them, assault them, and even murder them.

Until the beginning of the 1990s, travestis went to work each night not knowing whether they would return home at the end of the evening. They could virtually count on being arrested by either military police or the DJC vice squad. In both cases there was nothing legal about the arrests—prostitution is not criminal under the Brazilian legal code, and the travestis were almost never charged with any crime (on the few occasions when they were charged, the crime was *vadiagem*, vagrancy). Travestis arrested by the civil police were taken to jail, where they would have to spend at least one night, and sometimes as many as three, before they were released. If they were picked up by the military police, however—and especially if they were picked up by a paddy wagon of the Combat Battalion—travestis were routinely tortured. They were packed into the truck and repeatedly kicked and punched by the six to eight policemen who rode with them, not to jail but to the Praia do Flamenco, an (at that time) all but deserted beach about a forty-five minute drive outside of Salvador. Throughout this trip, policemen played a number of sadistic games with travestis. A favorite was to force them to sit kissing one another on the mouth for the entire journey. Another amusement was to command a travesti to put her hand, palm up, on the head of the travesti sitting beside her. A policeman then brought down his billy club with full force onto the travesti's hand. If she panicked when she felt the club falling and withdrew her hand, the blow landed on the head of her neighbor. Upon arriving at the beach, the policemen got out and formed two lines facing each other at the back of the paddy wagon. They then made the travestis descend one by one. As each travesti stepped down, she was forced to walk in between the policemen, who kicked her with their boots and beat her with their billy clubs. Beatings like this can have extremely serious consequences for travestis, because blows to the parts of their bodies in which they have silicone often cause the silicone to shift position. Hence, hips may slide down a travesti's thigh, breasts may descent into her stomach, and buttocks may splatter in all directions. Policemen knew this—because travestis, terrified of becoming deformed for life, told them—but they took no notice. On the contrary, the knowledge that they may have been destroying a travesti's life only seemed to increase the pleasure that many of them derived from the beating.

In the grand finale of these brutal horrors, the travestis were stripped and ordered to fight with one another. The spectacle of a group of naked travestis slapping one another was illuminated by the headlights of the paddy wagon and ogled by the policemen, who laughed at and mocked the travestis.

After the policemen had finally driven off, the travestis were left to try to find whatever remained of their clothes in the pitch blackness of the beach, and to try to get a lift back into town. Unless one or more of the travestis had managed to quickly stuff her night's earnings up into her rectum before she fell prey to the police, they couldn't take a taxi. All they could do was hitchhike back into the city.

For reasons that no one is quite certain of, the situation in Salvador for travestis has improved dramatically in the past five years. The dissolution of the vice squad has clearly helped. But even the Combat Battalion no longer rounds up travestis and abandons them naked and battered on the Praia do Flamenco. However, even though the organized police violence against travestis has all but ceased, hardly a day goes by that some individual policeman does not take it upon himself to harass travestis. I myself have listened as military policemen glided by in their dark cars and barked ominous threats to travestis working along the edge of the highway, and I have fled in panic with other travestis when a pair of military police approached a group chatting on a street corner and without warning butted a billy club into the stomach of the travesti standing nearest to them.

Travestis continue to be relatively powerless in the face of such police brutality. In the past, their most effective response to it was to slice open the veins of their inner arm and spray the policemen with blood. Travestis made sure to always have a razor blade somewhere on their person; sometimes they slid a small blade behind their upper lip or inside their cheek. If they were taken to jail and had no blade handy, they would attempt to use whatever they could find. A travesti once told me the story of how another travesti broke off the plastic top of her nail-polish bottle and sliced upon her arm with that, fleeing the police station as the policemen recoiled at the sight of her spattered with blood. This practice of self-mutilation (known among travestis simply as *se cortar*   to cut oneself) originated before the AIDS epidemic (Oliveira 1994 : 148–49; Mott and Assunção 1987). However, once it became clear that HIV was transmitted through blood, cutting oneself became all the more effective as a way of escaping from police or getting oneself released from jail.

With the relative easing of police repression, the incidence of self-mutilation has decreased dramatically in Salvador. Whereas travestis in their mid-thirties and upwards almost all have deep and numerous scars on at lest one of their inner arms, most younger travestis have never cut themselves. Their most common response to police brutality is to try to run away. Sometimes they will also threaten to go to a newspaper and publicly denounce a policeman who harasses or robs them or demands sex, but this threat rarely helps. Most often it simply elicits a threat in return—do it, the policeman responds, and the next time I see you on the street I'll kill you.

Violence against travestis remains so widespread and common throughout the country that it receives occasional attention in the Brazilian press—usually when a travesti corpse is discovered or when there is a wave of murders, such as when the *Folha de São Paulo* ran a series of reports after sixteen travestis in São Paulo were shot in the head during the first three months of 1993.

More common in Brazilian newspapers, though, are reports about crimes committed by travestis. These reports uniformly portray travestis as vicious, armed, drug-addicted, AIDS-spreading criminals who lure innocent men into dangerous situations and then assault them, often disturbing the public peace and causing pandemonium in the process. A newspaper article that appeared on 17 August 1995 in *A Tarde*, the largest daily newspaper in Salvador, is a kind of concentration of those themes. The only detail lacking in this article that frequently appears alongside texts about travestis is a line drawing depicting ridiculously masculine-looking males pulling at one another's wigs or brandishing menacing knives at frightened clients.

"Travesti Attacks Young Man with Razor in Pituba"

During more than 15 minutes of total pandemonium, motorists stopped their cars to observe the actions of the bloody battle provoked by the travesti known as "Karine," who frequents the Our Lady of the Light Square, in Pituba, to attract customers. The victim, who attempted to flee from well-aimed blows of a razor, was Roberto Carlos de Conceição Santos, 26 years old, from São Gonçalo dos Campos.

The event occurred at about 10 p.m. on Tuesday. The Our Lady of the Light Square was bustling with the presence of numerous travestis and prostitutes, who every night until daybreak afflict this dignified area of the Pituba neighborhood, not even respecting the presence of the soldiers stationed at the Military Police post there. "Karine," a lanky mulatta, 1.80 meters tall, in high heels, probably drugged, was inviting men to take part in amorous encounters. As incredible as it may seem, despite the threat of AIDS and a series of other dangerous diseases, men continue to frequent this locale to seek out travestis.

Chase

"Karine's" insistence finally attracted Roberto Carlos, who had already been in the area for more than an hour watching the travestis[!]. The two approach one another, according to a witness, and hold a quick dialogue. After this, the two disappear for several minutes, and, when there were fewer people about, "Karine" reappears, running after Roberto Carlos, armed with a razor. The young man attempts to flee, but receives a deep blow to his right shoulder, even cutting his shirt. Blood begins flowing quickly, and people begin to scream, attracting the attention of passersby and motorists.

Having already removed her high heels, "Karine" continues chasing Roberto Carlos and strikes him again, this time in the back. The young man throws himself into the middle of the road, with his shirt soaked with blood, and "Karine" keeps up her chase. A third deep cut is made on the right arm of Roberto, who is unable to continue fleeing.

Several days after this article appeared, I met Karine on the street at night and recorded an interview with her about the incident. Her version of the events differs dramatically from the newspaper's. "Look," she told me and several other travestis who had gathered to listen, "it's like this. I was there on my corner working, right? And he came up and asked for five reais [about five dollars]. I said I don't have five reais. And he said 'you don't, huh' and went away." The man, whom Karine knew to be a petty criminal who had previously robbed other travestis and female prostitutes working in the area, returned later, accompanied by another man and brandishing a club to which steel nails had been attached. He again demanded money, at which point Karine, feeling threatened, removed a small knife from her purse ("we have to defend ourselves, right?") and stabbed him. She was appalled at the report in *A Tarde*. "They lied," she explained. "It wasn't a razor. And he wasn't a client. He wasn't somebody who came to me wanting to pay for sex. He was a street criminal *(um marginal de rua)*." Karine was apprehended by the police after this incident, but they released her after she paid them a small bribe *(um acuezinho)*.

Since I did not witness the incident described by Karine and *A Tarde*, I can only speculate as to which of these two highly divergent accounts might be closer to "the truth." Based on everything I know about travestis, however, I find it extremely unlikely that a travesti would chase a client down the street and out into traffic just to stab him. As I document in chapter 4, travestis do indeed rob their clients very frequently. But they are not interested in injuring clients, they just want to rob them; and they have a number of well-developed ways of doing that—none of which involve running after them down city streets and stabbing them. I also know that it is not at all uncommon for men to try to demand money from travestis and female prostitutes in the area in which Karine was working. In addition to all this, *A Tarde* is infamous in Salvador for its regular, virulent attacks on homosexuals [7] The newspaper's profoundly homophobic attitude is evidenced fairly clearly by the tone in which the article about Karine is written. So my own educated guess, based on all this, is that Karine's version of the incident is the much more believable one, and that the piece in *A Tarde* is one of the many instances of journalistic reports about travestis where interest in promoting and reinforcing derogatory stereotypes overrides any concern to provide accurate information.

The article about Karine appeared in the crime pages of *A Tarde*. Such pages constitute a special section of every Brazilian newspaper. Generally speaking, whenever travestis who are not famous like Roberta Close appear in the news, they do so on these pages, where they are featured either as dangerous criminals or as corpses (often photographed in lurid close-up). An interesting linguistic difference in these two journalistic depictions of travestis is that whenever travestis are accused of committing violence, their agency is always clearly spelled out in headlines. So, for example, a headline will read, "Travesti attacks young man with razor in Pituba" *(Travesti ataca rapaz a navalhadas na Pituba)* or "Reporter robbed by travesti" *(Repórter foi furtado por um travesti)* or "Murdered with a knife in a car by a travesti" *(Assassinado a faca no automóvel pelo travesti)*.

In stark contrast, headlines in reports of violence against travestis are very frequently without agents. Typical examples are "August begins with the taste of blood: First victim is travesti" *(Agosto começa com gosto de sangue: Primeira vítima é travesti)* and "Three are killed at Ponta Negra" *(Três são mortos em Ponta Negra)*. Headlines reporting crimes against travestis also tend to attribute their deaths to instruments such as a knife, a gun, or a blow—not a person. So instead of saying something like "Man shoots travesti," a headline will read, "Floripedes, the travesti, murdered with blow" *(Floripedes, o travesti, assassinado a murro)*; "Death in Pigalle: Brazilian murdered with shots from a hunting rifle" *(Morte em Pigalle: Brasileiro assassinado com tiros de fuzil de caça)*; or "15 travestis die shot through the head in São Paulo" *(Em São Paulo 15 travestis morrem com tiros na cabeça)*. Thus, in the case of reports about violence committed by travestis, agency and responsibility are understood and foregrounded. Reports about violence inflicted on travestis, in contrast, often elide the agency of those responsible for the violence, or displace it into the weapon, so that the perpetrators of the crimes remain in the background (cf. Henley, Miller, and Beazely 1995).

Travestis in Salvador

At any one time, there will be between about 100 and 250 travestis living and working in Salvador. This variation is seasonal. Travestis are highly mobile individuals, and most travestis in their early twenties will have already worked at least for a while in three or four different, often geographically distant, Brazilian cities. Salvador is particularly popular among travestis during the summer months beginning in December. Throughout those months, the city is host to a large number of popular festivals that culminate in February in the famous Carnival, which vaults the city into a full seven days of nonstop partying. Travestis from all over the northeast of the country flock to Salvador during this period to cash in on the fact that so much partying puts many men in festive moods and predisposes them to spend their money on prostitutes.

Contrary to popular belief and scholarly accounts, however, which hold that travestis absolutely live for Carnival, because it is the only time of the year when they can display themselves publicly to popular acclaim (Da Matta 1984, 1991a; Kottak 1990:174; Parker 1991:146; Trevisan 1986), most travestis in Salvador do not actively participate in Carnival. Some of them do take the opportunity to dress up in homemade minimalist *fantasias* (costumes) that consist of glitter and a few feathers, and stand showing themselves off and keeping an eye peeled for potential clients on the steps of the city square (Praça Castro Alves) that is by tacit agreement a predominantly gay space during Carnival. Some travestis also visit one or two of the gay "balls" that occur throughout the week at discotheques and clubs. And a few even participate in a gay beauty contest that is usually held on the Monday afternoon of Carnival, on the same steps on which travestis most commonly congregate. But travestis do their best to avoid mingling with the throngs of people who follow behind, or crowd along the sides of the streets to see, the *trio elétricos*— the bands that are the main attraction of Carnival, and that parade along the city's main streets perched atop loudspeakers stacked up on eighteen-wheel trucks. Indeed, many travestis avoid going out onto the streets during Carnival altogether, because they know that, surrounded on all sides by crowds of people, they are extremely vulnerable to harassment and violence.

One of the myths Brazilians like to tell themselves about Carnival— one that frequently gets repeated and perpetuated in popular and scholarly analyses of the festival—is that it represents a world upside-down, in which anything goes, in which confusion and ambiguity are celebrated and in which deviance becomes normal (Parker 1991; Da Matta 1984, 1991a, 1997b; Sonia 1989:247–48). While this characterization may capture the experience of some of the participants in Carnival—particularly middle-class heterosexual males—scholars like Nancy Scheper-Hughes and Daniel Linger have recently shown that the breathless descriptions of Carnival to which tourists and academics are usually treated do not accurately reflect the experience of a great many other Brazilians. In the town in which Scheper-Hughes conducted anthropological fieldwork, for example, many of the poor women with whom she worked ignored Carnival, dismissing it as "nonsense" and "entertainment for men and children" (1992:495). And Linger (1992) devotes several chapters in his book to the violence that routinely occurs during Carnival celebrations and that makes many people wary of venturing out onto the streets during the festivities.

As far as travestis are concerned, in Salvador they are just as likely to be abused and attacked during Carnival as at any other time during the year. This was brought home to me most forcefully when I was walking back to São Francisco Street with several of the scantily clad travestis who had participated in the annual gay beauty contest. At one point we were passed by a *bloco de travestidos*—a group of men parading down the street dressed as women. Perhaps seeing real travestis threw the female drag of these men into new relief and suggested to them that their own getup might be interpreted by spectators not as performative parody of femininity, but as an inner desire for it.[8] Whatever the reason, the reaction of these men in dresses to seeing a group of travestis was to begin hurling at them exactly the same kinds of insults and abuse that travestis have all grown wearily accustomed to hearing from men at any other time of the year.

When Carnival ends, the festive atmosphere that has animated the city for several months dies down, and the streets on which travestis work tend to go through an extended period of being "bad" (*uó*). Customers become fewer and money scarcer. At this point, many travestis leave Salvador and migrate south to cities such as Brasília and São Paulo, which have local reputations as being good places to make money. The travesti population of Salvador returns to its normal size of just over a hundred individuals, and those travestis who remain continue working, complaining continually that the street is "dead" (*morta*) and that they would be better off working elsewhere.

A characteristic of the travesti population of Salvador is that it is largely composed of individuals who have come to the city from other places throughout northeastern Brazil. The northeastern states constitute one of the poorest regions in the country, and the people who live there are habitually stereotyped by Brazilians living in the powerful, more prosperous southern half of the nation as being backward, uneducated, and uncouth. The state of Bahia, in which Salvador lies, is connected with its own special set of associations and stereotypes. In its positive guise, Bahia represents Brazil's own tropical paradise; its predominantly black population constitutes a link to mysterious Africa, and it is depicted as the cradle of such quintessential Brazilian creations as candomblé (an Afro-Brazilian religion), copoeira (a form of self-defense originally developed by slaves), and Carnival. In this portrayal, Bahians are charming and sensual, even by Brazilian standards. In its negative guise, however, Bahia is seen by southerners as a poor, traditionalist, third-world-like backwater whose inhabitants are lazy, loud, obstreperous, and given over to excessive partying.

Salvador is the capital of Bahia and the third most populous city in Brazil. The city has expanded dramatically, more than doubling its size between 1970 and 1991—from 1,007,195 to 2,072,058 residents (CEI/CONDER 1994:186). Its size seems to act as a magnet, drawing immigrants from the rural parts of Bahia as well as from all over the northeast. Many of the travestis who live in Salvador are migrants: in the house in which I lived, for example, there were five travestis from the northeastern state of Pernambuco, one from the state of Rio Grande do Norte, one each from the states of Ceará, Paraíba, and Maranhão (this was Keila), and only four from Bahia. Although travestis told me that these days there are more and more native Bahian travestis appearing on the scene, they said that this composition of travestis was fairly typical, and that especially in the past, the majority of travestis in Salvador were not native at all but were from Pernambuco, particularly its capital of Recife. There is a large population of travestis in Recife—at least as large as Salvador's—but everybody is agreed that Salvador is a much more tolerant place than Recife. Hence, they told me, travestis who visit Salvador from Recife tend to stay, because not only are the culture and climate much the same as in their home state, but the level of freedom travestis enjoy is many times greater than anything they can hope for in conservative Recife.

In addition to being made up of people from many different (mostly northeastern) states, Salvador's travesti population is young. It is always hard to get a travesti to be truthful about her age, and most habitually lop off a number of years whenever anybody (including another travesti) asks them. Once travestis reach age thirty—which they all consider to be old (velha)—most of them simply stop supplying their age. It would be clear to even the casual observer, however, that the majority of travestis in the city are young—between the ages of about seventeen and twenty-six. Travestis between these ages, everyone is agreed, are at their auge, their pinnacle of beauty. And they spend a great many of their waking hours trying to foreground that fact, through bodily practices such as hair extensions, hormone consumption, and the injection of numerous liters of silicone into their hips, thighs, knees, and behinds.

One reason the majority of the travesti population is young is that travestis do not generally live very long. If the average life span of Brazilians is sixty-five years (Veras and Alves 1995), for travestis it is probably forty-five, or less. Many travestis die young from violence, from AIDS, or from other illnesses that are never officially diagnosed. Those who live into their forties and fifties can no longer earn much money as prostitutes, and as their clients become fewer and older, they find themselves forced to turn to other activities. Some travestis make a decisive move into drug dealing at this stage, gradually expanding their contacts and networks to the point where they can continue making a comfortable living even after they have all but stopped working on the streets. Others spiral downwards into depression and increased poverty, and support themselves as best they can by running errands, washing clothes, and cooking food for other travestis, who pay them small sums and let them eat some of the food they prepare. Still others generate income by performing specialized services such as silicone injections. In 1996, travestis who had good local reputations as bombadeiras, or "pumpers," could make a profit of more than 150 reais (about $150) for each liter they injected (see chapter 2). A final option for some older travestis is the most desirable: to have already earned enough money to purchase a house and perhaps a small bar or snack stand (uma barraca). If the house she has purchased is large enough, a travesti will often divide it up into tiny rooms and rent them out to others—often to young travestis—to live in and/or to bring customers to have sex in. If a travesti manages to buy a house before her "pinnacle" passes (and accomplishing this objective is one of the main reasons travestis these days all try to travel to Italy to work there for a while; see chapter 4), then she can look forward to a reliable source of income throughout her life.

Travestis in the area around São Francisco Street are fully integrated into the local community, and they maintain a wide variety of relationships with the men, women, and children who share the area with them. If they have lived there for any length of time, travestis generally know and are known by many of the other residents, who greet them, joke with them, stop to talk with them, or flirt with them as they pass on the street. Travestis are a continual presence on the street. At all hours of the day and night, they stand or sit in the doorways of their houses, watching for potential customers, talking loudly to one another about their lives and adventures, and commenting about the beauty or ugliness of some of the women—and the assumed or known penis size of virtually all of the men—who happen past them. Vocative cries of *bicha, mona,* and *viado*—all meaning "homosexual" or "fag," and all words that travestis habitually and (usually) nonpejoratively use in talking to one another—ring up and down the street at all times of the day. During the day, travestis perform some of their intimate personal grooming in full view of anyone who happens to pass by. Some sit on their front doorsteps rolling their hair up in curlers as they watch for customers, for example. And sunny afternoons often find three or four travestis standing next to one another, their buttocks pressed up against the warm facades of the houses, gazing into small compact mirrors with one eye and watching for clients with the other, chatting and laughing with one another and with passersby as they simultaneously tweezer out the hairs that have sprouted from their upper lips and chins.

The travestis on São Francisco Street are thus continually in one another's company. Many of them share tiny rooms with other travestis. In addition, throughout the day they drift in and out of each other's rooms to catch a television *novela*, to borrow a pair of shoes, to ask for help in injecting hormones, to smoke a joint, to gossip about men. At night they travel together on buses to work along the highway leading out of the city, and they help each other rob clients. They ask one another for advice about what clothes to wear to work at night, what product is best for getting the kinks out of their hair, which appliance store might be persuaded to give them credit enough to buy a television, which hormones work most effectively, how many liters of silicone they ought to inject into their behinds, and what drugs they need to buy to gain weight or to cure themselves of some illness they have contracted.

Despite all this interaction, cooperation, advice, and apparent conviviality, however, ties between travestis are in fact extremely fragile and are characterized by a marked degree of suspicion and distrust. "Tudo é falsidade" (It's all falseness), I was repeatedly corrected whenever I, at the beginning of my stay with travestis, naively commented on how well I thought that many of them seemed to get along with one another. And after my first couple of months living with travestis, I began to be pulled aside by individuals and told matter-of-factly, "Nobody here likes me" (Aqui ninguém gosta de mim). The first few times I was told this, I put it down to idiosyncratic paranoia, because it was travestis like Banana—who obsessively protects herself from the Big Eye, which she feels to be pursuing her at every turn—who were the first to impart such information to me. By the time I left Salvador almost a year later, however, virtually every travesti I knew well had at one time or another said to me privately, and seriously, "Nobody here likes me."

What I came to realize was that in the midst of the continual seemingly jocular and warm social interaction, travestis also habitually spread malicious gossip, seduce one another's boyfriends, and steal money and objects from one another. Keila once told me an archetypal story of betrayal, one that I heard repeated many times by many different travestis. The story always had the same structure; all that was altered in the different tellings were the names and the reasons and the forms of betrayal. The particular story that Keila told me involved a young travesti who arrived in Salvador with an advanced case of hepatitis and an extremely serious case of venereal warts on her anus. She was ashamed to tell anybody about her warts, but when she got to the point where she could barely even defecate, she sought the aid of another travesti, who brought her to Keila. "She came to my room and said she had something on her anus (um babado no edi)," Keila narrated. "I told her to show me. She said no. I said show me. She said no. I said 'What stupidity is this, viado? You're sick, let me look so that I can try to arrange somebody to tell you what to do.'"

Finally, the young travesti overcame her shame and agreed to take off her clothes and let herself be examined. A stench that nearly caused Keila to faint arose from the travesti's anus, and Keila, horrified at the sight before her, asked her how long she had had the warts, receiving the answer "more than a month." Keila told her where to go to get medicine, and the travesti went and procured it. Because she could not work during the time she was undergoing the cure, she slept on the floor in the rooms of other travestis, eating their food with the promise that she would pay back all debts as soon as she was able to get back on the streets. Finally, after several weeks, the travesti was cured. And what did she do then? "Robbed the bicha she was living with and skipped town," Keila concluded, disgusted.

Deceptive practices like this, and the telling of stories about them, are frequent occurrences among travestis. But travestis do not only betray and rob one another; they can also be violent. A travesti arriving in Salvador or any other city may have to square off with tough local travestis who may not appreciate the fresh competition, especially if the new arrival is pretty. If the new travesti is not capable of defending herself, or if she can make no allies among other local travestis, she may find herself mercilessly bullied and eventually forced to either leave town or work the city's least desirable streets. Even worse things can happen: a few years ago, it was briefly popular to throw sulfuric acid into the faces of travestis whom one did not like. Only a few travestis ever attempted this in Salvador, but in other cities the threat terrorized travestis for some time. In the city of Belo Horizonte, in the southern state of Minas Gerais, a travesti known locally as the Monstro do Ácido (the Acid Monster) managed to maim more than thirteen travestis with sulfuric acid before she was finally apprehended by police in August 1994 (*Diário da Tarde*, 13 October 94).

Individual travestis do sometimes form deep and lasting friendships with one or two other travestis. But often a travesti would tell me that she had no real friends and that she distrusted all travestis—often following this statement with a detailed example of some travesti who she had thought was her friend, until that travesti betrayed her by spreading gossip, snatching away a boyfriend, not looking after her when she was sick, stealing money, or reneging on a loan. Travestis use a number of words to describe the way that travestis "are" in relation to one another, and continually recurring among those words are the terms *recalcada, invejosa,* and *despeitada*—all of which carry similar connotations of envy, resentfulness, and destructiveness. These words are used jokingly in their conversations with one another, but also deadly seriously in their private comments on the behavior of other travestis. And hearing them used again and again in travesti talk, I came to realize that while Banana's obsessive concern that other travestis are trying to turn the Big Eye her way and take away her customers, her looks, and her material goods is exaggerated, it is not unusual. On the contrary, by the end of my stay in Salvador, it sometimes seemed to me that travestis regarded one another as their own worst enemies. Travestis live and work together, but many of them seem to see themselves in continual competition with one another. The objects of that competition are scarce and valuable resources—boyfriends, clients, beauty, femininity, money—that travestis must work extremely hard to obtain and that they seem to feel themselves to be forever on the verge of losing to other, more belligerent or more beautiful travestis.

Perhaps the distrust that travestis so widely feel for one another, and the practices that reinforce and perpetuate that distrust—the gossip, the violence, the robberies, the betrayals, the conscious seduction of others' boyfriends—are a result of the fact that travestis live in a violent world that gives them absolutely nothing and teaches them that if they want to survive and prosper, they need to snatch every possible opportunity to further their own lives and goals, even if that means betraying others who have trusted and helped them. Maybe such practices arise from the fact that travestis are so disliked and discriminated against by other people that many of them have internalized that dislike and discrimination and turned it against one another. One travesti suggested as much when she told me firmly, "Travestis themselves are prejudiced (*preconceituosos*). They themselves don't like other travestis."[9] Or maybe the distrust of other travestis is one more instantiation of the "basic mistrust of the world" that the Brazilian anthropologist Roberto Da Matta has argued characterizes Brazilians' attitudes towards one another (1991a: 163; see also McCallum 1996: 218–19; Sarti 1995).

However much the fragility of travesti social relations may be explained in terms of larger socioeconomic patterns of inequality and general cultural propensities for wariness towards others, a final reason why many travestis live much of their lives distrusting their colleagues and feeling disliked by them may lie in the nature of the travesti project itself. Perhaps travestis do not spend much time attempting to forge deep and lasting ties with one another because travesti culture is in many ways an individualistic youth culture, generated through the practices of individuals who either are young or want to remain young. It is a culture enacted and perpetuated by individuals whose major preoccupation is not their social lives, but rather their own appearance. It is a culture in which dazzling beauty counts for more than dazzling social skills, and in which number of boyfriends and clients and sexual conquests in the form of *vícios* is more highly valued than number of friends. It is a culture that centers on attraction, sex appeal, and femininity. And it is, most importantly, a culture in which all those qualities are practical accomplishments—the products of conscious effort and intense physical manipulation, often beginning early in life and continuing as long as a travesti lives.

Two

Becoming a Travesti

Tá vendo, a dor da beleza? You see the pain beauty requires?
—Xuxa to me, as I sit witnessing a travesti having a liter of
industrial silicone injected into her lower body

The scene: Tânia's room, a three-by-four-meter windowless box decorated in an eclectic combination of glossy photographs ripped from the pages of both homosexual and heterosexual pornographic magazines, and cartoon paintings of pink and blue baby elephants swinging on swings and splashing on the beach. The only source of light is a single, bare, sixty-watt lightbulb suspended from the ceiling on a wire. Against the far wall, taking up most of the space in the room, stands a big queen-size, four-poster bed that Tânia sleeps on (and works on). And stretched out on her stomach on this bed, smoking a cigarette and naked except for a pair of panty hose tied around her waist, is Tina, a twenty-seven-year-old travesti.

At the moment, Tina has four needles sticking out of her left buttock. For the past two and a half hours, she has been getting "pumped" (*bombada*) full of silicone by a travesti visiting from the northern city of Recife. Now, at almost 2:30 in the morning, Tina's inner thighs, outer thighs, hips, and right buttock are finished, and the large holes left from the thick needles have been sealed with dabs of superglue and covered with tiny cotton balls. All that remains to be done is the left buttock. The liter of industrial silicone that Tina had brought with her is almost empty, and Keila is sitting on a chair beside the bed sucking the remaining silicone up into syringes and handing them to Carlinhos, the *bombadeira* (literally, the "pumper"). Carlinhos takes a syringe from Keila, double-checks to see that there is no air in it, screws it into one of the needles extruding from Tina's buttock, and, sweating slightly from the heat and from the exertion of the past few hours, bears down on the syringe—using both hands and all her strength to force the thick, clear plastic down through the needle and deep into Tina's flesh.

As one syringe empties itself into Tina's buttock and Carlinhos reaches out to take another one, Keila wonders how Tina is doing:

Keila: Tá doendo muito nesse lado não, né?

Tina: Não.

Keila: É porque ela botou dois.

Tina: Mas o outro minha filha, Ave Maria. Da outra vez que eu for bombar, eu vou comprar mais né/pra botar mais né?

Keila: Não bicha. Dois frascos é suficiente.

Tina: Quêm?

Keila: Os dois frascos é suficiente.

Tina: Os dois frascos?

Keila: É. Os dois frascos de Xylocaina que você comprou. Você não pode botar anestesia demais, que endurece muito a carne. Muito mesmo.

Tina: É depois/depois é capaz de dar problema, né?

Keila: É. ⌜porque a carne fica dura
       ⌈e . . . ⌊
Tina: ⌊   ⌊É
       ⌊e dá problema.

Keila: Tem gente que não tem/

Tina: Aí doeu um pouquinho só.

Keila: É porque já/

Tina: Falta quantas seringas?

Keila: Umas três.

Tina: Uma, né?

Keila: Acho que umas três.

Tina: Aí mulher, um pouquinho só. Dá três ainda? Ave Maria. É porque é grosso, né?

Keila: Um pouquinho/um pouquinho dá para encher essa seringa. Quer ver como ainda vai ficar duas?

K: It's not hurting much on this side, is it?

T: No.

K: That's because she [Carlinhos] injected two [cc's of anesthetic].

T: But the other side, girl [lit., my daughter], Ave Maria. Next time I get pumped, I'm gonna buy more [anesthetic] you know/to be able to inject more, you know?

K: No, bicha. Two bottles are sufficient.

T: What?

K: The two bottles are sufficient.

T: The two bottles?

K: Yeah. The two bottles of Xylocaina [novocaine] that you bought. You can't inject too much anesthesia, because the flesh will get really hard. Really hard.

T: And then/then it might cause problems, right?

K: Yeah ⌜because the flesh gets hard
      ⌈and . . . ⌊
T: ⌊   ⌊Yeah
      ⌊and causes problems.

K: There are people who don't have/

T: That just hurt a little bit [when Carlinhos began injecting another syringe].

K: That's because already/

T: How many syringes are left [to be injected]?

K: About three.

T: One, ah?

K: I think about three.

T: But woman, there's just a little bit [of silicone left in the bottle]. That's enough for three [syringes]? Ave Maria. It's because [the silicone] is thick, right?

K: Just a little/a little is enough to fill up this syringe. You wanna see how there will still be enough for two more?

Tina: É babado, viu? Ser mulher
é tanta coisa. É güentar um pouquinho de dor.

T: It's amazing, isn't it? It's hard to be
a woman. It means being able to
stand a little pain.

The liter of silicone that Tina had injected into her hips, thighs, and buttocks on this night was not her first—she was not lying on Tânia's bed with what travestis called a *corpo virgem*, a virgin body. Before she arrived to be injected that evening, Tina already had two and a half liters of silicone in her lower body. And when I met her again, a few days after this session—as she was standing on the street in front of her room, ostentatiously jiggling her newly augmented bottom to the rapid beat of a *pagode* tune playing loudly on somebody's radio—Tina told me that as soon as she had the money, she was going to inject two more.

The injection of industrial silicone into her body is one of the final steps that an individual takes in her transformation into travesti. It is the most dramatic step and also the most irrevocable one. Although some people maintain that it is possible to remove at least some of the silicone (the travesti Fernanda Farias de Albuquerque, for example, writes that silicone can be removed if a doctor uses "extremely sophisticated instruments" and "opens, delicately, muscle upon muscle, to separate the silicone from the tissue" [Albuquerque and Janelli 1995 : 150]; and travestis themselves use a method known as *drenagem* [drainage], which consists basically of an incision made into the body and a piece of bandage stuffed in and left hanging out so that blood and silicone can drip out), silicone injected directly into the body bonds with internal tissue, making it virtually impossible to ever extract. Thus, when a travesti makes the decision to undergo *uma aplicação de silicone* (a silicone application), she is taking a step that affects her for the rest of her life.

The experiences and the thoughts that lead travestis to take that step begin in a childhood recalled as a period of erotic play with other boys and attraction to other males, always culminating in a series of sexual experiences in which the young travesti is anally penetrated by playmates or by older boys or men. Once this happens, boys who become travestis begin to experiment with female clothing in an increasingly open manner, and they begin modifying their bodies, in various ways, in a more feminine direction. As these modifications become more apparent, these boys either leave or are expelled from their family homes. Away from home, they are freer to fully explore what they experience as their feminine nature. They meet older and more experienced travestis, and perhaps lovers and clients, who offer them advice about how to enhance and perfect themselves as feminine. They thus begin ingesting great quantities of female hormones and living full-time in female clothing and accessories. By the time they end up like Tina, laid out on a bed before a silicone "pumper," they have been living as travestis for several years, and they have saved up the money necessary to permanently acquire the physical features that they define as hallmarks of femininity—features they desire to make them attractive in the eyes of the men that they depend on to make them feel like "total women."

Early Memories

> I was the cow. Genir, the bull; Ivanildo, the bull-calf. Shorts and tank top stripped off in a hurry inside the woods. Far away from everybody, it was a secret. Genir mooed and ran after me. A game of jostling, pulling, and panting. He mounted the cow from behind, possessed by a demon on top of me. Moving, a little animal mounting the leg of its master. Little boy's penis and rubbing. Ivanildo, the bull-calf, clumsy little cousin, always sticking his nose into the chaos of entangled bodies. Dampened and sucked below my stomach. Oh! Ivanildo, look for the teat! My little teat. Swallowed, mutilated. Tickles and a shiver of happiness. With Genir wet and spent and out of breath, the game had finished. And me, exhausted. But Ivanildo always started again. Look, there's the sheep and the ram, the tomcat and the pussycat. One Sunday, Uncle João appeared out of nowhere and discovered us. He gave us a thrashing, then he told [my mother] everything.

This description of erotic play between young boys appears on the second page of Fernanda Farias de Albuquerque's autobiographical account *A Princesa* (Princess; Albuquerque and Janelli 1995). It is preceded by a short mise-en-scène in which the narrator informs us of her family background: she was the youngest of four children, but her siblings were all much older; they married and moved away by the time she was six, which meant that Fernanda (at the time, Fernando) grew up in a house alone with her widowed mother. After that brief introduction comes the passage just quoted, which is the first indication we are given of the identity of the narrator, who we know from the book's subtitle is a travesti. That identity, we are led to infer on page 2 already, is intimately bound up with attraction to other males.

Only five pages later, same-sex erotics makes another appearance. Little Fernando, now seven years old, is hiding on the street outside his house, calling out to grown men passing by. He wants them to show him their penis. After several unknown men hurry by, unable to discover who is calling out to them, Fernando sees Seu (i.e., Mr.) Arlindo, a man he knows well, appearing in the distance. As Seu Arlindo walks by, Fernando calls out:

Seu Arlindo, let me see your dick! But what the devil is this you are saying? Where are you hiding, you devilish child? He came, looking in my
direction. I summoned my courage and, with a sheet on my head, I stood
up in the tall grass. It's me, little Fernando! What do you want, boy? Arlindo, let me see your dick! If your mother hears you, she'll kill you! [My
mother] isn't at home, she went away to be with [my sister] Alaide when
she has her baby. If you show me, I'll make you a chicken dinner and give
you liqueur.

Read in the light of autobiographical accounts of male-to-female
transgendered individuals who write about their childhood in the United
States or Europe, passages like these are striking. No North American or
European memoirs of transgenderism mention early erotic interest in
members of the same sex as a motivating force in the perception of oneself as transgendered. Quite the opposite; that erotic feelings for males
might be a motivating force for wanting a sex change is consistently and
explicitly denied. Transsexualism is about gender, we are reminded time
and again in those accounts, not about sexuality.[1]

What is therefore particularly noticeable (and, I believe, particularly
Brazilian) about Albuquerque's remembrances of her childhood is that
they foreground sex. In recounting the games she used to play in the
woods and her attempt to get grown men to show her their penis, Albuquerque makes it very clear that erotic interest in males was not a
peripheral or subsidiary dimension of her self-understanding as a travesti—it was an early and central one. Her narrative does segue into
brief descriptions of early identification with female roles, and she tells
us, for example, that when little Fernando's mother told him that babies
arrive in an airplane from God, he lay on a bed and pretended to be a
mother waiting for the plane to arrive. When his widow neighbor told
him stories about princes and their brides, Fernando refused to play the
role of the prince: he wanted to marry a prince, he told the neighbor,
not be one. Albuquerque also mentions that she was identified early on
as o veadinho, the little faggot, and teased by playmates, including the
boys who played with him/her (gender becomes problematic here) in
the woods. But what is most significant is that all these memories of being feminine are bound up with—indeed, they are narratively *preceded
by*—erotic interest in other males.

This is precisely what I found to be the case among the travestis
whom I asked to tell me about their childhood memories. No one I spoke
to omitted erotic attraction to males as the single most significant factor
in their self-discovery as travestis. On the contrary—although virtually
every travesti to whom I posed the question "When did you first discover you were different from other boys?" told me in an almost mantric

fashion, "I liked to play with dolls" (*Eu gostava de brincar de boneca*), they immediately moved on to their attraction to, and their desire to be attractive for, other boys. Forty-one-year-old Carlinhos, the travesti who was pumping Tina full of silicone as this chapter began, told me during an interview:

Carlinhos: Mais eu sempre tive essa tendencia de fazer essas artes femininas. Tudo meu eu era feminino. Eu nunca achava uma mulher bonita. Eu só achava os homens. Passava horas sentada no muro lá de casa olhando os homens passando. Aqueles boys: "Oi Carlinhos"—faziam questão de falar comigo: "Oi."

Don: [laughs]
Carlinhos: Assim bem pintosa, né?

Keila: Lógico.
Carlinhos: Sem aquela mentalidade que a gente tem hoje, né não? Mamãe me botava pra dentro: "Menino, vem pra dentro!" Entendeu? Se eu ia pra rua tinha algum comicio, eu não ia pro comicio, porque era só, "Viado, viado, viado, 'bota agua no fogo,' pega a bicha." E eu assim-ô [jiggling her shoulders provocatively like a stereotypically vampy woman].

Don: Quando era criança?
Carlinhos: Quando era criança. Eu sentei pra mostrar que era mulher, eu remexia mais que as mulheres. Eu tinha que fazer aquele remelexo mais que as mulheres. E eles: "É, é, é, é." [Don and Keila are laughing.] Essas coisas que passavam na

C: But I've always had this tendency to do these feminine things. Everything about me was feminine. I never thought women were beautiful. I only thought that about men. I used to spend hours sitting on the wall in front of my house watching the men who passed by. And those boys [in the neighborhood would call out to me and say] "Hi Carlinhos"—they would always talk to me: "Hi!"

D: [laughs]
C: [I used to sit there] all effeminate, you know?

K: Of course.
C: Without the knowledge that I have today, you know? Mom would come and make me go inside: "Boy, come inside!" You understand? Whenever I walked around on the street when there was some big meeting in town, I never went to the meeting, because everyone would shout, "Faggot, faggot, faggot, 'put water on to boil,' grab the bicha."[2] And me [walking around] like this [jiggling her shoulders provocatively like a stereotypically vampy woman].

D: When you were a child?
C: When I was a child. I wanted to show that I was a woman, I jiggled my shoulders more than the women did. I had to do this jiggling of my shoulders more than the women. And they [the boys and men who saw me] went: "Oh,

minha mente. E hoje quando eu deito que eu vou pensar, né não?

oh, oh, oh." [Don and Keila are laughing.] These things that flew into my head. When I think back on the things I did, you know?

Note the way in which Carlinhos defines "the tendency to do feminine things" in terms of not finding women attractive and of "only [thinking] that about men." Thirty-five-year-old Banana's answer to my question about when she first realized she was different from other boys was similar to that of Carlinhos: "At eight, nine, ten years old," said Banana, "I felt an attraction, a strong attraction, to men." Nineteen-year-old Cintia also gave a typical answer:

Keila: Quando foi que você percebeu que não era menino? Que não gostava das coisas . . . de menino . . . gostava sempre das coisas de mulher?
Cintia: Ah, desde os, de criança mesmo/desde os sete anos.
Keila: Quantos anos? Sete anos?
Cintia: Desde os sete. Já gostava de coisa de menina. Brincava de boneca, brincava de . . . coisinhas de menina, só brincava cum menina . . . Não brincava com, meni/só brincava com esses dois menino . . . durante a tarde. Que de manhã eu estudava. De tarde eu brincava com eles . . . Aí pronto, era um roça-roça, um esfrega-esfrega, era um beija-beija na boca [laughs]. Pronto.

K: When did you realize that you weren't a boy? That you didn't like . . . boys' things, [and] always liked women's things?
C: Ah, since, since childhood/since I was seven years old.
K: How old? Seven years?
C: Since I was seven. Already then I liked girls' things. I played with dolls, I played with . . . girls' playthings, I only played with girls . . . I didn't play with bo/I only played with these two boys . . . in the afternoon. Because in the morning I went to school. In the afternoon I played with them . . . And there you are, it was all squeeze-squeeze, rub-rub, kiss-kiss on the mouth [laughs]. There you are.

The kind of erotic play that Cintia describes here often leads to direct sexual activity at an early age. When I asked twenty-nine-year-old Elisabeth what her first memories were of not being like other boys, she replied:

Elisabeth: Ah, eu era de criança . . . de criança mesmo, de pequeno mesmo, que eu gostava de ir com os meninos, né? Né, ir brincar com os meninos.
Don: Mas brincar como?

E: Ah, I was a child . . . just a child, really little, that I liked to go with the boys, you know? You know, go and play with the boys.

D: But play in what way?

Elisabeth: Ah, brincar, pode falar? [laughs] Ah, gostava, gostava de fazer sexo com os meninos, né, brincar de trocar com os meninos, de/entendeu?

Don: É?

Elisabeth: É, eu adorava, era meu hobbie preferido [laughs]. Era brincar de me esconder cum os meninos, dento dos matos, das bananeiras, né?

E: Ah, play, can I say it? [laughs] Ah, I liked, I liked to have sex with the boys, you know, play sex with the boys, to/you know?

D: Really?

E: Yeah, I adored it, it was my favorite hobby [laughs]. To play hiding with the boys, in the woods, in the banana palms, you know?

A few minutes later in the same conversation, talking about the same playmates:

Elisabeth: . . . aí eu dava pra eles, adorava dar.

Don: Dar mesmo?

Elisabeth: Claro, dar, é, dava mesmo, assim, era uma pessoa muito dada [laughs].

E: . . . and I let myself be penetrated by them, I adored being penetrated.

D: Really be penetrated?

E: Of course be penetrated, yeah, I let myself be penetrated, like, I was a very penetrated person [or "generous person"—this is a pun on the word *dada*, and Elisabeth laughs at this].

When I asked Mabel how she realized that she was different from other boys, she told me that she *tinha o jeito*—had an effeminate manner. "I used to play with dolls," she told me. "I used to play that I was the mother and the boy was the father." She also said that she remembers her father saying to her mother, "Look Mara, Cecéu [i.e., Mabel] is half 'that way,' I think he's gonna get all limp-wristed in time and become a bicha" (*Olha Mara, o Cecéu, ele é meio assim, eu acho que ele vai desmunhecar com o tempo e vai ser uma bicha*)

After this brief preamble, Mabel launched into a story about her and the boy next door:

We went to school together, we went for walks together, we did everything together, we played snooker together, we went to the beach together, we went to the movies together—all of this, nothing more, but he was always flirting with me. He knew that I would be a bicha and he wanted to be my master, you know? (*Ele sabia que ia ser bicha, que, queria o, o ser dono de mim, tá entendendo?*) It was a deep friendship, but after a while, I couldn't stand it any longer. I wanted to feel what it felt like to have a man on top of me, to see what an ejaculation was (*já me deu vontade deu sentir um homem em cima de mim, eu ver como era um gozo*), you know, an orgasm, so I went to him and said "Paulo, today I want to do it" (*Paulo, hoje eu tô querendo*). And he went "That's great, Mabel"—just like that, "That's great."

Mabel told Paulo that they couldn't go back to her house, because her family was there. Paulo said he had the same problem. So Mabel suggested that they go down to the river.

> We got there and he took hold of me, took hold of me—I had never been kissed before. He took me and hugged me. He understood and I didn't, you know? He kissed me on the mouth, he caressed me, you understand, he caressed me, he hugged me, kissed me. His little dick was hard, his prick, and I took it, I did aaaaa . . . oh, what's it called, wait let me think of it . . . a "blow job" (um boquete). I did a blow job on him [i.e., Mabel sucked Paulo's penis]. He liked it, the blow job. OK, then I turned my back to him, you know? I had sex with him . . . He/he didn't fuck me, the first time, I didn't manage that. He put a little bit in, then I started to feel pain. Later he put in more, and I/later, I dilated completely for him (delatei pra ele todo)[3] . . . and after that I was married to him for three more years.

Mabel was eleven years old when the events she describes here took place. Her "husband," Paulo, was thirteen. The story Mabel tells of this first sexual encounter recounts a kind of experience that she shares with all other travestis. Whenever travestis think back on their childhood and on the signs that they now can single out as indicating they were destined to become travestis, they always focus most directly and most elaborately on erotic attraction towards males and on the enjoyment they derived from erotic play with their male playmates. In other words, they focus explicitly and at great length on homosexual desire as a motivating force in their self-realization as travestis. This early homosexual desire is bound up with the performance of female or effeminate roles (playing with dolls, acting out the role of mother in play, being "limp-wristed"), and it is the combination of these two factors—homosexual desire and effeminate behavior—that seems to guide travestis towards their first sexual encounters, where they invariably assume the sexual role of the one who is penetrated.

The male who first penetrates a travesti is sometimes, as in the cases of Mabel and Elisabeth (who says she was already practicing her "favorite hobby" at age seven), a peer playmate or a slightly older friend or acquaintance. Often, however, the male who first penetrates the travesti is markedly older—he is already um homem mesmo, "a real man." Fernanda Farias de Albuquerque recounts that the first man to attempt to penetrate her, when she was seven, was Seu Arlindo, the man who accepted her invitation to show her his penis for a chicken dinner and liqueur. Seu Arlindo was thirty years old. He did not succeed in penetrating little Fernando, and with the boy "immobilized on the double bed . . . [b]etween his knees, smaller than a bird . . . crying," Seu Arlindo "had a bit of grey matter [in his head, and] didn't force the entrance" (Albuquerque and

Janelli 1995:31–32). A few months later, however, Fernando, now eight years old, followed Paulo, a sixteen-year-old youth he knew, down to the river. Paulo asks him:

> Little Fernando, is it true that you're a viado? Viado. That word again, venomous like coral, like a snake in the desert. It resounded wherever I went. I didn't get angry, I didn't respond.
>
> He approached me, I knew what was about to happen. I didn't run away. I managed to speak in a little thread of a voice, a tiny voice: let me alone, I don't want to! For me it was still a game, me the cow. He did it with force and penetrated me. It was the first time. Stomach and head contorted in torture. He became furious with my pain. I saw the water rapidly become tinted red. I became white with fear. I vomited and cried with pain, with remorse. [I remembered the words my mother said:] "If you do devilish things, you'll end up in prison or in Hell." A fever rose up in me suddenly, seized me. I was shaking with fear, with shame. What did you do to me? Paulo grew pale as well. But you wanted to, he said. It was true. I wanted to. It hurt but I wanted to. Simply and unacceptably, that is my memory. It happened like that.

Compare this memory to Keila's account of the first time she was penetrated by a male:

> I was already eleven and a half years old, almost twelve, I was/I/every day, early in the morning, I went to buy milk for my mother, and I went down a street where a guy lived who was a soccer player, I don't know if he still is today. My town had a soccer team that was really good called Atlético, and he played. Silva was his name, José Silva. He was an athlete, twenty-six years old, he had a strong body, his legs really muscular. And he was a public servant. He worked at the post office.
>
> But I saw him as a handsome man. I didn't have any attraction for him because he was a man. I never, I never dreamed he would try anything outrageous with me, even if he knew that I was a little homosexual, a bicha, whatever. And there was a curiosity because everybody in town knew and talked about how his father, that man, could tie a big bottle of beer to his penis and lift the bottle up full of beer. This was something everyone in town talked about. And if everyone talked about it there must have been some shred of truth to it. I don't know for what reason, but I was curious about this man, because I thought that if his father does that, then the son ought to have the same thing. But I never approached him, since I was a very shy person . . . But I always passed by down the street where he lived.
>
> And from one day to the next he began to look at me in a different way. I would walk past and he would greet me, when I went and when I came back, because when I went by to buy milk he was already awake, since he worked early in the morning at the post office.

And he: "Hi Carlinho [Keila's male name], everything fine?" Me:
"Everything's fine." I would go past. When I returned: "Hi, *tudo bom?*" Me:
"*Tudo bem.*" One day, I walked past in the late afternoon, and he did like:
    "Carlinho, come here."
    I went, "What?"
    "I have some magazines here in my room, you wanna see them? You
like comic books?"
    I said, "Yeah."
    And he: "Well come in then so I can show them to you."
    He was only dressed in a towel, he called me and I went inside his
room—his mother was in the kitchen. I went in, he threw the comic books
on the bed and I started looking at them. All of a sudden, he takes off the
towel and is going to put on his clothes. But he didn't take off the towel to
get dressed, he took it off for me to see what/him naked. And I was pretty
curious, I was reading the comic books and when he got naked I sat, looking at that big thing, half paralyzed. Look, I had never seen a man totally
naked before. I'd seen boys naked . . . but I'd never seen a man naked.
    I became panic-stricken with a man of that size in front of me, hand-
some, because he was a really handsome man and is still today I'm sure if
he hasn't lost/if he hasn't died. And I became paralyzed. And him too, he
let me look. I noticed that his penis was really . . . developed. It wasn't
hard, it was soft, but it was enough to know that—I already had an understanding that if that penis got hard, it would be a phenomenal thing,
enormous.
    OK, I stopped looking at his body and started to page through the
comic books. But I was nervous, I couldn't stand it anymore, I wasn't calm
anymore, I wasn't seeing the comic books I was reading anymore, I was
seeing him in the comic books. And he noticed that I was nervous. But his
mother came and called out to him, "José, come here." He: "Wait here, I'll
be back." But when he went to his mother, I ran out.

A few days later, when Keila passed by José's house as usual, he told
her to come to the post office where he worked "'cause I want to talk to
you." Keila went, and she saw him at the window of the post office mo-
tioning for her to come in, but she didn't:

> I felt a strong attraction, but I also felt afraid. I was really attracted, I
> wanted that man, because he was handsome, because I had seen/the first
> man in my life that I had seen naked and I wanted him. But deep down, I
> was scared—of gossip, I was scared of him, as a man, and all those things.
> I was thinking and thinking—imagine, a child not even twelve years old,
> discovering the tendency that he will have—what to do? I was disturbed
> for a while.
>   But one fine day, I'm going past, he's in his doorway. He said, "And
> you've already read my comic books?"

I said, "Yeah."

"You wanna read some more? I have some more."

I felt like I couldn't breathe. I thought: Now I'm gonna do it, and I said, "Is Dona Clarice [José's mother] at home?"

He said, "She's in the kitchen, but come in and I'll lock the door."

I said, "No, you don't have to lock the door, leave the door open."

When I got in he was just wearing shorts, and I saw that he wasn't like he had been in the towel, his penis started to get hard inside his shorts. And he was looking at me, and it seemed like he was looking at me with an intensity that grew stronger every minute. After a couple of minutes, I saw that the head was coming out the top of the shorts.

It was on top. I got/I got nervous. He grabbed me, when he grabbed me he took my head and put it here on top. On top of the shorts. And he went, "Open your mouth and put it in your mouth."

He pulled down his shorts. When he pulled down his shorts I opened my mouth, but my mouth wasn't big enough for that thing. It was a thing more or less like this, this size [twelve inches], and thick, really thick. And I was/my mouth could get in this much of his penis, but then no more, not at all, it wouldn't fit. And he wanted to force it, to fill up my mouth with that hard thing. I couldn't cope, I couldn't breathe. And he yanked off my shorts, I was only wearing shorts, I wasn't wearing a shirt, and he rubbed I think it was some kind of cream he had, and he tried to penetrate me. But all at once. When he tried to put it in I let out a huge scream: Uai!!!! And his mother heard this in the kitchen. He stayed there, trying to cover my mouth with his hand, but it didn't work because I had already screamed, and I ran out . . . I jumped out of the window and ran, ran down the street.

I got to my house despairing, screaming. My mother ran up to me to see what was wrong. I locked myself in the bathroom, my mother asking, "What happened?" Me: "Nothing nothing nothing." When I looked everything was bloody, blood was running down my legs. I was trying to wipe it off and I couldn't stop it. I think he tore some part, tore something and I saw so much/I was panicking because I saw so much blood and I didn't know where it was coming from. I thought that a piece of glass had gotten into me because it was burning, it seemed like something was cut, and I thought that just to be mean, maybe he had something sharp on the end of his penis and that when it entered me it was left inside. I was in a panic for about fifteen minutes inside the bathroom, with the door locked and my mother banging on it from the outside. Me: "No, it's nothing, no."

I calmed down a bit and said, "It's nothing. I'm here cause I have to . . ." And I stayed in the bathroom. I stayed for a long time throwing water on it, and the more water I threw on it the more blood came out. I tried to stand up and open up my butt to see if something was cut open. And a lot more blood ran out. I stayed inside even longer, pressing on the place it was bleeding from, not feeling pain, but feeling a burning sensation. I inserted my finger to see if there was anything inside, didn't see anything, I just felt this burning, and I realized it wasn't some thing that cut me.

I started to regain control and finally the blood stopped. I took advantage of that, took a shower and left the bathroom. My mother asked, "What happened Carlinho?" I went, "Nothing. I had a really bad pain in my stomach and went to the bathroom, that's why I arrived crying."

I went to my room and took a mirror and saw the thing—I could see that it was as if there was a little cut, there was a cut that I opened up with my hand and saw. I put some Mercurochrome on it for a couple of days and in a week it was fine.

And what did I do then? I went back and wanted to do it again!

I did. I said, "Listen, I'm gonna do it with you, what you want, we'll do it, on the bed, but calmly. If it doesn't work, don't force it, because I've never done this, it's the first time."

I think that this made him even a lot more anxious. But he had such a need, he wanted to so much that he didn't succeed, it wouldn't enter, it was like there was something blocking it. It wouldn't go in and it would start to hurt. I don't know how much would go in today—a whole arm probably. But before only a little bit would go in and no more. Because he tried to force it, I felt pain and it didn't work. So I would say, "It's not working," and he pulled it out and rubbed it against my butt and ejaculated on my back.

This went on for a month—him doing those things, like that, two times, three times, once a week, when after two months, he succeeded in penetrating me. Almost all. Even then not all of it entered, four inches or so were still not in because they wouldn't go in. He tried to force it and force it, but it didn't work. Also, a little while later, he left town . . .

But that was my first experience. I still remember it today, I never forgot it, the first time with him. But it was really horrible the first time, really painful. It was tremendously painful.

Among the many similarities between Keila's remembrance of her experiences with José Silva and Fernanda Farias de Albuquerque's recollections of her encounters with Seu Arlindo and later with Paulo is that, despite the fact that their first experience of penetrative sex was painful and in many ways quite terrifying, both boys sought out similar experiences soon afterwards. A few months after having almost been raped by Seu Arlindo, Fernanda followed Paulo down to the river, knowing "what was about to happen." Similarly, a week after Keila had fled bleeding and screaming from José Silva's house, she was back again, saying, "Listen, I'm gonna do it with you."

Two further details about these stories are noteworthy. First, in neither account is there any indication that the sexual roles assumed by Paulo and Fernanda and by José and Keila were the outcome of discussion or negotiation. After asking little Fernando if it was true that he was a viado, Paulo approaches the boy in the river and penetrates him without further ado. José attempts the same with Carlinhos (Keila), who has willingly entered his room. In both cases, the sexual roles played are assumed, predetermined.

The second significant detail is that in both cases it is made abundantly clear that the males who penetrated the boys—roughly, with no sexual foreplay or preparation—exhibited no interest whatsoever in the sexual satisfaction of those boys. Furthermore, neither Fernanda nor Keila makes any mention of her own sexual satisfaction. When Fernanda affirms Paulo's claim that she "wanted to" by asserting "It was true. I wanted to," she is clearly referring to the act of penetration itself, not the attainment of orgasm. And since Keila kept returning to José Silva during the course of their several-months-long sexual relationship, I assumed that she did so because José satisfied her sexually. But no. Throughout their relationship, José never kissed Keila or touched her penis, and she never experienced orgasm while he was penetrating her ("I had my first orgasm when I was fifteen [i.e., three years later], always by masturbating," she told me). This absence of orgasm during sex with lovers is a recurring feature of travesti relationships with men. No account of early sexual experiences that I have collected or read makes any mention of the travesti ejaculating. Mabel's narrative of her encounter with her Paulo at the river, for example, is typical here in that, although it is appreciably more romantic and tender than the experiences described by Fernanda and Keila, it focuses on the actions performed by Mabel to satisfy Paulo, and it makes no mention of whether Mabel experienced orgasm (I later asked her—she didn't). This absence of orgasmic experiences with men whom travestis consider to be their lovers is something that continues throughout their lives and that eventually comes to constitute one of the most important lines of division between boyfriends (with whom travestis generally *do not* experience orgasm) and clients (with whom they often do). I will have a great deal more to say about this division in the chapters that follow. For now, it is enough to be alerted to the fact that the pleasure travestis derive from being anally penetrated is not directly and immediately sexual. The joy of anal penetration, for them, springs from other sources.

After hearing Keila's narrative of her encounter with José Silva, I felt compelled to ask her, coming as I do from a culture where children as young as Keila (not to mention Fernanda, who was seven to eight years old at the time of the encounters she describes) are widely considered to not yet have a sexuality—and certainly not a *homo*sexuality—if her experience with José wasn't traumatic. "Well," she told me, it was a disaster the first time, that's for sure, there's no doubt about that. But what happened is that the curiosity became even greater. Because this was something that I wanted, I went looking for it and I found it and it hurt me and I could have never wanted to do it again. But just so you see how it is an unconstrained desire that you have inside: [The first time] made me want to not do it again. But the desire was much greater than the fear (*me deu vontade de não fazer. Mas o desejo foi muito maior, que a vontade*).

Keila went on to say that after her experience with José, she did feel "a little restrained (*reprimida*), a little depressed (*depressivo*), because I was thinking what people would think of me.⁴ I was traumatized in that sense, about what people would say."

Keila had good reason to be worried about what people would say. In small, rural towns like the one in which she grew up, the stigma of being a viado, a faggot, weighs heavily on anyone classified in that way. Unending verbal abuse, as well as the physical humiliation of having people throw stones and rotten fruit whenever one walks past on the street, is the price that individuals in small towns are likely to pay for being known to be a viado. Sometimes the penalty used to be (and in some places probably still is) death. Angélica, at nearly sixty years of age the oldest travesti in Salvador, told me that when it became known that she had, at age thirteen, *deu seu cu* (given her ass) to a neighborhood adolescent, her brothers, concerned about the reputation of the family, took up arms and went looking for her to murder her. "Even my mother was against me: 'Kill the son of a bitch'" (*Mata esse desgraçado*). Angélica escaped only because a caring neighbor hid her in her house and told her to run away at daybreak, when she knew the brothers were all at home sleeping.

Nothing so horrendous happened to Keila. Her relationship with José Silva never reached public attention, and even when, about a year later, she began hanging out with three other young viados in town and wearing increasingly androgynous styles of clothing at night on the street, she was never physically attacked or threatened with death. Her local reputation as a viado did result in some verbal harassment and rumors that contributed to her eventual decision to leave town and seek her fortune in larger cities. But it also resulted in a deluge of requests, by males of all ages, for sex—requests to which Keila usually acceded.

Leaving Home

Keila's trajectory more or less mirrors that of all other travestis I know in Salvador. The crucial turning point for Keila in her self-awareness as a travesti ("Imagine, a child not even twelve years old, discovering the tendency that he will have") was being attracted to a male. And that attraction led inexorably to her being anally penetrated. Once this happened, Keila, like the majority of other travestis in Salvador, began to come out (se assumir) as a viado. She attached herself to the male who first penetrated her, as often happens, and she began having a great deal of sex with males, *always* as the one who is penetrated. Like other young travestis on the verge of puberty, Keila at this point chose a female name for herself, and she began gradually modifying her clothing styles and appearance in a more feminine direction. Young travestis will wear—often only at night, away from home and in the company of their bicha friends—*shortinho curto* (tiny shorts pulled up so that the bottom of the buttocks visibly protrudes) and baggy shirts that they tie in a knot above the navel. They will also try to let their hair and nails grow out, they will begin to experiment with lipstick and cosmetics, and they may begin to pluck their eyebrows and shave their legs.

This is the stage at which a great many travestis either leave or are expelled from home. Some travestis decide to leave home on their own. Keila, for example, left at age thirteen, because she felt that if she stayed, her "homosexual tendency . . . would shame my father and mother" (*Eu tava tendo uma tendência homosexual, que eu tinha certeza que, na época, ia envergonhar meu pai e minha mãe*). Mabel left home at fourteen because her older brother harassed her when he discovered that she was having sex with Paulo. "Suddenly he called me names, mistreated me, hit me, beat me . . . he even took me to a bordello, took me to a red-light zone, so that I could have relations with a woman." Magdala left home because after her first sexual experience with an older boy, at age twelve, she "began to get to know other bichas. And I began to change my way of dressing, my way of speaking." Her father would not tolerate this, and so, when she was sixteen, she made the decision to move out.

Many other travestis to whom I spoke, however, did not decide to leave home. They had no choice. Once their families became aware of their homosexuality, they were expelled violently. Old Angélica is to this day convinced that she would have been murdered by her brothers if she hadn't fled. Another travesti, twenty-year-old Adriana, is the only travesti I know who was clearly abused as a child. Her mother was a prostitute, and Adriana, together with her younger sister, was raised on the streets of Recife. From as far back as she can remember, Adriana was sent out to beg. And if she returned to her mother empty-handed, "there was the stick. It beat us bloody." One of the most common means for Adriana to receive money was by performing sexual services for men. As she grew up, Adriana began wearing feminine clothes and experimenting with makeup. She did this far away from her mother, because her mother, although she must have known how Adriana was earning the money she brought home every day, would not tolerate any hint of homosexuality. Adriana says that once when her mother caught her and her cousin rubbing their penises together, she "grabbed us and beat us horribly" (*Mamãe pegou e deu um pau horrores na gente*). When Adriana finally "came out" as a travesti at age twelve, "I was thrown out. *Ave Maria*, that was one of the saddest moments in my life," she told me, crying. "This is one of the greatest remorses I have because I was put out, thrown out, with just a plastic supermarket bag with my clothes."

When I asked Tina whether she remembered when she began to notice that she was different from other boys, she answered, "Of course I remember. Do you know what I did? I told my mother and my father. And they took me and threw me out of the house. I said, 'I'm not going to leave this house. I'm staying in this house.' And you know what he [Tina's father] did? One Friday? [laughs] Got a moving van and brought it to the house, took everything out, and left me and the house. Took the furniture and everything."

This story seemed so fantastic that I didn't believe it the first time I heard it, but other travestis told me that they did believe it. Tina was a notorious liar, they all agreed, but she had told this particular story in the same manner so many times that it had to be true. The story ends with Tina shaving her eyebrows, getting hold of a radio, and turning the house into a bordello, until her father returned a few days later and took her to FEBEM (Fundação Estadual do Bem Estar do Menor), a kind of state reform school that everyone agrees is like an abusive prison. At the gates of FEBEM, Tina says, she gave her father a big push and ran away into the streets of Recife.

At the time this happened, Tina was twelve years old.

Hormones

Gone from their homes and in need of money to support themselves, travestis now enter the next phase of their transformation. This is when they begin to "fulfill themselves" (*se realizar*) as travestis by letting their hair grow, wearing increasingly feminine clothing (at least at night), and beginning to engage in other female bodily practices, such as shaving their legs, plucking their eyebrows, and tweezering the hair from their upper lips and chins.[5] Travestis who have not already begun to do so will now also start to modify their bodies through the ingestion of female hormones. And travestis who had not already begun surreptitiously prostituting themselves while they were still living at home learn that they can do so and earn money.

Exactly what a travesti does when she leaves home seems to depend a great deal on where she goes. If she goes to a small town, she will get a job—almost always, it seems, as a domestic servant. She will work at this job during the day, dressed in male clothing and called by her male name. At night, however, she will dress in much more androgynous or feminine clothing, and she will go to the square in the town where groups of bichas congregate to socialize. (To judge from the accounts of the travestis I have spoken to, all Brazilian towns of any size seem to contain such a square and such people to populate it.) She will quickly become part of this group of bichas; she will hang out with them, be called by a female name by them, and learn from them. If it is possible to earn money as a travesti prostitute in the town, she will eventually discover this—often by unexpectedly being given money after sex—and she will occasionally attempt to earn money in this way. But even today, in small towns it is virtually impossible to earn a living as a travesti prostitute. Hence, even if a young travesti living in such a town does now and then earn some money selling sex, she will remain dependent on her day job for the bulk of her income. On the other hand, a young travesti who lives in, or leaves home to travel to, a large city such as Recife or Salvador is much more likely to "fall into the life" of a prostitute—*cair na vida*, as travestis say—almost immediately.

In either case, the period when a travesti leaves home is marked by a progression away from the masculine attributes of her childhood and towards more feminine attributes. It is at this point that many travestis understand they can modify their bodies to become more feminine.

The most common source of information about body modification is older travestis. Banana's experience is typical:

When I was thirteen years old and already working, I saw my first travesti. I was working in the evening. I remember it like it was today. I saw a bicha, a chest out to here. She was pretty . . . more or less. And I asked. I was always an inquisitive person, you know, I asked a friend of mine—what is that? Because I saw the breasts, but it didn't look like a woman. You understand? It was really something, that chest. And so I asked. And the guy said, "It's a viado."

"Viado?"

And one day, I went down and talked to her

[She asked me] "What do you want?"

"Why are your breasts like that?"

And she said, "It's hormones, I take hormones."

"What are hormones? What are they?"

And she said, "It's a medicine to avoid pregnancy" (*É remédio de evitar filho*).

Uh-huh. I thought about that and I said, "I'm gonna be a travesti like her. Just like that one, I'm gonna be a travesti."

Magdala recounts something similar:

When we see a travesti for the first time, what an impact! When I saw one for the first time, I didn't believe it. I was walking with my sister across the town square, and there were three. There was a blonde with blonde hair down to here, and there were two more. I thought she was a woman, but she had a kind of strange way (*um jeito estranho*), it was like outrageous—you know, strange. But days later . . . I'm sitting alone in the square, on the first day I left/I decided to leave home. I sat down in the square, the Praça da Bandeira, and a travesti passed by me. I looked and said, "Oh, what a beautiful woman." But a strange beautiful woman. I perceived something more in her. She was a woman, but she had something different, that didn't fit.

This travesti presumably sensed Magdala's fascination with her, because she came and sat down next to her, and the two quickly became friends. She gave Magdala her first female name, Kelliane, and showed Magdala a bar where travestis, homosexuals, and men who were attracted to them gathered. She also told Magdala about hormones.

Older and more experienced travestis encourage young travestis to take hormones, because they know that the younger they begin, the more effect the hormones will have. Adriana, for example, who began taking hormones at age twelve, never developed beard growth. A travesti who is almost legendary in this respect is Chispita, who grew up in a house in which most of the tenants were travestis. She began injecting hormones at age eight. Travestis who knew Chispita (she was run over by a car and killed at age thirteen) always say, impressed, "There was nothing boyish about her, she was a real girl (*era menina mesmo*)."

I witnessed the kind of encouragement that young travestis receive from older ones when an eleven-year-old boy wearing androgynous clothing and white nail polish suddenly appeared on the streets where travestis worked and began prostituting himself. This boy told the travestis that his name was Babalu (after a sexy female lead in a *novela* showing on television at the time).[6] When they asked him if he was a travesti, his reply was "I'm beginning" (*Tou começando*). No one questioned or challenged this choice. Instead, the travestis were supportive and showered Babalu with advice ("Are you still living at home? Move out") and tips on how to become more attractive for men ("Bicha, you should take hormones. You're really young. Hormones would really do wonders" [*fazer muito efeito*]).

Aside from older travestis, the ones who encourage young travestis to start modifying their bodies through hormone ingestion are males who have sex with them. Adriana received her first boxes of hormones at age twelve from a pharmacist who, she said somewhat demurely, "liked me."

Chispita at age twelve. (From Keila Simpsom's private collection.)

Martinha, a forty-year-old travesti who grew up in the old red-light district in Salvador and who began prostituting herself without the knowledge of her family when she was nine, told me that she discovered hormones at age fifteen from one of her clients, who was a doctor. The doctor told her that she could grow breasts by injecting hormones, and he himself gave her her first few injections. This occurred in her mid-1970s, when hormones were still quite new in Brazil.

Hormones constitute something of a dividing line between "true" travestis (*travesti mesmo*) and what travestis and others call *transformistas*—a word that literally means "transformers." Transformistas are homosexual males who live their lives during the day dressed in male clothing, answering to a male name, and acting in a male fashion. At night, however, they sometimes don wigs, dresses, and makeup, either to visit gay clubs and perhaps perform there—miming to the music of Whitney Houston or one of the several gravel-voiced Italian female singers who are popular in gay circles in Salvador—and/or to prostitute themselves. Although some travestis maintain cordial relationships with individual transformistas, there is a general feeling among travestis that transformistas look down on them and regard them as vulgar.[7] For their part, travestis are suspicious and distrustful of transformistas, whom they regard as frauds—both when they are in female drag (because they are not women or travestis) and when they are dressed as males during the day (because they are not men either, travestis reason, in a logic that will become increasingly apparent in later chapters). In defining the difference between travestis and transformistas, travestis point to the fact that they live in female dress twenty-four hours a day. In addition, they modify their bodies—at the very least through the consumption of hormones, which produce visible breasts that are not easily concealed should one wish to appear masculine.

The hormones that travestis take are either medications designed to combat estrogen deficiency (e.g., Benzoginoestril) or they are, as the travesti whom Banana spoke to in the town square told her, contraceptive preparations (such as Perlutan). All these preparations contain estrogens and other hormones that either "reproduce the characteristics of the natural estrogen cycle" or, if they are contraceptives, "suppress the secretion of hypophyseal gonadotropins . . . modify the cervical mucus, the endometrium, and the tubal motility . . . and . . . permit the evolution of a cyclical and predictable endometrial menorrhea, resembling normal menstruation."[8]

These hormones come both in tablet form and in ampoules that are injected into the body using the syringe that comes provided in the box. The tablets, such as Anacyclin, are oral contraceptives designed to be taken once a day. Travestis commonly take as many as five a day. The hormonal products meant to be injected are all extremely powerful and are supposed to be taken by women once a month. Travestis inject them *once a day.* For example, in 1995 Balão was on a hormone regime that consisted of the injection of a month's worth of hormones into her buttocks every day for fourteen days. Then she stopped for fourteen days, commencing again at the end of that period. She continued in this way for many months, until her breasts were acceptably larger and her hips and face noticeably rounder. Other travestis inject a month's supply of hormones into their buttocks every other day for years. One travesti (who had stopped taking hormones several years previously because, she said, the only effect they had on her was to make her fat) told me that many travestis, when they begin taking hormones, buy oral contraceptives to take over the course of fifteen days but end up taking all fifteen pills at once, thinking that they will wake up in the morning with breasts the size of watermelons. What they in fact wake up with is a body racked by hellish pains and uncontrollable spasms of vomiting.

There are at least twenty different hormone products on the market in Brazil, and travestis have tried them all. The packages in which the preparations are sold all state, in big white letters against an orange background, "Sold under medical prescription," and the accompanying instructions contain the warning, usually in bold print, that the product should be used "only under medical supervision." But in practice, these products are available over the counter at any pharmacy, and a month's supply can be purchased for the equivalent of less than five dollars.[9]

Travestis value hormones because they are inexpensive, easy to obtain, and fast working. Most hormones produce visible results, in the form of enlarged breasts and noticeably rounder bodily features, after only about two months of daily ingestion. In some individuals, they also produce a white fluid in the breasts that some travestis will use to gain access to the cars of clients who are looking for women. Tina, who was famous among travestis for her daring assaults on clients, used this fluid to this effect. "Yes, I'm a woman, I have three children and I'm nursing a newborn baby. Wanna see?" Tina would say, and spray the client who had wondered with the fluid in her breasts, usually to his rapture. Once in the car, she pulled her little scissors out from her panties and demanded money.

A problem with the hormones, however, is that they can, especially after intensive and/or prolonged consumption, result in serious side effects. The instructions accompanying Perlutan, for example, one of the most popular products among travestis, list as possible side effects "chronic headaches, nausea, vomiting, tension in the breasts, intermenstrual hemorrhaging, dysmenorrhea, amenorrhea, vaginal itching, emotional and libidinal swings, weight gain, sensitivity to light. In case of extreme headaches, visual impairment, phlebitis or thrombophlebitis, or hypertension, intake of contraception hormones should be discontinued."

Travestis taking hormones sometimes complain of nausea, headaches, heart palpitations, burning sensations in the legs and chest, extreme weight gain, and allergic reactions. Those who take hormones in tablet form suffer from chronically upset stomachs. Keila told me that during the years when she was taking only one tablet of Anacyclin a day, she felt chronically nauseated. When Magdala took hormones, her skin broke out in open sores that left scars when they healed. Pastinha thought that the hormones she once took nicely affected her legs (*fazia efeito nas pernas*), but no matter how much she took, her breasts never "came out" (*o peito num saía*). In addition, they were attacking her heart, Pastinha said, and would have killed her if she had continued injecting them.

In addition to such uncomfortable and potentially fatal side effects, travestis also believe that it is unwise for them to ejaculate while they are taking hormones, because they think that hormones are expelled from the body in that way. Each ejaculation, therefore, means progressively smaller breasts.

As it turns out, however, the doses of female hormones that travestis ingest make it difficult for them to achieve erections and to ejaculate, so the risk of ejaculating out all the hormones one consumes or injects would not be a serious one anyway. However, losing the ability to achieve an erection can be a considerable problem, since the overwhelming majority of travestis who take hormones are also working as prostitutes. And because many clients want to be *penetrated* by the travesti (this is a point to which I shall return in detail), travestis unable to achieve erections will lose clients.

For all these reasons, what usually happens after several years of taking hormones is that most individuals stop, at least for a while, and they begin injecting silicone into their bodies.

Silicone

A sorte da gente á que a gente tem silicone. Our good fortune is that we have silicone. I have heard travestis affirm this with one another time and again. For travestis throughout Brazil, silicone is a miraculous product—some of them refer to it as "revolutionary"—that makes it possible for them to acquire feminine bodily attributes that in many cases are, they say, more beautiful than those possessed by most women. Among travestis in Salvador, silicone (they call it *silicone* or *óleo*, which literally means "oil") is a continual topic of conversation and commentary. Travestis all know exactly how much silicone other travestis have in their bodies, where they have it, when it was injected, by whom, and in what city. They regularly display their own silicone-filled body parts to one another, ordering others to feel them, and they comment on and feel the silicone-filled parts of others.

The following conversation occurred one night when, in the company of Keila, I was out visiting travestis at their various points of prostitution. We approached two travestis—tall, thin, elegant Bianca, and her friend Madonna, a blonde who took her name from the famous American entertainer. After a few minutes of conversation about what the street was like that evening, whether working the local pornographic movie theater was worth the effort these days, and the whereabouts of other travestis who had disappeared from the street where Bianca and Madonna often worked, Bianca turned to Keila and asked her:

Bianca: Você bombou, foi Keila?	B: You've already [been] pumped, haven't you Keila?
Keila: Vou bombar amanhã, domingo.	K: I'm gonna get pumped tomorrow, Sunday.
Bianca: Vai botar mais um litro?	B: Are you gonna put in another liter?
Keila: Vou botar mais um pouquinho, só porque eu fiquei com duas baixinhas do lado, aí tem que botar.	K: I'm gonna put in just a little, because I was left with these two indentations here on the side, so I have to put in more.

[Keila is referring here to two large, craterlike indentations on one side of her buttocks. These are the result of her tripping and knocking her buttocks against a stone wall shortly after she had undergone a silicone injection several months previously.]

Madonna: Sempre tem que botar uns retoquezinhos.	M: One always has to do a little touching up.
Keila: Tem que dar um retoque. Precisa de um copo, um copo e meio.	K: I have to have a touch-up. It needs a glass, a glass and a half.
Madonna: Vários retoques tem que dar.	M: One needs to touch up every now and again.
Keila: É. E eu tenho silicone em abundância agora, aí eu faço. Porque eu me arrependo de ter posto um litro e meio de silicone em mim. Mas eu queria botar. Eu queria ter botado de meio e meio, um e um. Mas já tenho.	K: Right. And I have an abundance of silicone [that she has purchased] right now, so I'm gonna do it. Because I regret having put in a liter and a half [all at once]. [Keila thinks if she had put in less silicone last time, she could have avoided

Madonna: Você tem quantos?

Keila: Três. Agora eu quero botar no peito mas tou com medo. Tu tem no peito quanto?

Madonna: Eu tenho um litro no peito.

Keila: Um litro?

Madonna: Meio em cada peito.

Keila: Viado, mostra. [Madonna lifts up her shirt, and Keila reaches up and squeezes and feels her breasts.] Mas tá bem. Eu tenho o maior medo de botar. Eu tenho silicone ⌈sesenta mil barra.

Madonna: ⌊Tenho três copos em cada peito.

Keila: Sesenta mil, que tenho medo de botar.

Madonna: Só é ruim a dor.

Keila: Mesmo com anestesia dói?

Madonna: Dói. Mesmo com anestesia.

Don: Verdade? E depois?

Madonna: Depois passa.

Keila: Eu bombei o peito de Pastinha, ela não tinha nada não. Eu botei um copo de silicone em cada peito dela.

Madonna: Porque vai doendo, vai rasgando por dentro. Como dói. E aí fica com aquele falta de ar, aquele negócio aí. É ruim.

Keila: Mais despois não sente não?

Madonna: Não, depois não. O negó-cio na hora que tá bombando e o repouso.

the indentations that resulted from her tripping.] But I wanted to do it [i.e., inject a liter and half at once]. I would like to have put in a half liter at a time, or a liter at a time. But I've already got it in now.

M: How much do you have?

K: Three [liters]. Now I want to put it in my breasts, but I'm afraid. You have how much in your breasts?

M: I have a liter in my breasts.

K: A liter?

M: A half [liter] in each breast.

K: Viado, show me. [Madonna lifts up her shirt, and Keila reaches up and squeezes and feels her breasts.] They're good. I have the greatest fear of putting it in. I have silicone, ⌈sixty thousand *barra*.

M: ⌊I have three glasses in each breast.

K: Sixty thousand, that I'm afraid to put in. [Sixty thousand *barra* indi-cates how gelatinous, i.e., how thick, the silicone is.]

M: The only bad part is the pain.

K: Even with anesthesia it hurts?

M: It hurts. Even with anesthesia.

D: Really? And afterwards?

M: Afterwards it goes away.

K: I pumped the breasts of Pastinha, she didn't have any [silicone in her breasts previously]. I put one glass of silicone in each of her breasts.

M: Because it hurts, it tears inside. How it hurts. And you get that kind of feeling like you can't breathe, that feeling. It's bad.

K: But afterwards you don't feel it?

M: Afterwards no. Just when you're getting pumped and when you're recovering.

A few minutes later, Madonna told Keila that she had the three glasses of silicone injected into her breasts at three different sittings:

Madonna: Bombei três vezes. Aliás bombei quatro vezes. Eu botei um copo, aí depois eu botei dois, aí foi pra botar os três, eu não aguentei. Saiu sangue, como doeu.

Keila: Eu tou morrendo de vontade de bombar mas tou morrendo de medo.

Madonna: Mas depois que bota, é como quadril. A gente faz um/a gente faz aquele medo, depois que botam, viram um vício. Aí quer botar botar botar botar botar.

M: I got pumped three times. No, actually four. I put in one glass, then after that I put in the second, then I went [the first time] to put in the third glass, and I couldn't stand it. Blood came out, it hurt too bad.

K: I'm dying to get pumped, but I'm scared to death.

M: But after you've put some in [your breasts], it's like when you put some in your hips. We have that/ we have that fear, but after it's in, it becomes an addiction. We want to put in more and more and more and more and more.

Numerous themes that occur continually in travesti conversations with one another are touched on in this brief stretch of talk. Bianca's opening question to Keila about whether she has already been pumped is a display of the kind of knowledge that circulates among travestis. Bianca has not personally spoken to Keila for several months, but through the travesti grapevine, she knows that Keila has been planning to inject more silicone into her body. Her follow-up question about whether Keila is going to put in "another liter" is a further display of the kind of knowledge that travestis have about one another's bodies. Bianca's question is also an oblique reference to the fact that the most common amount of silicone for a travesti to inject in one sitting is one liter.

The necessity for touch ups that Keila and Madonna discuss is another recurring theme in travesti talk about silicone. Because silicone is injected directly into the body, it often binds with tissues unevenly, sometimes producing rippled skin that resembles cellulite. Also, the first few days after a silicone injection are sensitive ones, and any sudden jolt to the body (such as when Keila accidentally banged her buttocks against the stone wall) may cause the silicone to retreat deeper into the tissue, thereby sucking the skin inwards and producing large, craterlike indentations.

To even out such ripples or indentation, travestis undergo periodic re- toques (touch-ups). These consist of small amounts of silicone injected directly into the indentations, in the hope that the newly injected silicone will settle on top of the old and cause the skin to rise. Some travestis become obsessed with these touch-ups. I once heard a bombadeira shout in exasperation at a travesti who had marked little xs with eyebrow pencil on at least twenty different parts of her body where she wanted a touch-up. The bombadeira tried to inject silicone into these parts, but the travesti already had so much silicone in her body that no more would go in. "Bicha," the bombadeira finally cried out, "stop this. Women don't have absolutely smooth bodies. *Nobody* has an absolutely blemish-free body."

After the talk reaffirming that "one always has to do a little touching up," the conversation moves on to silicone injections in the breasts. Keila is typical among travestis in that she has a number of liters of silicone in her lower body, but none as yet in her breasts. The vast majority of travestis over twenty years of age have some silicone in their bodies, in amounts ranging from a few glasses (travestis measure silicone in liters and water glasses [*copos*], six of which make up a liter) to up to twenty liters. Most have between two and five liters. The majority of travestis who have silicone, however, have it in their buttocks, hips, knees, and inner thighs, not in their breasts.[10] This strategic placement of silicone is in direct deference to Brazilian aesthetic ideals.

Throughout Brazil, the hallmark of feminine beauty is not first and foremost large breasts, as it tends to be in North America and Europe. Instead, the symbol and essence of feminine allure are fleshy thighs, expansive hips, and a prominent, teardrop-shaped *bunda* (buttocks). The salience of the bunda in Brazilian culture is evident to even the most casual visitor to the country. The conspicuous display of bundas during the annual Carnival celebrations is well known. But even during the rest of the year, bundas are omnipresent. They are displayed with great flair at beaches, where the tiny bathing-suit bottoms known throughout the country as *fio dental* (dental floss) cover women's genitals but nothing else. Many young women, especially when they go out to dance in the evenings—but even when they are relaxing during the day—are careful to arrange their shorts or skirt so that the bottom of their bunda is clearly visible. A gesture used by men throughout the country to express a desirable female body is to cup both hands at waist level, spread the fingers, and bounce the hands lightly up and down, as though jiggling the bottom of a bunda. Television commercials for virtually anything, it seems, usually manage to include at least one shot of a woman's bunda. Viewers watching any female entertainer performing on television will be treated to repeated shots of her bunda—usually filmed from knee level, so one actually looks up her (inevitably short) dress. The credits of a popular television *novela* shown in the afternoon in 1996 begin and end with a shot from behind of a woman in tiny shorts bending over at the waist to extract something from her gym bag. A major dance success in 1995 and 1996 was a tune called "Na Boquinha da Garrafa" (Onto the mouth of the bottle), by a group called Companhia do Pagode. The refrain of this song calls for women to place a bottle of beer on the ground between their legs and to gyrate and click their bundas as they slowly descend . . . onto the mouth of the bottle. Continuing this trend was the group É o Tchan's smash hit "Dança do Bumbum" (Dance of the bottom)—a song that in late 1996 was breaking all sales records and that was responsible for catapulting one of the group's exuberantly bottomed dancers, Carla Perez, to national fame. The list could go on and on.

The Brazilian preoccupation with the bunda has been noted by numerous commentators. The anthropologist Richard Parker calls the emphasis on the bunda in Brazil "remarkable" and observes that "aside from the genitals themselves, nothing so dominates the language of the body in Brazil [as the bunda]" (1991:116). Fernanda Farias de Albuquerque writes that it is easy to tell the difference between Brazilian and Italian travestis in Italy—just look at their bundas (Albuquerque and Janelli 1995:143–44). The Brazilian filmmaker and essayist Arnaldo Jabor goes so far as to nominate the bunda as the symbol of his country (1993:214).

Because erotic attention in Brazil is focused on a woman's bunda, travestis desiring female forms worry most about that, and they inject silicone into their breasts only later, if at all. Most travestis taking hormones already have at least small breasts. And in addition to the fact that large breasts are not crucial capital on the erotic market, many travestis believe that silicone in breasts (but not elsewhere in the body) causes cancer. They also know that silicone injected into breasts shifts its position very easily. They are fearful that it will flow into the heart; and every travesti is, furthermore, acquainted with several unfortunate others whose breasts have either merged in the middle, creating a pronounced, undifferentiated swelling known as a pigeon breast (peito de pomba), or whose silicone has descended into lumpy protrusions just above the stomach. In addition to all this, travestis delay having silicone injected into their breasts because they are convinced, as Keila repeatedly conveys to Madonna, that silicone injections into the chest are extremely painful.

The realization that silicone injections hurt is a thread running through the conversation between Keila and Madonna. Keila repeatedly emphasizes how scared she is to inject her breasts, and Madonna repeatedly acknowledges that great pain is indeed involved. This kind of conversation is one of the ways in which travestis prepare themselves for silicone injections. Young travestis who have "virgin bodies" will interrogate older travestis in the manner that Keila questions Madonna, and

Tina showing off her bunda

they will gradually steel themselves for the moment of truth when they are lying on a mattress and the bombadeira raises a syringe and asks, "Vamos?" (Shall we start?)

What is important to understand is that travestis do not inject silicone into their bodies on a whim. Those who decide to undergo a silicone application always have thought about silicone for months and even years, and they have saved up the money they need to buy the silicone and pay the bombadeira. They have also usually been taking hormones for a long time, and perhaps taking medication to gain weight, in order to give their skin the added elasticity they believe it will require in order to stretch out to accommodate the silicone.[11]

All this means that the majority of travestis do not begin injecting silicone into their bodies until their late teens. Anyone wanting to start before about age fifteen would tend to be dissuaded by others, since travestis know that silicone injected into a body that is still growing shifts position easily, and if a travesti continues to grow after she has injected silicone, she may end up with a bunda halfway up her back. There is a growing tendency, however, for travestis to begin injecting silicone at increasingly early ages, because silicone, even more than hormones, produces immediate (and permanent) effects. Nowadays it is not uncommon for travestis to have their first silicone injections when they are as young as sixteen or seventeen. These travestis will continue injecting silicone periodically until about their mid-twenties. Then they leave off for a while, often beginning again in their mid-thirties, when they feel they are losing their beauty and that a liter or two of silicone will help to restore it.

Silicone in Brazil

Given its widespread use and its central place in the lives of travestis, it is hard to believe that silicone is actually a relatively new phenomenon in Brazil. By all accounts, it is not more than about fifteen years old. Fernanda Farias de Albuquerque claims that the first silicone injections occurred in the southern city of Curitiba in 1981. A travesti named Daniela, who had worked for a time as a prostitute in France, returned from Paris, rich—and bearing with her a number of liters of silicone, which made her even richer (Albuquerque and Janelli 1995:150). Martinha in Salvador also told me that Curitiba was the birthplace of silicone injections in Brazil, and that anyone who wanted silicone in the early 1980s had to save up their money to travel there. Martinha said that the silicone brought back from Paris was not the industrial silicone used today, but was extracted from "marine algae." Banana also remembers that silicone imported directly from Paris was different. She didn't know what it was made of, but it was "rose-colored, pretty," and she had two water glasses of it injected into her hips in 1987.

News of the arrival of silicone appears to have spread very rapidly among travestis throughout Brazil. It was certainly well known in Salvador by 1984, when the sociologist Neuza Maria de Oliveira interviewed a number of travestis living in the city. She found that while none of the Salvador travestis she interviewed had any silicone, "the great majority have a tremendous desire to subject themselves to the process [of silicone injections]." Even at this early stage in the history of silicone injections, several travestis could describe for Oliveira how the injections were done and how much they cost (1994:129–30).

It appears that quite soon after the news about silicone began to spread among travestis throughout Brazil, enterprising individuals started searching for ways of obtaining silicone that did not involve importing it from Paris (something that in any case became virtually impossible to do after 1982, when France imposed visa restrictions on Brazilians wishing to enter the country and simultaneously expelled hundreds of Brazilian travestis who had been working there as prostitutes). Somehow, these individuals discovered industrial silicone. Industrial silicone differs from surgical silicone in that it is nonsterile and impure. It is widely used in manufacturing plants to make things such as automobile dashboards, and in construction work as a sealant. If purified, surgical silicone—which in the case of breast implants is inserted into the body encased in a protective envelope—has been linked to severe health disorders including inflammatory arthritis, autoimmune disease (in which the immune defense reacts to the body's own tissues as if they were foreign bodies), lymphadenopathy (disease of the lymph nodes), and connective-tissue diseases, it is not hard to imagine the serious health consequences that might result from the injection of several liters of impure industrial silicone directly into bodily tissue.[12] On the label glued to the plastic bottles in which the product is packaged, users are advised to take the following precautions:

PRECAUTIONS:
Use in a ventilated space
Avoid breathing in fumes
Avoid extended contact with skin
Should be kept out of reach of
    children
Keep away from fire and heat

FIRST AID:
INTOXICATION FROM FUMES: Move to
    open area
CONTACT WITH SKIN: Wash with soap
    and water
CONTACT WITH EYES: Wash immediately
    with water for 15 minutes
INGESTION OF PRODUCT: SEEK MEDICAL
    HELP

The industrial and building supply outlets that manufacture this silicone will not sell it openly to travestis because they know that they inject it into their bodies, something that they say is illegal.[13] However, at least one or two travestis in any city containing a silicone-manufacturing plant will be well connected enough to be able to buy it under the counter. These travestis control the market and charge whatever they want for their silicone. This means that knowledge about how and where to buy industrial silicone is an extremely carefully guarded secret. Any travesti possessing such knowledge will usually impart it only at great cost (the telephone number of contacts in Salvador and several other cities had cost one travesti the equivalent of five thousand dollars in the mid-1990s), and usually only if she plans on leaving a city and never returning. Whenever they sense a demand, these travestis contact their supplier at the plant and travel there in great secrecy to buy several liters, which they then resell at a hefty profit to individuals wishing to inject it into their bodies. In February 1995, I accompanied a travesti friend to an industrial outlet where she had a contact. That contact sold her five liters of silicone at a price of thirty reais each (approximately thirty-five dollars at the time). She resold this silicone for between seventy and one hundred reais a liter. By the end of 1996, the price had soared to two hundred reais a liter on the travesti market.

In the form in which travestis buy it, silicone is like a clear, thick, odorless oil. Its viscosity makes it difficult to inject into human bodies; the travestis who work as bombadeiras use veterinary needles the thickness of dull pencil points, and all their strength, to force the silicone into the travestis they have been paid to "pump" (bombar). These bombadeiras are always self-taught. Although some have been given some casual instruction by a more experienced "pumper," a travesti's usual route to becoming a bombadeira is seeing someone else do it (or having it done on herself) and feeling that she can do it better. Carlinhos, the bombadeira who pumped Tina, told me that she began injecting silicone into people when a woman pleaded with her to inject a liter into her, reasoning that since Carlinhos had already been pumped herself, she must remember how it was done:

I had been pumped some five years, no, less than that, three or four years previously, and she: "You know how to do it mona, do it. You can do it because you've already seen it being done." I said, "But man I've never done it before." I kept delaying it so as not to do it. "Ah, I don't have needles, don't have this, don't have that"—I was afraid to do it. And then, the day came, it had to be done and that day, and I thought, sheez, let's do it. So I went and had the woman lie on the bed, marked where to insert the needles, and I did the woman. The woman went home, the next day the woman was beautiful, and she brought two more women . . . OK I could already see, if I insert the needle into that woman in this way, fill up that hole, then I'll insert this one in the same position and fill it like this, you know?

Carlinhos told me that she thought one reason she was so successful as a pumper is because she knows something about anatomy—in her day job at a hospital in a city in northern Brazil (she is the only travesti I know with a steady day job), she is responsible for tagging corpses and sending them on to funeral parlors or to operating rooms for autopsy.[14]

Because bombadeiras are largely self-taught, they vary dramatically in their methods and in their bedside manner. Carlinhos, for example, is a careful and methodical bombadeira who is always concerned to keep herself informed about the state of the travesti she is pumping. Another experienced and well-known bombadeira in Salvador whom I was able to observe is much more brusque and businesslike, and she seems in a great hurry to get the application sessions over with as quickly as possible. Whereas Carlinhos continually asks if the injections are hurting, and slows down or momentarily stops if they are, the other bombadeira says little to the travestis she pumps; even when they scream in pain, she continues bearing down with all her weight onto the plunger of the syringe, trying to force the silicone through the needle. Horror stories circulate among travestis about bombadeiras in other cities who are only interested in money and care nothing for the travestis they pump. These bombadeiras send travestis who have just been pumped on their way, with no instructions about how they should care for their new bodies. They lie about how much silicone they have injected—saying they used six glasses, for example, when it was only five (and thus keeping a glass of silicone for themselves; this is called "breaking the glass," *quebrar o copo*).[15] They are even known to put alcohol in the syringe, in order to create abscesses in travestis they for some reason don't like.

Travestis wanting to get pumped with silicone will rely on other travestis' experiences with bombadeiras in order to choose one for themselves. But the single most important factor in the choice of a bombadeira is the results she produces. Whenever a travesti appears with new silicone in some part of her body, one of the questions that everybody will ask is who "did" (*fez*) her. If other travestis feel that the body a particular bombadeira has "done" is especially successful, they will attempt to get that bombadeira to do them as well. In the larger cities of Rio and São Paulo, some well-known bombadeiras apparently display photos of travestis they have "done," and they ask their clients to choose from the photos a body they would like to have. Fernanda Farias de Albuquerque recounts that when she was going to get pumped for the first time, she arrived at the house of the bombadeira and saw "so many pictures, so many photos of famous travestis who had passed through her hands! They were beautiful bodies, to die for" (Albuquerque and Janelli 1995:148). She asked the bombadeira to "do" her just like Perla, a travesti displayed on the wall

When a travesti has decided who she wants to pump her, she arranges a time and place with the bombadeira. Silicone applications occur in either the travesti's or the bombadeira's room, depending on the preference of the bombadeira. It is also the latter who decides how the silicone will be purchased. If she has direct access to a *fonte* (source) of silicone (i.e., a contact at a silicone-manufacturing outlet), she will insist that travestis purchase the silicone directly from her. "I like to know what I'm putting into these bichas," one bombadeira once told me. In other cases, the travestis are expected to bring silicone that they have purchased elsewhere to the application session. They also may be asked to bring syringes and needles of two different sizes (small, thin ones for the anesthetic and large, thick ones for the silicone), one or two bottles of Xylocaina (the Novocain-like drug used as a local anesthetic), rubbing alcohol and toilet paper to clean the needles and wipe off the excess silicone, a pair of panty hose to tie around the waist if the area to be pumped is the lower body (this is to prevent the silicone from rising into the heart), and/or cloth bandages if the silicone is to be injected into the breasts (at the end of the session, the bandages are tied, like a halter between and around the breasts, to prevent them from merging in the middle and creating a pigeon breast), a small tube of superglue to seal up the holes made by the thick needles, and cotton balls to put over the superglue-filled holes.

Tina's Silicone Application

When Tina arranged with Carlinhos to pump her, she requested that the silicone application not begin until quite late at night, so that she would have a chance to work that evening and perhaps rob a client or two. She arrived on the appointed evening after 11 P.M., with a plastic supermarket bag containing the silicone and all the implements she had been instructed to bring. When I greeted her in the doorway of the house where the application was to take place, I was very surprised to notice that Tina seemed not to be under the influence of any drugs. Almost always, I knew, she liked to unwind after a night of work with one or two big joints and/or a few lines of coke. I had certainly expected her to take something to numb her sensitivity to the pain she was about to undergo. But no. In this she differed slightly from her bombadeira, Carlinhos, who, an

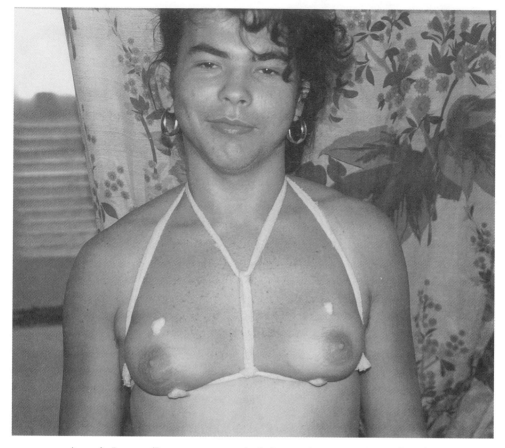

A newly "pumped" travesti wearing the halter used to prevent a *peito de pomba* (pigeon breast)

hour earlier, had happily smoked from a large joint being passed around in the room of another travesti. It was there that Carlinhos had told me that when she pumps somebody, she works with that person's face in mind. If the travesti has the face of a girl, she told me, she would not consent to give her a *bundão* or a *peitão* (a huge ass or enormous breasts). It is important, Carlinhos stressed, for face and body to match. If they don't, then one could end up looking like Jô Mamãe, a travesti in her forties with twelve and a half liters of silicone in her body. Jô's body, Carlinhos (and everybody else) explained, was quite buxom and attractive. Her face, however, looked like an old man's. "De longe é um presépio, de perto uma presepada," Carlinhos joked, using a proverb that means roughly "From far away she's a vision; close up she's a sight." (Jô Mamãe responded to these kinds of comments by saying that other travestis were jealous of her beauty, and she always retorted with a disdainful flick of her hair extensions and a biting riposte of her own: "Eu não tenho culpa se a natureza foi mãe para mim e madrasta pra vocês," which means "I can't help it if nature was like a mother to me and like a [wicked] step mother to you.")[16]

Since Carlinhos lives in a city in the north of the country and was only in Salvador on one of her frequent short visits, she had no room of her own to use for Tina's silicone application. And since Tina was sharing a tiny room with several other travestis at the time, her room wouldn't do. The session therefore ended up taking place in the room of a mutual friend, Tânia, where Carlinhos was staying during her visit to Salvador (Tânia was later treated to free touch-ups in return for this hospitality).

Seeing that Tina had arrived, Carlinhos went into Tânia's room and spread a white towel on the big double bed, thus covering the sheets festooned with line drawings of men and women in different copulatory positions that Tânia told me she had stolen from a motel room. Tina entered the room and handed her plastic bag to Keila, who was going to assist Carlinhos throughout the silicone application. Keila sat down on a little stool next to the bed, and on another little stool in front of her she spread out the contents of the plastic bag. She opened the bottle of silicone that Tina had brought with her and poured some into the water glass on the stool in front of her, filling the glass to the brim with the oily liquid.

Now Tina pulled off her dress and stood before Carlinhos naked. Keila helped her tie the pair of nylons she had brought with her around her waist. Tina then told Carlinhos in what parts of her body she wanted the silicone, and Carlinhos marked the places in which she would be injecting it with a pink eyebrow pencil. She used no measuring device; she just looked at Tina's body and marked the spots with little xs: four going down each of Tina's inner thighs, four on each outer hip, and four on each buttock.

Tina then lay down on her back on the towel. Carlinhos positioned herself next to Tina on the bed, poured some rubbing alcohol on her hands, and rubbed them together (Keila, as assistant, did this too). She then poured some alcohol on a cotton ball and wiped the first area to be injected—Tina's right inner thigh. Taking up the thin syringe, she extracted some Xylocaina from one of the small bottles that Tina had bought and asked her "Vamos?" Tina closed her eyes, bit down on a little stuffed teddy bear that she had found lying on Tânia's bed, and told

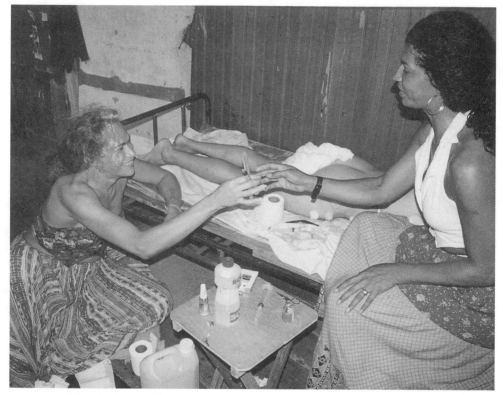

A bombadeira and her assistant

Carlinhos, "Vamos, bicha." Carlinhos plunged the needle into each little *x* marked on Tina's thigh.

As soon as she had emptied the syringe of anesthetic, Carlinhos reached over to Keila to be handed the large, 10 ml syringes that Keila was filling with silicone. Keila filled a syringe by dipping it into the glass of silicone and sucking up the liquid. Wiping off the bottom with a piece of toilet paper, she then screwed the thick needle onto the bottom of the syringe and pushed the plunger until some of the liquid began to ooze out. Keila wiped this away with toilet paper and handed the syringe to Carlinhos.

Carlinhos double-checked the syringe and then plunged it deeply into the first little *x* on Tina's thigh. Once it was fully inserted, Carlinhos braced herself and took hold of the plunger with both hands. Using all her strength, she emptied the contents of the syringe into Tina's thigh. This took about thirty seconds. When she had finished, Carlinhos left the syringe where it was, poking out of the thigh. She was then handed a second syringe by Keila; she inserted this one in the second little pink x and emptied it, again leaving it in. She continued in this way until all four marks had syringes poking out of them.

At this point Carlinhos unscrewed the first syringe, leaving the needle it was attached to still embedded in Tina's thigh. She handed this syringe to Keila, who put it in the water glass and started to suck up silicone into it. As Keila was busy doing this, Carlinhos removed the other syringes from the needles, leaving them all sticking out of Tina's thigh like metal porcupine quills. Carlinhos laid the syringes on a plate that Keila had in front of her and waited for her to finish filling the first syringe. After wiping it off with toilet paper, Keila handed the first syringe back to Carlinhos, who screwed it back onto the first needle and injected its contents. This procedure was repeated with the other three syringes. At any one time there were four needles sticking out of Tina's thigh, with at least two empty syringes attached to them.

Each point on the thigh was injected four times. After the fourth time, a clear swelling began to appear under each needle. But the swellings were separated under the skin—they did not merge, and they looked like four big bumps or bites. After the last injection, Carlinhos removed all the needles. She then unrolled a piece of toilet paper big enough to cover the entire area that she had injected (about ten inches). She put the paper over the thigh and then, with her thumb and forefinger, began massaging the area (*fazer massagem*) quite hard-handedly, as though she wanted to break down the silicone inside the body. What she was doing, she told me, was trying to smooth the silicone out, so that it would merge and leave the skin smooth, not bumpy. This massage lasted for five minutes. Towards the end, Carlinhos removed the toilet paper (which was to absorb the blood and silicone that came seeping out the holes) and rubbed and squeezed and kneaded the area around the holes, as though she were squeezing a pimple. Clear silicone and a tiny amount of blood oozed out.

Finally, Carlinhos poured some alcohol on a cotton ball and wiped the area, then poured some alcohol on her hands and vigorously rubbed the thigh for about a minute. She was now ready to seal the holes left by the thick veterinary needles. For this she used the superglue that Tina had brought with her (had Tina forgotten the glue, nail polish would have been used). Carefully, Carlinhos squeezed one drop of the glue out onto a hole and put a little piece of cotton on top of it. She continued in the same way until all four holes were closed and covered with tiny white cotton balls. The whole procedure, from the injection of the Xylocaina to the sealing with superglue, had taken fifteen minutes.

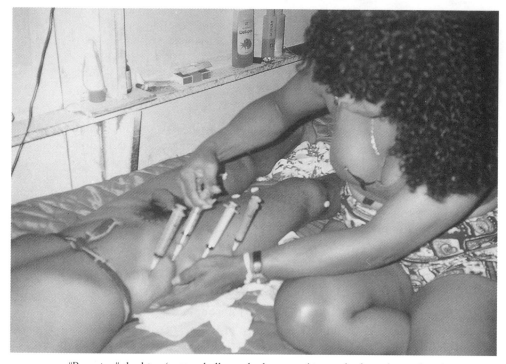

"Pumping" the hips (cotton balls on the knees and inner thighs indicate that these
have already been "pumped")

Now Carlinhos repeated the entire process on Tina's left inner thigh.
From there she moved on to the right hip, left hip, right buttocks, and,
finally, about two and a half hours after she began, Tina's left buttocks.

Despite the fact that a travesti is taking a step that will modify her
body for the rest of her life, the atmosphere during a silicone application
is not marked in any special way. Some travestis prefer a minimum number of people in the room, and all keep the door shut. But travestis who
want to talk to the one being pumped, or to the bombadeira or her assistant, often enter and leave the room at will, and comment freely on the
session. The travesti being pumped smokes and maintains a running conversation with the bombadeira and anyone else who wanders in to see
what is gong on. If there is a television in the room, it will be turned on.
During Tina's session, *Gone with the Wind*, dubbed into Portuguese, played
in the background: Atlanta burned as Tina's bunda grew.

Tina's silicone application began at 11:10 at night and finished, finally,
at 2:15 A.M.—three hours later. When the liter of silicone that she had
brought was gone and the final drops of superglue had been applied,
Tina stood up. Now Keila helped her arrange two cut-up plastic grocery-

Enlarging the bunda

store bags around her buttocks, like a big diaper. This was to help *esquentar* the silicone—to "heat it up" so that it would "dissolve" (*dissolver*) and smooth out faster. On top of these bags, which she was instructed to keep on for a day, Tina pulled up a pair of panty hose that she had brought with her. This was to help keep the silicone in place and prevent it from running down her legs and collecting in her ankles. When the bags and panty hose were in place, Tina pulled her dress over her head, listened while Carlinhos warned her not to eat pork for the next few days, said good night, and was gone.

Two nights later, Tina was sufficiently recovered to be out working the streets again, her new bunda and hips generously displayed in the shortest shorts I think I have ever seen in my life.

The Dynamics of the Body

Until now, I have presented the bodily practices and modifications that travestis engage in as fairly unproblematic and self-evident. As boys, travestis discover that they are attracted to males, and these erotic feelings

are bound up with and often followed by—narratively, at least—effeminate behavior and an interest in female objects (dolls) and activities (acting out the role of mother in play). Once their attraction to males cul-
minates in their being anally penetrated, these boys begin engaging in
bodily practices that feminize them and that culminate, in their turn,
with the injection of numerous liters of industrial silicone into their
bodies.

The question I want to raise at this point is: why? Why do the individuals who engage in these kinds of bodily practices do so? Why
exactly do they want rounded features, expansive bundas, and hormone-
produced breasts? Why do they transform themselves in *this* manner?
And if the goal is to approximate female bodily forms, what do they
think about their male genitals?

When I asked travestis why they modified their bodies in the ways
they did, the reason they habitually cited was the most self-evident one:
"to mold my body, you know, to be more feminine, with the body of a
woman," explained Elisabeth, the twenty-nine-year-old travesti with one
and a half liters of silicone in her hips and one water glass of silicone in
each breast. I persisted: But why do you want the body of a woman?

When I first began asking individual travestis that question, I expected
them to respond by telling me that they wanted the body of a woman because they felt themselves to be women. That was not the answer I received. No one I spoke to ever offered the explanation—even when I,
confused and exasperated, sometimes suggested it—that they might be
women trapped in male bodies. On the contrary, there is a strong consensus among travestis in Salvador that any travesti who claims to be a
woman is mentally disturbed. A travesti is not a woman and can never be
a woman, they tell one another, because God created them male.

Any individual is free to embellish and augment the male body parts
that God has given them, but their sex cannot be changed. Carlinhos, for
example, who has five liters of silicone in her buttocks, hips, and thighs
and large silicone implants in her breasts, once explained to me: "I'm not
removing anything that He gave me. I'm just improving things. He gave
me a chest—I made it bigger. He gave me a bunda—I made it bigger.
He gave me thighs—I made them bigger. I'm making what He gave me
in life more beautiful." Banana summed up the thoughts of most travestis
on the subject when she told me, *tout court:* "I was born a man and a man
I will die. How could I ever be a woman if I was born a man? If I castrate
myself and put in a cunt (*botar uma buceta*), that'll turn me into a woman?"

The impossibility of ever changing the sex with which one was born
is what makes travestis suspicious and dismissive of transsexuals. Although there are no transsexuals, to anyone's knowledge, currently

living in Salvador, travestis know that transsexuals exist, and transsexualism is a topic that regularly arises in travesti conversations and commentaries. Transsexualism as a phenomenon is referred to in terms of the operative procedures that make it possible. So travestis talk of *tirar o sexo* or *tirar o pênis* (remove the genitals/penis), *fazer transplante* (have a transplant—just who the donor of this "transplant" might be, or how it might be obtained, is not something I ever heard anyone consider), or, most commonly, *botar uma buceta* (put in a cunt). Transsexuals are usually called *bichas operadas* or *bichas castradas*, that is, operated or castrated bichas. Some travestis refer to them as *bichas mutiladas*—mutilated bichas. Sometimes, in order to distinguish them from travestis, transsexuals are called, simply and directly, *bucetas* (cunts). This name is heard, for example, when travestis are looking at pictures in a magazine article about travestis and transsexuals and someone wonders if a particular individual portrayed is a travesti—"É travesti?" No, someone will reply, "é buceta." What transsexuals are *never* called is "women."

Whenever the topic of transsexualism arises in travesti conversations, the general reaction is incomprehension. No one can understand the point. Since putting in a cunt, as Banana says, will not turn one into a woman, then why do it? Amputating one's penis will only make one unable to experience any sexual pleasure ever again. And this prospect horrifies travestis. Banana, when I discussed sex-change operations with her, scoffed at the idea. "Remove my penis and become useless (*inutilizada*), without being able to cum? Someone who is neutered (*uma pessoa neutra*)? No. It's already enough, this sin that I have of being a viado," she laughed. "Isn't it? And beyond that, castrate myself? No. I could have millions of dollars and I wouldn't want to do it." Adriana told me something similar:

Adriana: E todo travesti tem que ter o direito dele, né, o pênis—o direito do travesti é o pênis. Sem o pênis ninguem goza.	A: And every travesti has to keep what's his, you know, the penis—it's right for a travesti to have a penis. Without a penis nobody cums [i.e., experiences orgasm].
Don: Não, claro.	D: No, of course not.
Adriana: Sem o pênis ninguem goza.	A: Without a penis nobody cums.
Don: Não.	D: No.
Adriana: E se o homem, ele/ele/se o homem, ele já veio/ele já veio com a tendência de ter um pênis, é porque a natureza que fez ele um homem, fez ele com um pênis. Então ele tem que continuar com o pênis dele.	A: And if a man, he/he/if a man, he already came/he already came with a tendency to have a penis, it's because nature made him a male, made him with a penis. And so he has to continue with his penis.

Adriana continued by telling me how much she loves to *gozar* (ejaculate) and that she thinks a penis is "the best thing in the world" (*a melhor coisa do mundo*).

Martinha also highlighted her own sexual pleasure when she talked about the idea of a sex-change operation. "And never cum again?" she asked, incredulously. "I love to fuck, I love to be fucked, I love to suck, love being sucked, love playing different roles—can you imagine? You'd be like a hole in a banana tree, some man just putting it in-out, in-out." Jô Mamãe echoed and extended this sentiment, announcing once in a conversation with other travestis that she thought sex-change operations were ridiculous. Since you couldn't ever *gozar* (cum) again, you would be transformed into an *objeto*, an object—a numb hole who existed only for the pleasure of others. Jô was holding a shoebox when she made this comment, and to illustrate her point, she threw the shoebox down on the mattress she was sitting on. "Like this," she said, hitting it with her hand to depict the action of someone having sex with an empty, unfeeling box.[17]

Not only do sex-change operations not produce women, and not only do they rob one of all possibility of experiencing sexual pleasure, travestis believe, but they also invariably result in insanity. Travestis share a number of vaguely articulated but firmly held ideas about human physiology and how various internal organs are connected and influence one another. One such idea is the already mentioned belief, widely held among travestis, that if a travesti ejaculates while she is taking hormones, her breasts will get smaller. Another, similar belief is that a sex-change operation makes it impossible for semen to ever leave the body. Instead, the semen travels up to the brain, where it collects and forms "a stone" (*uma pedra*) that will increase in size until it eventually (ten to fifteen years was the most time any operated travesti could hope for) provokes *uma trombose* (a thrombosis), which causes madness.[18]

Most travestis who talked about this process were vague on the details. "I'm not a doctor, you'll have to ask a doctor exactly how it happens," several responded when I pressed for more precise explanations. They only knew *that* it happens, and they could all cite several examples of transsexuals who had gone crazy, such as Luciana Buceta (Luciana Cunt) in Recife—who, everyone says, goes around town forever exposing her buceta to anyone who wants to see it (and, frequently, to people on the street who have no desire to see it at all). But one travesti who had thought about this a lot told me that the reason semen goes up to the brain is that the testicles are not removed during a sex-change operation—they are merely inserted inside the body. Furthermore, a surgically inserted vagina is made of the "nerves" (*os nervos*) of the penis turned

inside out and put inside the body. Hence, this travesti reasoned, the semen that normally would travel through the penis to leave the body travels through the inverted penis *into* the body, eventually lodging itself in
the brain and building the stone that results in insanity.[19]

What is evident in travesti talk about transsexuals is their firm conviction that one can never change sex. If you are born with a tendency
to have a penis, as Adriana, rather originally, put it, then you are a man,
and, as Banana says, you will die a man. But if this is the case, and if travestis do not feel themselves to be transsexuals—people who in North
America and Europe have come to be understood as "women trapped in
men's bodies"—then, again, why do they adopt female names, clothing,
hairstyles, and bodily practices; why do they call each other by feminine
pronouns; and why do they inject substantial quantities of industrial silicone into their bodies in order to achieve stereotypically feminine bodily forms?

Travestis themselves give two answers to that question. The first concerns the desirability of a feminine body on the sexual market. Pastinha
is a travesti in her mid-twenties with two liters of silicone in her buttocks
and a quarter liter in each of her breasts. When I asked her why she had
injected silicone into her body to make it look more feminine, her reply
was immediate:

Pastinha: Hm, para ganhar dinheiro,
né? [laughs]

Don: É?

Pastinha: É. Porque tem que ter um
corpão pa poder ganhar dinheiro,
né? Porque se num tiver/por/
porque os home gosta de ver . . .
Travesti é cum corpão pa poder
ganhar dinheiro.

Don. Sim . . .

Pastinha: Aí eu botei pra isso. Porque
quando eu cheguei pra aqui eu
num tinha nada disso.

Don: Mas só para ganhar dinheiro?
Não tem outra, é, razão? Só
para/só para ganhar dinheiro?

Pastinha: É, só pa botar/Porque . . .
quando um home vê um travesti
dum corpão assim, né, aí pára o
carro e diz, "Ah, eu vou sair com
aquela dali que tem o corpão." Aí,

P: Hm, to earn money, you know?
[laughs]

D: Really?

P: Yeah. Because you need a beautiful
body to be able to earn money, you
know? Because if you don't have/
be/because men like to see . . . Tra
vestis have beautiful bodies to be
able to earn money.

D: Yeah . . .

P: So I put in [my silicone] for that
reason. Because when I arrived
here [in Salvador] I didn't have
anything [i.e., any silicone].

D: But only to earn money? There's
no other, ah, reason? Just to/just to
earn money?

P: Yeah, just to put/Because . . . when
a man sees a travesti with a beautiful body like that, you know, he'll
stop his car and say, "Ah, I'm gonna
go with that one over there who

depois que eu botei que melhorou pra mim.	has the beautiful body." And so, after I put in [my silicone] things got better for me [on the street].
Don: É.	**D:** Uh-huh.
Pastinha: Porque antes deu botar, minha bunda era chulada assim, batida [claps her hands together].	**P:** Because before I put in [my silicone], my butt was flat like this, smashed [claps her hands together].

The link between beautiful feminine bodies and success in prostitution that Pastinha expresses here is a continual theme in travestis' talk about bodies and in their presentation of their bodies. Those with no feminine forms, any travesti will tell you, earn little money. Travestis like to describe to others the admiration and awe they felt the first time they saw a *bicha plastificada*—a "plasticized bicha"—and realized that they, too, with the help of silicone, could have ample feminine forms and hence earn more money. At night when they work on the street, travestis who have acquired pronounced feminine features use them to attract the attention of passing motorists, and they dress (or, rather, they undress) to display those features prominently. Those who do not have prominent feminine forms do their best to hide this lack, by dressing in large, loose blouses and skirts and wearing wigs. A few especially "butch" (*machuda*) travestis pad their buttocks with pieces of foam rubber and their bras with toilet paper or water-filled condoms.

One travesti who did this for years was Magdala. Magdala was unusual among the travestis in Salvador, partly because she had had something of a career before she began prostituting herself (she had a tiny hair salon with a bicha friend, who ended up stealing everything and disappearing) and partly because she didn't start living full-time in female dress until about age twenty-three. Although everybody I spoke to defined Magdala as a travesti, because she lived with travestis, dressed primarily in female clothing, and had hair that reached below her shoulders, she did not see herself as having absolutely committed herself to being a travesti.[20] She seemed to regard herself more as a transformista than as a "real travesti" (*um travesti mesmo*). The major sign of this lack of commitment to being a real travesti, she told me herself, was her almost total lack of silicone. At thirty-five years of age, Magdala had no silicone anywhere in her body except for 10 cc's in her cheeks and chin. Furthermore, she didn't take hormones, because they made her break out in an ugly rash. With her long hair, painted fingernails, bespangled fingers and forearms, and languid, expansive gestures, Magdala looked like a tautly muscled, gangly, effeminate homosexual. When I interviewed her in late 1995, she was going through a depressing period in her life. She was finding it increasingly hard to earn money as a prostitute. This was, she said, because she did not have the feminine forms that clients wanted. And for this reason, she was considering taking the step of injecting silicone into her body and "becoming a real travesti":

Magdala: Tou querendo me jogar a ser travesti, porque eu não tou conseguindo . . . ganhar dinheiro na pista sem ser travesti mesmo.

M: I'm wanting to throw myself into becoming a travesti [and injecting silicone], because I'm not succeeding . . . in earning money on the street without being a real travesti.

Don: É.

D: Uh-huh.

Magdala: Tá entendendo?

M: You know?

Don: É.

D: Yeah.

Magdala: Os homens gostam de ver [corpo, peito, entendeu?

M: Men like to see [bodies, breasts, you know?

Don: [de ver peito. É.

D: [to see breasts. Yeah.

Magdala: Eu faço aquela linha mas num . . . eh . . . tem alguns clientes . . . Entro em alguns por causa da neca, né, que eles gostam, [mas . . . eu num sei. Peito que [eles gostam/

M: I try to look like that but I don't . . . eh . . . I have some clients . . . I get in some cars because of my dick, you know, that they like, [but . . . I don't know. The kind of [breasts that they like/

Don: [É.

D: [Yeah.

Magdala: Num chamo muita atenção. Quer dizer, eu chamo muita atenção mas os carros que param . . . a maioria já me cohece, num pára porque . . . sabe que eu num tenho seios, nem tenho/

M: I don't stand out. That is to say, I stand out, but the cars that stop . . . the majority already know me, and they don't stop because . . . they know that I don't have breasts, don't have/

Don: É.

D: Uh-huh.

Magdala: entendeu . . . silicone, essas coisas, que eles gostam. Mas da/da/daqui pra a frente eu vou pensar direitinho o que é que eu vou fazer realmente.

M: you know . . . silicone, these things that they like. But look/look/looking ahead, I'm gonna think a lot about what I'm gonna do.

Don: É.

D: Right.

Magdala: Porque . . . se eu tou de machuda, não tou conseguindo nada. Então vamos virar logo travesti pra ver o que é que dá, né?

M: Because . . . being "butch," I'm not getting anywhere. So let's turn into a [real] travesti and see where it gets us, right?

By the time I returned to Salvador a year later, Magdala had indeed turned into a real travesti. She had injected five liters of silicone into her hips, inner thighs, and bunda, and she was planning on injecting three

more. With the help of other travestis, she had found a brand of hormones that didn't give her allergic reactions, and was on a regime of four
birth-control pills a day. The hormones were making her look chubbier
and giving her breasts. Magdala had also changed her clothing style
from a rather conservative, buttoned-up way of dressing to the much
more relaxed style (halter tops or small bodices, short skirts or tiny
shorts) preferred by most travestis. She told me that she had many more
clients, had been through a few attractive boyfriends, and was earning
lots more money. She seemed much happier and more self-assured than
she had been the previous year.

In their talk about their bodies, Magdala, Pastinha, and all other travestis I know are extremely explicit that a beautiful body full of silicone—what Pastinha calls a *corpão*—translates into cash in the Brazilian
sexual marketplace. Because of this direct link that travestis themselves
foreground between prostitution and the body modifications they un-
dertake, what tends to happen with scholarly analyses of travesti bodies
is that they stop here and propose the explanation that travestis modify
their bodies in the ways they do because they are the tragic dupes
of a destructive system of sexual exploitation and degradation. The
Australian feminist polemicist Sheila Jeffreys used Brazilian travestis as
an example of the most pernicious kind of sexual oppression, one in
which "the demands of the sex industry" force individuals to fatally alter
their bodies "so that they can earn more money in the sex industry"
(1996: 88). And Neuza Maria de Oliveira argues something similar in the
study of Salvadorean travestis that she conducted in the early 1980s. Although Oliveira's book is extremely nuanced and sympathetic towards
travestis, her conclusion is that "the travesti . . . constructs a body suit-
ing the taste of the client through a corporeal discipline that rests upon
a sexuality that is politically and economically conservative. It is a body
that is docile and useful for the streets of prostitution, just like a factory product. A commodity product body *(Um corpo produto mercadoria)*"
(1994: 129).

While it is important to not lose sight of the fact that the overwhelming majority of travestis throughout Brazil work as prostitutes
and, hence, are indeed sensitive to the demands of the sexual marketplace, it is also important to notice the ways in which analyses like those
offered by Jeffreys or Oliveira are an artifact of a perspective that sees
travestis solely as prostitutes and sees their bodies as existing only in relation to "the taste of the client." It is a perspective that ignores the fact
that travestis generally begin remodeling their bodies in an increasingly
feminine direction several years before they begin prostituting them-

selves, and it neglects to inquire how a travesti understands and uses her body in other, nonprofessional contexts (such as in her relationships with her boyfriends). This perspective also elides the crucial dimension of travestis' subjectivity in the construction of their bodies ("docile"?). Does a travesti really regard her own body as nothing more than a "factory product"? This seems rather unlikely (and unfair). After all, individual travestis probably spend more time than most people thinking about, caring for, planning, and fashioning their bodies. To reduce all that time and all that engagement to a deluded desire to construct a commodity for "the sex industry" is to understand only part of the story.

For, as important as it may be, attractiveness to potential clients is not the only reason that travestis modify their bodies. When I asked them why they did so, they also mentioned a second reason (many of them mentioned *only* this reason): they modify their bodies because they feel themselves to be "feminine" (*feminino*) or "like a woman" (*se sentir mulher*).[21] This quality or characteristic of being feminine is talked about in very specific ways.

When I asked Elisabeth what it meant when she told me she felt like a *mulher*, a woman, she answered: "I like to dress like a woman. I like when someone/when men admire me, you know? I like to be admired, when I go with a man who, like, says, 'Sheez, you're really pretty, you're really feminine.' That makes me want to be more feminine and more beautiful every day, you see?"

Luciana told me that for her, feeling like a woman meant "to feel good, with men—I feel good when I'm with men, you know, but it's kind of strange because there are only a few men today who will take you/who will accept you totally, twenty-four hours a day, who will go out places with you, have you like a woman, make you feel like a woman, take you anywhere at all. I've had men like that, you know? They made me feel *mulheríssima* (like a total woman)."

Adriana's definition of feeling like a woman is similar to Elisabeth's and Luciana's:

I feel like a woman, like, let's suppose when I put on a dress, a discreet dress and I pass by a lot of people and no one notices [that Adriana is a travesti]—I love doing that. I love dressing well. I love dressing up in clothes that look good on me, clothes that make me look more, you know, feminine, you know? Feminine . . . And I feel like a woman when I'm with my boyfriend. When he treats me well, I feel like a woman in front of him, you know?

When I asked Magdala when she felt most like a woman, her response was direct:

A man. Who treats me well. Who treats me with affection. You know? That's when I feel most like a woman, most content . . . I had a boyfriend like that, who treated me like that, in that way. He was good with me, attentive. He treated me well, didn't try to cheat me or use me (*não me gigolava*), because I think that's really important, that one's boyfriend doesn't pull a gigolo number on one, you know, because the majority of them . . . come with certain interests (*vêm interessados*). He was wonderful with me. I'm sure he did have some [monetary and material] interests, but it wasn't too bad. We had a period of time together, it was a good phase, I felt more like a woman, more married. Happier. But on the other hand, I'm very jealous. And there were problems because of my jealousy.

Banana echoes all these sentiments when she, too, foregrounds the role of a male in making her feel like a woman:

I feel like a woman (*Me sinto mulher*) when I desire a person, you know, when I desire that person, that makes me feel good, I feel like a woman with him, you understand? If I succeed in getting that person, let's say that I want the man in this picture [Banana points to a photo of a naked man that she has ripped out of a pornographic magazine and pinned on her wall], and I succeed in getting him, being a/you know, if I succeed in getting him, I'm gonna feel fulfilled, a woman, you understand? And walk with him anyplace. You know?

I asked Banana what it was about her, exactly, that she felt to be feminine.

When I have money/when I have . . . I like money, I like being a person . . . I like nice things—only the best will do, from perfumes to shoes, only the best will do. I don't like junk, because, if I were to buy something— let's suppose that there are two things, two bottles of perfume. This one is expensive, and this one is cheap. Even if I only have money enough to buy this one [the cheap one], I'm not going to want it. I'm gonna save my money to be able to buy that [expensive] one.

But is that an attribute of women? I wondered.

Yeah. Because women are vain. Well, some of them. Because there are others who crawl out from under [claps her hands]. I like elegant women (*mulher fina*). I think cultured women are beautiful, not these shabby wrecks (*esses traste*) that live around here on São Francisco Street, you know? These wrecks around here, no. But those society people, cultivated, I like them, I think those women are elegant, really pretty, dressed well, nice shoes, you know? Only the best will do, I'd like to be one of those.

This answer is similar to the reply I received from Tina when I asked her what she most liked about women:

What I like about women is dresses. Tight dresses, high heels, I like that. Bodices. A good make-up, pretty, those shiny make-ups that stand out. That's what I like about women.

Cintia answered the question in almost exactly the same way:

The things I most like about women . . . I like to wear the clothes, the clothes I think are pretty . . . I think a woman's breasts are pretty, I would like big, hard breasts . . . I like the body, I admire it a lot . . . the hair . . . There's lots of things about women that we like, you know?

Characteristic of all these replies is that "woman" is spoken of in terms of her appearance, her behaviors (buying "only the best"), and, consistently, her relationships to men.[22] In stark and complete contrast to North American and European transsexuals, who lay claim to a female subjectivity and who discuss their desire to be women in terms of predispositions and essences, travestis do not speak of women in terms of internal states and biologically generated feelings. Noticeably absent from travesti talk about feeling like a woman is any reference at all to reproduction or to any kind of maternal feelings or essences. Virtually the only essences I have ever heard travestis attribute to women are vanity, jealousy, the propensity to gossip, and the proclivity for passionate love. These are all qualities that travestis consider themselves to possess, and they are all qualities that are directly related to males: vanity being the certainty that one is attractive to men, jealousy being jealousy that one's man might be sleeping around, gossip usually being gossip about how someone else's man is sleeping around, and passionate love being love always directed towards a male.

Because women are seen in this way, it is easy for travestis to construct the argument that whatever a woman can do, a travesti can do better. Hence, travestis are, they will tell you, generally better dressed, better coiffed, and better maintained than most women, and they have better taste. They are also better lovers, better prostitutes, and better spouses. In addition to permitting travestis to see themselves in this way in relation to women, the interpretive framework within which they comprehend women compels them to regard those dimensions of biological women's lives that do not mesh with their perceptions of what "woman" is not as a competing reality, but rather as the sad fantasies of misguided individuals. This was made particularly clear to me once when Martinha explained why she would never want to be a woman:

| Martinha: Eu acho a vida de mulher totalmente diferente da nossa, e eu acho a nossa que encara mais a | M: I think that the life of a woman is totally different from our lives, and I think that our [lives] face |

realidade. Nós vemos a realidade da vida como ela é, e elas não. Elas vivem num mundo de fantasia. É.

⌐Casar/
Don: └As mulheres?

Martinha: É, as mulheres. É casar, ter filho, viverem do marido, entendeu?

Don: É.

Martinha: É nós não. Nós temos a realidade. A gente enfrenta a realidade da vida.

Don: É.

Martinha: Né? No fundo no fundo ela/a gente teve/certas vezes eu mesmo tenho até pena dela, porque eu convivo com muitas aqui e vejo muitas, muitas mulheres . . .

Keila: É realmente as mulheres muitas vezes se tornam muito submissa, elas gostam de deixar os homens dominá-las e isso ⌐não é bom não.
Martinha: └É.

Keila: Eu não gosto desse lado de ser mulher por isso, porque eu sempre acho que elas vão sempre ser inferior aos/aos homens.

Martinha: ⌐Por mais que ela . . .
Keila: └E a gente é travesti, a gente num é mulher, a gente já foi homem, a gente agora é mulher. É por isso que é bom a gente ser travesti, por essa mágica que a gente tem de ser/

⌐Já foi homem. Agora elas, as mulheres, jamais vão ser homem pra tentar saber o que, o que é ser homem.

Martinha: └Ela nunca tem a malícia que a gente tem nem nada.

reality. We see reality like it is, they don't. They live in a world of fantasy. They do.

⌐Marriage/
D: └Women?

M: Yeah, women. It's all marriage, have children, live off their husband, you know?

D: Yeah.

M: And us no. We have reality. We face the reality of life.

D: Yeah.

M: Isn't that true? Really deep down, she/we had/sometimes I even feel sorry for them, because I live with a lot of them here [in this house] and I see lots and lots of women . . .

K: Yeah, really—lots of times women become really submissive, they like to let men dominate them, and this ⌐isn't good.
M: └Right.

K: I don't like this side of being a woman for that reason, because I think that they'll always be inferior to/to men.

M: ⌐No matter how hard she . . .
K: └And we're travestis, we're not women, we were men, now we're women. This is why it's good being a travesti, for this magic that we have being/

⌐We were already men. And they, women, are never going to be men, to try to know what it is, what it is to be a man.

M: └She'll never have the spark that we have, never.

Because the idea of "woman" that travestis elaborate is discussed entirely in terms of specific appearances, behaviors, and relationships to males, and because any evidence that real women do not look or act in the expected ways is taken as evidence that travestis understand femininity in better and more realistic ways than women do, femaleness becomes something wholly within the reach of anybody who wants it badly enough. To feel like a woman, travestis need not engage with the lives of real women. They need only acquire the appropriate attributes and the requisite relationships. As I have documented throughout this chapter, those attributes are precisely what individual travestis spend many years of their lives acquiring, as they move from furtive, nocturnal appearances in androgynous clothing, through increasingly open displays of female clothing and bodily practices such as letting hair grow, plucking eyebrows, and shaving legs, through the consumption of hormones that give them breasts and rounded features, and finally to the injection of industrial silicone that provides them with permanent and prominent bundas and other female bodily features.

Appearances, however, are only part of the picture. In order to truly feel like a woman, a *mulher*, a travesti needs more than a skirt and a bunda. She also requires relationships to males, males who, at best, make her feel like a total woman—who make her feel, in Luciana's word, *mulheríssima*.

Three

A Man in
the House

A recurring and extremely serious problem with scholarly studies of prostitution is that they generally only tell us about the professional lives of the women who earn their living through sex work. Unlike most other people, who are readily acknowledged to have a life outside or beyond what they do at work, a prostitute tends to be defined completely in terms of the work that she does.[1] She is generally thought of as a prostitute twenty-four hours of the day, even when she is not working. This understanding of prostitutes is reinforced by study after study that either makes no mention of a prostitute's private life or discusses her private life in a way that only serves to highlight her identity as a prostitute. Often we are told or led to believe, for example, that the boyfriends of prostitutes are their pimps, and that the prostitutes are together with them out of necessity, delusion, or fear—or for all those reasons at once (see, e.g., Barry 1979:86–120, 1995:198–219; and Høigård and Finstad 1986: 203–69).

Even work that is sympathetic to prostitutes and concerned to nuance understandings about them and their lives tends to mention their private lives cursorily, and then primarily to draw contrasts with their professional lives.[2] So in Sophie Day's sensitive writing about London prostitutes (1990) or in the careful monograph by McKeganey and Barnard on prostitutes in Glasgow (1996), for example, discussion of boyfriends is restricted to an account of how the women interviewed reserve specific parts of their bodies (for example, their mouths) and specific sexual activities (e.g., kissing and oral sex) for their boyfriends, whereas other parts and activities can be made available to clients. We are told nothing about how the prostitutes' boyfriends are chosen or how the women interact with them in nonsexual contexts. Similarly, in Shannon Bell's respectful and revealing interviews with prostitutes (1995), in Gail Pheterson's theoretical and activist writings (1989, 1996), in the recent special section of the journal *Social Text* that concerned prostitutes (vol. 37, winter 1993), and in the newly published collection of feminist writings by sex workers (Nagle 1997), what is discussed is the practice and politics of sex work, not private lives.

What all this means is that in the many studies, interviews, and books about prostitutes, we learn an enormous amount about how prostitutes think about, interact with, and relate to clients. But with only a few exceptions—such as Serena Nanda's work on Indian *hijras* (1990), Annick Prieur's writings on Mexican *jotas* (1994a, 1998), or Jeferson Bacelar's monograph on the domestic lives of Brazilian female prostitutes (1982)—we learn next to nothing about how they think about their private relationships, how they make themselves attractive for the individuals they wish to have as partners, and what role those partners play in the prostitutes' life more generally.

In living with travestis in Salvador, I discovered very quickly that boyfriends (generally referred to as *maridos*, which literally means "husbands," but also called *bofes*, *ocós*, *homens*, and *machos*) are a continual and central consideration in their lives. Boyfriends take up an enormous amount of a travesti's thought, time, and talk—not to mention her money. Travestis are forever orienting themselves to their current boyfriends, their ex-boyfriends, and their prospective boyfriends. The activities of boyfriends provide endless fodder for gossip and conflicts among travestis. When talking to other travestis, they discuss various men, commenting on what qualities a male must possess in order to be considered eligible as a boyfriend. They are forever trying to figure out how to attract some male who they have decided has those qualities, or they are trying to get over their bitterness at having been left and possibly robbed by some male who they *thought* had those qualities. When they are courting a potential boyfriend or have snagged one they want to keep, a great deal of their life and their income revolves around him and his comfort, and they shower him with money, presents, and drugs—until the day they tire of him, at which point they send him packing and install a new man in their room. If there is one topic about which all travestis have strong opinions, it is boyfriends. Without understanding the role that boyfriends play in the lives of travestis, it is impossible to understand any dimension of their lives.

Of Men and Viados

The topic of boyfriends will always provoke discussion among travestis. Late one night I was sitting with several travestis as they stood working along a street in a suburb of Salvador. Present were Keila; Michelle, a forceful travesti in her late twenties; and Treze, a young travesti who was unique in Salvador in that she had a relationship with a young man who dressed up in female clothing and prostituted himself at night, often alongside Treze. As we were talking, this young man, in full female drag, passed by on the other side of the street. Treze pointed him out and asked me if I had already met her "bicha." I said that I had, and I asked her if it was true that they were living together as a couple. The answer she gave to this question led to an extended discussion of boyfriends:

Treze: Eu não preciso de um homem para me satisfazer Don (   ) para ter problemas, sabe? Ele só em cima de mim, com despesas, não quero não.

Don: É?

Treze: Quero não, quero nada de diabo de homem na minha vida. Pra comer o que é meu? Óia.

Michelle: ⌈Não é assim também não mona.

Treze: ⌊"Ói, meu amor, bote uma saia." O quê?! Os homens de hoje querem o quê Keila?

Keila: Que a gente lhes sustentem.

Treze: Pra travesti tá na rua pra dar na mão. Pra dar na mão, né?

Michelle: ⌈Né todos assim não mona. Né todos assim não.

Treze: ⌊Eu: "Bota saia ali. Vai ganhar também junto comigo."

Michelle: Não que não é todos não.

Treze: "Ganhe junto comigo. Pare o carro roube a maricona junto comigo. Vá. Olhe: a primeira maricona que sair volte no meu pé pra azuelar."

Michelle: ⌊Ah mona, mas é porque você mora com viado.

Treze: Lógico. É com viado mesmo. É por isso que eu não quero homem.

T: I don't need a man to satisfy me, Don (   ) to have problems, you know? Him only hanging onto my coattails, with expenses, I don't want it.

D: No?

T: I don't want it, I don't want any damn man in my life. To eat up everything I have? I'm so sure.

M: ⌈It's not like that, mona.

T: ⌊"Oi, dear heart, put on a dress" [Treze told the male living with her]. What!? Men today want what, Keila?

K: That we support them.

T: For travestis to work the streets to support them. To support them, right?

M: ⌈They're not all like that, mona. They're not all like that.

T: ⌊I [said]: "Put this dress on. You're gonna go and earn [money] together with me."

M: They're not all like that.

T: "Earn [money] together with me. Stop cars, rob old faggots together with me. Go on. Look: the first old faggot you go with, bring him back to where I'm standing ⌈so we can rob him."

M: ⌊Ah mona, but that's because you live with a viado.

T: That's right. I live with a real viado. That's why I don't want a man.

Michelle: Olha, você quer que todos more com viado.

Treze: Não.

Michelle: Vamos se amigar todos agora, né mona?

Treze: Eu disse apenas que eu não quero mais homem na minha vida. Pra comer o que é meu? Não minha filha.

> ┌ Homem, todos é podre.

Michelle: └ O meu não toma nada que eu tenho, sabe mona?

Treze: Homens são podres Keila.

Michelle: O meu é otimo. O meu tem um mal—ele é preguiçoso. Mas ele não é ruim não. Ele não é do tipo de chegar/eu chegar com dinheiro ele pegar minha bolsa pegar meu

> ┌ dinheiro, ele não faz isso não.
> │ Ele nunca fez isso. Agora é
> │ preguiçoso.

Treze: └ Eu ter um homem pra tá assistindo televisão vinte quatro horas de cu pra cima Keila? Em cima da cama, só close? E eu me fu dendo na pista, chegar em casa . . .

M: Listen, you want all of us to live with viados.

T: No.

M: Let's all marry each other, huh mona?

T: I just said that I don't want another man in my life. To eat up everything that is mine? No, girl.

> ┌ All men are rotten.

M: └ Mine doesn't steal anything of mine, you know, mona?

T: Men are rotten, Keila.

M: Mine is great. Mine has one fault—he's lazy. But he's not horrible. He's not the type who comes home/I come home with money and he takes my purse and takes

> my ┌ money, he doesn't do that.
> │ He's never done that. But he
> │ is lazy.

T: └ I should have a man to have him sitting watching television twenty-four hours a day with his ass up in the air, Keila? Reclining on the bed striking poses? And me fucked out on the street working, get home . . .

This conversation continued, Michelle protesting that her boyfriend respected her and that if travestis had the kind of boyfriends that Treze was talking about, it was their own fault: "Tudo é o comportamento do viado"—It all depends on how the travesti comports herself. "If you let him behave like that," Michelle explained, "he'll grow used to it and always behave like that." She elaborated:

Michelle: O meu tem um mal: ele é preguiçoso. Mas ele nunca me dá na minha cara, ele não dá na minha cara, porque se ele der, ele toma. Se ele pegar arma pra mim, eu pego pra ele também—eu não deito pra ele não. Que ele tem medo, ele tem medo de mim, sabe? Ele não me tira como viadinho, não, que eu não sou viadinho.

M: Mine has one problem: he's lazy. But he never hits me, he never hits me, because if he hits me, he'll get hit back. If he pulls a gun on me, I'll pull one on him—I'm not gonna let him walk all over me. He's afraid, he's afraid of me, you know? He doesn't take me for a stupid little viado, 'cause I'm not a stupid little viado.

Keila: Eu não vejo Maurílio mais. Eu vi ele uma vez só/

Michelle: Só fica dentro de/Keila, quando esse homem tá comigo, ele é dentro de casa o dia todo. Só sai de noite pra trabalhar—lá no sindicato, lá no Kimuqueca. E de noite, vai pra casa. Não anda em meio de jeito nenhum. Trabalho ele nunca vai ter, pelo menos, minha filha, morrer de fome, não vai, né?

K: I never see Maurílio [Michelle's boyfriend] anymore. I only saw him once/

M: He's always inside the/Keila, when this man is with me, he's inside the house all day long. He only leaves in the evening to work—there at the union building, at Kimuqueca [a restaurant where Maurílio stands some evenings and collects change from people who park their cars along a stretch of sidewalk he watches]. And when it gets late, he comes right home. He doesn't hang out with homosexuals at all [the implication being this is why Keila has not seen him in a while]. He'll never get a job, but at least he won't die of hunger [because Michelle earns money prostituting herself], right girl?

Purposely or not, Treze hit a sore spot here when she began disparaging men as rotten and saying that all they really wanted from a travesti was an easy life and a meal ticket. And the sore spot, as the sarcastic and heated response to Treze's pronouncements indicates, belonged to Michelle. Other travestis were of the opinion that Michelle's boyfriend, Maurílio, exploited and bullied her, and her ardent and detailed assurances that Maurílio respected and even feared her indicate that Michelle was aware of that opinion and felt compelled to defend herself against it.

More than as an accurate account of her relationship to her boyfriend, Michelle's response to Treze can therefore be heard as a kind of description of what a travesti-boyfriend relationship should be like. In this ideal, the boyfriend will be supported economically by his travesti girlfriend, but he will wait to be given money—he will not just reach into her purse when she comes home and take it. Furthermore, he will not hit her or threaten her with firearms—indeed, he will be frightened of her. He will occasionally leave the room where the two live together, perhaps to earn some pocket money; but he will avoid the company of homosexuals, and he will spend most of his time "inside the house" in the company of his travesti girlfriend.

Treze presents the flip side of this idealization—a male who does nothing except lay at home watching television "twenty-four hours a day . . . striking poses," while his travesti girlfriend is getting "fucked out

on the street working." In this depiction of a travesti-boyfriend relationship, all a boyfriend does is hang on the coattails of a travesti in order to
consume everything she earns. The only thing the boyfriend wants from
the travesti is to be supported by her. "All men are rotten," Treze repeats
several times, dismissing Michelle's rose-colored tale even as she is busy
presenting it. Treze's own solution to the problem she identifies is to
refuse to enter into relationships with "men." Instead, her relationship is
with a viado, a faggot like herself, who puts on a dress and goes out at
night together with her, helping her earn money through prostitution
and robbery.

Treze's choice of partner was regarded by other travestis as idiosyncratic and bizarre, something that is evident in Michelle's snide barb that
Treze thinks travestis should all marry one another. The oddness of
Treze's personal life was also reflected in the way other travestis generally behaved towards her: she had a reputation among them as being a
bicha mole—a soft, weak fag—and other travestis picked on her and took
advantage of her, driving her away from where she wanted to stand to
attract clients, or demanding small sums of money from her to buy themselves beer or something to eat. And then there was her name. Although
she always said it was Rogéria, everyone called her Treze, which means
"Thirteen" and has the same link to bad luck in Brazilian Portuguese as it
does in English.

When I first heard travestis voicing their dislike of Treze, and when
the connotations of her name were made explicit to me, I was surprised.
I found Treze to be funny, perceptive, and intelligent. I liked her. So
whenever I saw her in the company of other travestis, I began keeping
my eyes open for some indication that she was somehow disagreeable or
socially inept, or that she was the fey *bicha mole* that everyone said she
was. I never saw it. I finally came to the conclusion that other travestis
bullied Treze and disliked her not because she was dramatically different
from any of them, but because her choice of a viado as her partner threw
into relief their own choices and prompted them to reflect on, and in
some cases defend—in the long-winded and rather forced manner that
Michelle does here—the fact that they were living with, or searching
for, a man who consumed a great deal of their time, energy, and money.

For the fact of the matter is that Treze, for all intents and purposes, is
right. Not only is her description of travesti relationships with boyfriends a fairly accurate summary of what I observed myself in relationship after relationship, but it is also what travestis themselves readily tell
one another—particularly when they find themselves at the tail end of a
relationship. Treze's offense is therefore not so much that she tells it like
it is—lots of other travestis do that. Her impropriety is that she has

altogether opted out of the affective framework that lends meaning to travestis' personal relationships. She has removed herself from the social system that provides travestis with the males they choose as boyfriends. Just as sex-change operations make no sense to most travestis, Treze's choice of a viado as a partner is irrational, disturbing, perverse. Indeed, one of the harshest insults one travesti can scream at another—immediate fighting words—is "Seu marido é viado": Your boyfriend is a faggot.

Keila's Passion

Keila was in the throes of passion. During the week of Carnival, she had suddenly begun falling in love with Tiane, a tall, muscular, tattooed, illiterate, thirty-year-old man who looked and acted like a nineteen-year-old adolescent, spending every day playing soccer on a nearby beach and getting high with his friends. Keila knew Tiane well—for six years he had been the live-in boyfriend of her best friend, Marília, who had died after a long illness a few months previously—but she had never felt anything for him. She had lived in the same house with him, seen him daily, and spoken to him occasionally without contemplating the possibility of having him as her boyfriend. Now, though, without any warning and for some completely inexplicable reason, she was experiencing what she told me was desperate, sincere, and blind passion.

It had begun with an electric exchange of looks as they passed one another on the street during Carnival, and quickly progressed into brief, meaningful greetings as Tiane passed by Keila as she was working on the street at night. From Tiane's old mother, who lived in a back room the size of a cupboard in the same house as Keila, Keila began hearing that Tiane wondered if Keila could spare a few reais for him to buy himself food and beer on the street. Keila gave his mother the money to pass on to him. She also bought him several new shirts and pairs of shorts, which she again conveyed through his mother.

Tiane's mother was the intermediary at this point because initially, Keila's passion for Tiane had to be kept secret. The reason for this was partly because Keila shared her tiny room with Edilson, her boyfriend of the past seven years, and partly because a toothless older travesti living in the house on São Francisco Street—Rita Lee, who took her name from a famous Brazilian rock singer—had recently let it be known to everybody that Tiane was hers. She demonstrated this by ostentatiously buying and preparing food for him and calling him into her room to eat, closing the door behind him and emerging later with a content smile, even when it was obvious to everyone in the house that all she and Tiane had done in her room was argue.

For the first few weeks of her infatuation, Keila didn't know what to do. She couldn't openly speak to Tiane—not near the house where she lived, because Edilson or Rita Lee or someone else would surely see, nor on the street where she worked at night, because one of the other travestis working the same street would certainly observe such a conversation and report it to others. All she could do was keep sending him small sums of money through his mother and exchange brief, coded words as they passed one another on their way to or from the communal bathroom or the communal refrigerator at the back of the house, where they both had rooms (Tiane had been sleeping in his mother's room since the death of Marília). During these quick encounters, Keila twice whispered times and places for Tiane to pass by on backstreets near where she worked. Both times she waited in vain—once he didn't show, and once he passed by with friends saying he would return later, but never did. A third time she asked *him* to suggest a time when he knew he would be able to come. He didn't show up that time either. Keila began to despair.

While all this was going on, Keila was helping me buy furniture for the room I had rented in the house where she (and Tiane and Rita Lee, among many others) lived. Trudging across Salvador's old town, grasping the front end of a queen-size mattress I had just purchased, Keila told me that she was on the verge of giving up on Tiane. After having attempted to meet with him three times and having him not show, she was tired and annoyed. She was going to drop him, she announced firmly. Well, maybe after she gave him one more chance. She would ask him straight out the next time she saw him—did he want her or not? She needed a definite answer. "It will hurt me if he says no," she said, "because I am impassioned with him—I'm going crazy, I think about him all the time. But the hurt will go away. And if he definitely says no, he doesn't want me, then I can stop thinking about him. If he gives me the answer I want, though," she continued, "then he will have to stop playing with me."

The next day, as we were lugging my new table and four little stools up steep, potholed hills, Keila, beaming and laughing, told me that she had asked Tiane and he had given her "the correct answer." So now they had arranged to meet later that night outside a backstreet hotel to which Keila sometimes took clients

I heard the denouement to Keila's passion the following day, as we picked our way through crowded streets carrying a roll of carpet that I had decided I needed to put down to make it more difficult for the roaches to crawl up through the cracks in my floor. Keila had arranged to meet Tiane outside the hotel at eight o'clock the previous evening. At nine o'clock, he passed by in the company of a friend. "Where are you going?" Keila hissed at him discreetly. Up the street for a drink, he answered.

He returned at eleven o'clock. Keila was still waiting. They took a hotel room and sat talking for several hours. They did not have sex, Keila told me; they just talked about whether Tiane really wanted to begin having a relationship with Keila. He told her he would. Before they left the hotel room, he also told her that his birthday was coming up in a few weeks, and he would really like a present of an expensive pair of stylish overalls that he had had his eye on for some time.

The end of this story is both happy and sad. A few days after her discussion in the hotel room with Tiane, Keila announced to Edilson that it was over and that she was leaving him. She installed herself in my newly furnished and carpeted little room for a couple of days, then moved her belongings to a room in a house several blocks away. Tiane began to sleep and take his meals with her regularly. After several weeks of living isolated from other travestis and the milieu she had lived in for seven years, Keila decided that she wanted to return to her old house. She rented a small room right above Edilson, and moved in there with Tiane. Edilson took all this very badly, and he began to drink heavily and spread rumors that Keila had AIDS. He made several attempts to find another travesti girlfriend, but no one was interested. Edilson did what he could to make Keila's life miserable for a few months, then he had to move, because he had sold the last of his belongings and could no longer pay his rent.

Rita Lee, who had only been together with Tiane for less than a week, continued to regard him as her boyfriend whom Keila had snatched from her. She grew enormously bitter and also began to drink continually. Her health failed, she grew increasingly desiccated, and she was unable to work the streets at night. She, too, eventually became unable to pay her rent, and she was duly evicted. Unable to support herself and unwanted by her family, who live in a suburb on the outskirts of Salvador, Rita Lee ended up in a hospice for AIDS patients, where she died in early 1996.

The Selection and Socialization of Boyfriends

The story of Keila's passion reveals a number of characteristic features of travesti-boyfriend relationships. First of all, there is the object of Keila's infatuation—a handsome young man with no apparent income who spent all his days playing soccer and getting stoned. For six years he had been the boyfriend of a travesti who had lived in the same house as Keila, a relationship that ended only when Marília died.

Tiane could be the pattern from which all other travesti boyfriends were cut. The males that travestis choose to be their boyfriends are

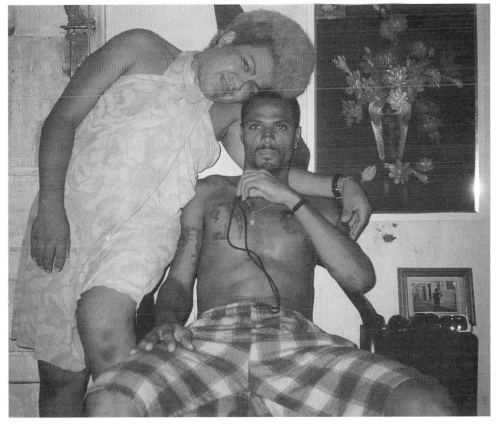

Keila and Tiane

always handsome, muscular, usually tattooed young men between the ages of about sixteen and thirty. They almost never work, and if they do, they virtually invariably seem to work as security guards for buildings or parking lots. Just as invariably, the majority of those who do work stop working soon after they establish a relationship with a travesti. Sometimes they stop at the insistence of the travesti; most often they don't need to be told, but quit of their own accord.[3] A travesti usually meets such a man because he lives in the same area, because he is the brother or cousin or friend of another travesti's boyfriend, or, finally, because he is himself already the boyfriend of a travesti. Once a male becomes known as the boyfriend of a travesti, he immediately sparks the interest of the others, who will wonder what he has that his travesti girlfriend wants. Keila explained this to me once with the help of a concrete example:

> A man can pass by travestis and they won't even notice him—no one notices him, no one wants him, no one sees him. But if he gets together with

a travesti, everyone is going to size him up, because he has something different. Because if he's been passing by here and no one has noticed him, but she wanted him—well let's see what he has.

Look at the case of Carla's boyfriend. That little black man (*aquele neguinho*) who lives with her. Carla's boyfriend lived on the street. Nobody even looked twice at him—he used to come around here selling used shorts, used shoes. He was a friend of ours, but nobody noticed him. And Carla took him and made him her boyfriend. I don't know who the fortune-teller was among travestis, with her crystal ball, but some travesti discovered that he had an enormous dick (*um picão*). In her crystal ball, she saw it. And so, the gossip started among travestis that he had an enormous dick, and everyone suddenly wanted him to find out why he was together with Carla—he could only be with her because of some quality that he had. And how to discover that quality? Have sex with him.

If "that quality" that a particular boyfriend has is a particularly attractive one (and for many—most—travestis, an unusually large penis can constitute such a quality), then the boyfriend will be the object of much attention from other travestis, who may try to win him over by giving him presents and money. There is thus continual, and sometimes quite fierce and brutal, competition among travestis over a limited number of boyfriends. (The only fights I have witnessed between travestis have been about boyfriends.) Many of these boyfriends, once they have formed a relationship with a travesti, remain in the boyfriend pool for many years, where they circulate among travestis until they either settle down with one or—as in the case of Keila's ex-boyfriend Edilson—grow too old and unattractive to be of much interest to anyone, in which case they disappear from the travesti milieu.

The most unusual way for a travesti to meet a male who later becomes her boyfriend is as a paying client. This apparently sometimes happens—in her book *A Princesa*, Fernanda Farias de Albuquerque mentions that several of her boyfriends were met whom she first met on the streets as clients. But in this, Fernanda seems somewhat exceptional. I know of no travesti in Salvador who has formed a relationship with a man whom she met as a paying client. Travestis can meet their boyfriends while working on the street, but usually only in the capacity of what they called *vícios*, a word that means "vice" or "addiction" and that signifies men with whom they have sex for free because they are attracted to them. (*Fazer um vício*—do a vício—also signifies the action of having sex with such a man.) A particularly manly and breathtaking vício can eventually become a boyfriend, but not, it would seem, a man from whom the travesti has accepted money for sex.

There are three reasons why travestis are not interested in making their clients into boyfriends. The first is that they are suspicious of a man who has paid for sex and then attempts to develop a relationship with them. They think that he is only interested in free sex and in ingratiating himself so that he will become part of the pool of boyfriends who circulate among travestis. In addition, the very fact that the travesti accepted money from him in the first place (instead of treating him as a vício and having sex with him for free) means that she does not find him desirable enough to enter into consideration as a boyfriend. And finally, a great many clients pay travestis to penetrate them. While travestis often enjoy penetrating clients and some of their vícios, they will not tolerate, for reasons to be discussed in detail below, a male who enjoys being anally penetrated *dentro de casa*—in the house.

Another very characteristic feature of Keila's passion for Tiane is the fact of her being impassioned—*apaixonada*. This is an emotion that travestis feel they share with women. Like themselves, women can become *perdidamente apaixonadas* (desperately impassioned) with men and do anything and everything to attract and keep the object of their passion. Men, travestis say, rarely become impassioned, and when they do, it is always for a woman—never for a travesti. As far as I was able to determine, this is a viewpoint shared by all travestis; I never heard a travesti describe her boyfriend's feelings for her in terms of passion, even though they regularly used that word in talking about their own emotional engagement. Quite the opposite—I repeatedly heard travestis tell one another that in fact, boyfriends don't even particularly like travestis. Right after Keila had left Edilson and begun living with Tiane, Carlinhos advised her to be careful: "Men don't love us," she warned, "men don't love us" (*Homem não ama a gente, homem não ama a gente*). Banana told me something very similar. "Men don't like us," she said. "They like women. For a woman they'll go out and sell popsicles on the street if they have to, and for us, even if we're on our deathbed, they won't work. Either they'll find another travesti [who will give them money on the sly], or they'll leave." Martinha bemoaned the fact that "men are mean and spiteful (*maldoso*) to travestis. Unfortunately, we're homosexual, we like them. But they create a lot of malevolence (*maldade*) around us." When I asked Magdala what she thought about the men that travestis had as boyfriends, she began her response with "Look, Don, it's really sad . . ." And in a conversation between me, Angélica (the sixty-year-old travesti), and Boca Louca, Angélica's middle-aged female prostitute friend, passion was talked about in the following terms:

Angélica: Os homens nunca se apaixona. São crocodilos, né?	A: Men never get impassioned. They're crocodiles, you know?

Boca L: São crocodilos.

Angélica: São falsos. Assim como eles faz com as mulé, faz com os viado também.

Boca L: Faz com os viados também, a mesma coisa ⌈com uma mulher faz.

Angélica: ⌊Com as mulé ele faz, que têm buceta eles faz, quanto mais ⌈com os viado.

Boca L: ⌊Faz com, é, com os viado.

Don: É, é, é.

Boca L: Porque homes, é difícil considerar, ⌈sabe?

Don: ⌊É.

Boca L: Já a mulher e o viado, se apaixona, e eles quasilmente, larga as, uma mulé aqui, agora pega outa lá adiante. E o viado, quando gosta, é de um só.

Don: É.

Boca L: O viado e a mulé também, quando se apaixona é por um só.

Don: É.

Boca L: E eles, home, não. Ele só se contenta pegar uma, pegar outra, pegar outra, pegar outra, pronto.

BL: They're crocodiles.

A: They're false. The things they do to women, they do to viados too.

BL: They do it to viados too, the same thing ⌈that they do to women.

A: ⌊They do it to women, to them who have cunts they do it, you can imagine how they do it even more to ⌈viados.

BL: ⌊Do it, yeah, to viados.

D: Uh-huh, uh-huh, uh-huh.

BL: Because men don't take anyone into consideration, ⌈you know?

D: ⌊Yeah.

BL: Women and viados get impassioned, but they [men] easily leave one woman here, take another one there. And viados, when they like a man, it's only one.

D: Uh-huh.

BL: Viados and women too, when they get impassioned, it's only for one [man].

D: Uh-huh.

BL: And them, men, no. They're only content taking one, then another, then another, then another, that's it.

Here, men are considered to never become impassioned with anyone—female or travesti. This viewpoint is probably a common one among lower-class women in Salvador, many of whom share with Boca Louca the experience of being abandoned by the fathers of their children (the father of Boca Louca's four children left her, she told me, for another woman while the children were all still tiny. He contributed nothing to their upbringing). But even though all travestis know that men routinely abandon women, they would all agree with Banana that at least they can feel, even if only temporarily, some kind of passion for them. Furthermore, there is a concrete, tangible reason for this, travestis say: "God made woman for man and man for woman" (*Que Deus fez a mulher pro homem e o homem pra mulher*).

This saying recurs with surprising frequency in travesti talk. I heard it used in discussions about gay marriage, which many travestis dismiss as a *safadeza*—a strongly condemnatory word meaning something like "atrocity" or "abomination"—and in discussions about lesbianism, which travestis find unnatural and threatening.[4] It also regularly appears in discussions about boyfriends. At one point during Keila's conversation with Carlinhos about her fresh relationship with Tiane, for example, Carlinhos told Keila not to delude herself into thinking that the relationship would last forever. Keila responded:

> Eu sei que não vai, eu sei que não vai, eu sei que nada é definitivo. Justamente quando são homem e mulher, o que nasce um pro outro, o que Deus determinou que fosse homem pra mulher, eles se separam mais dia menos dia, imagina dois homens com cabeças iguais que pensam diferente. Eu sei que não vai durar, claro.

> I know it won't last [forever], I know it won't, I know that nothing lasts forever. When men and women, who were born for one another, since God determined that men should be for women, separate sooner or later, imagine two men with the same [male] head who think differently. I know it won't last [forever], of course not.

Because travestis believe that men were not "determined" for them and hence do not become impassioned with them, it is useless for them to try to appeal to a man's emotions when they are trying to hook him. In other words, a travesti does not assume that a man to whom she is attracted will also become attracted to her if she flirts demurely and tries to ingratiate herself with him. Her assumption is the opposite—that the man she is after will never fall in love with her. So instead of attempting to seduce him through sex appeal, a travesti will travel a much more direct road to her man's heart (to the extent that he has one, in this understanding of male emotions). That road is one paved with money and material goods.

From its inception, any travesti-boyfriend relationship will be characterized by the transfer of money and presents from the travesti to the male. For example, money and gifts began to flow from Keila to Tiane (via his mother) before the two had even had their first long conversation. Words were not needed at this point, however—the fact that Tiane requested money from Keila, and the fact that she gave it, signaled that a relationship was in the offing. Indeed, gift giving by a travesti to a male both marks a relationship and signals to others that a relationship is under way. Keila's ex-boyfriend Edilson told me that he began to suspect something was amiss when he noticed that Tiane suddenly had begun sporting expensive-looking new clothes. Who bought them for him? he wondered to himself, suspecting it might have been Keila. And when Keila was still in the initial stages of her relationship with Tiane, before anyone knew she was interested in him, Rita Lee confided to me that she thought Keila was after "her man." The reason she cited for this suspicion struck me as ridiculously trivial and paranoid, but I later realized that within the travesti framework for understanding relationships with boyfriends, it was actually profoundly meaningful. The reason was this: one evening when he was staying in Rita Lee's room, Tiane demanded a soda pop. Rita Lee had no money at all and told him so. He left the room and returned a few minutes later with a soda pop. "Where did you get that?" she asked him. "Keila gave it to me," was his portentous response.

That money and gifts are crucial to all travesti-boyfriend relationships is a recurring theme in talk about boyfriends. A poor travesti has no boyfriend. A wealthy travesti, on the other hand, can pick and choose. Carlinhos reminded Keila of this in the conversation they had about Keila's new life with Tiane. Telling Keila to be careful, Carlinhos turned to me and explained:

Carlinhos: Ela sabe que no caso dela ele é uma pessoa maravilhosa. Mas se der mais, do que ela pode oferecer aqui, ele vai.

C: She knows that in her case, he [Tiane] is a marvelous person. But [Carlinhos's point is:] if someone gives him more than she can offer him, he'll leave.

Keila: Claro que sim, lógico.

K: Of course he will, of course.

Carlinhos: Chegar um travesti agora da Itália, pegar ele no canto e encostar, dizer assim: "Vamos, eu vou alugar um apartamento ali, você vai ter um carro,"

C: If a travesti who has returned from working in Italy should turn up, take him and lean him up against a corner and say: "Let's go, I'm gonna rent an apartment over there, you'll have a car,"

Keila: Ele vai, lógico que vai.

K: He'll go, of course he'll go.

Carlinhos: ele parece que nem viu você.

C: he'll act as though he's never even seen you.

Keila: Eu sei.

K: I know.

Carlinhos: Sabe disso né?

C: You know this, right?

Boyfriends know this too, of course, and one of the ways they keep their travesti girlfriend giving is to either imply or say outright that other travestis are giving them, or are willing to give them, more. Early in their relationship, for example, Tiane let Keila know that some unnamed person had mentioned to him that she would give him much more than Keila was giving him if he left Keila and came to live with her instead. Keila asked him what he had replied to this. Nothing, he shrugged. Keila then tried to get out of him the identity of the travesti who had made such an offer. But Tiane wouldn't say, since Keila has a *cabeça quente*, a hot head, and would certainly have flown at the guilty travesti (that the person in question was a travesti was taken for granted by Keila—a woman would never offer to support a man in that way, she reasoned). In the end, Keila thanked Tiane for imparting this information and brought up the incident later in a conversation with me to indicate that he was enjoying being together with her. My own interpretation of this interaction was very different—I saw it as a way for Tiane to make Keila feel insecure and compel her to keep up the flow of money and goods.

How much a travesti gives her boyfriend depends entirely on what she earns. Rita Lee, who was too old and sick to earn much money as a prostitute, courted Tiane by giving him the only thing she had to offer—a place to sleep and one cooked meal a day. At the other end of the continuum are travestis who spend enormous sums on their boyfriends. Luciana once returned home from Italy with a sizeable amount of money hidden under some cold cream and bought her boyfriend of the time a car. Likewise, Tina, who could sometimes return from an evening of prostitution with more than five hundred reais—all of it stolen—showered the young men she was courting with beer and marijuana and cocaine. Because I was working so intensely with Keila during the first few months of her relationship with Tiane, we talked a lot about the relationship. It quickly became very clear that she bought him some kind of present almost every single day. The present could be a slice of fancy cake for the equivalent of $2, or a handheld video game for $5, or a shirt for $10, or a wallet for $12, or some soccer socks for $15. In two particularly expansive weeks several months into their relationship, Keila bought Tiane a pair of soccer shoes with spikes ($60), a pair of pants and a shirt ($60), another pair of athletic shoes that he had asked her for ($119), a wallet and a baseball cap ($30), several T-shirts and pairs of shorts ($40), and a ticket to a rap concert ($30). In other words, in two weeks Keila spent the equivalent of over $300 on Tiane—this, in a country where the average salary at the time was just over $100 *a month*. And this in addition to paying the rent for the room, washing Tiane's clothes, preparing him meals, and providing him pocket money for entertainment, beer, snacks, and marijuana.

It is important to note here that despite this unidirectional flow of money and goods from the travesti to her boyfriend (when Keila told me she was going to buy Tiane the pair of overalls he requested at their first meeting for his birthday, I asked her what he was going to give her for her birthday, which was right around the same date. "Um beijinho," she laughed—a little kiss), it would be wrong to view the boyfriends of travestis as their pimps. Boyfriends are not pimps. They do not force unwilling individuals out into a life of prostitution on the street in order that they may live the high life.[5] Nor do they keep tabs on their travesti girlfriends while the travestis are working; indeed, the vast majority of boyfriends maintain no involvement at all in the professional life of the travesti. As long as she keeps paying the bills, boyfriends seem happy to leave the work side of life completely to the discretion of their travesti girlfriends. Many boyfriends go so far as to get up, turn off the television, and leave the room if their travesti girlfriend suddenly enters with a man and announces, "Vou trabalhar" (I'm gonna work). The only problems that can arise in this arrangement occur if a travesti claims to have no money despite the fact that she has been going to work nightly. At this point the boyfriend will suspect either that she has been doing vícios—having sex for free with attractive males (something that in fact occurs quite frequently while travestis are on the streets working)—or that she is paving the way for a relationship with another male by siphoning money off her income in order to begin the flow of presents and cash that will eventually result in a new boyfriend. In either case, the boyfriend will feel his own status threatened, and he will protest.

Whenever travestis talk about their relationships with their boyfriends and about the presents and money that they give them, they always stress their own agency. They all emphasize that they chose their boyfriends, not vice versa, and they all maintain that they elect to support them and give them things because they want to. "I *like* giving," Keila insisted whenever I expressed dismay at the fact that she was forever buying Tiane presents. She and other travestis commonly denote their giving by the verb *agradar*, which means "to please"—they give to please their boyfriends, not because they feel forced to.[6]

But is this magnanimity really entirely uncoerced? Are travestis really so generous by nature that they happily give a substantial amount of their hard-earned income to males who not only are not impassioned with them, but who don't even do anything to help them at work or around the house? An outsider coming from a culture where intimate relationships are supposed to be based on reciprocal feelings of love and on mutually supportive efforts to generate income and maintain a household might easily see travesti accounts and practices of giving as delusions—fantasies of agency that travestis spin in order to mask the harsh fact that they are being exploited by greedy, manipulative gigolos.

There are two reasons why a perspective that portrays travestis as the deluded victims of mercenary males would be too simplistic. The first is that travestis actively socialize young men into expecting money and goods from them. The majority of travestis I know in Salvador have a great weakness for adolescent boys, whom they refer to as *boys* or *boyzinhos*. The boyzinhos who are most attractive to travestis are generally muscular youths between the ages of fourteen and seventeen. There is no shortage of such youths in Salvador, and in any of the areas in which travestis live, there will be scores of tough-looking young men hanging

A travesti and a vício she met while working

around on the streets, doing little except socializing with one another and smoking and/or selling marijuana and other drugs. In many cases, these young men have grown up in the area, and travestis may have known them since they were children. When a travesti sees a boyzinho to whom she feels attracted, she will call him into her room and offer him a beer and/or some marijuana, and then she will have sex with him. Afterwards, she will give him the equivalent of a couple of dollars, to buy himself a *lanche*—a hot dog or some other snack—or some marijuana.

Although not all boyzinhos whom travestis beckon into their rooms follow them there, many do, often warning the travesti afterwards not to mention a word of the encounter to anyone else (she, of course, agrees, and then immediately blabs all the details to any travesti willing to listen). Through interactions like these, travestis treat themselves to a steady supply of attractive young men. And those attractive young men come to learn at least two things. Some of them undoubtedly learn that sex with a travesti can be erotically fulfilling. And they all learn that sex with travestis translates into cash. Keila's former boyfriend, Edilson, told me during an interview that he learned early on that "viado dá dinheiro"—viados pay: [7]

Edilson:: Eu sempre gostei de/de dinheiro, é porque . . . a gente, pobre . . . no bom sentido . . . sem formação . . . viado pra a gente, é . . . é uma fonte de renda.

Don: É.

Edilson: Sempre, desde pequeno que eu aprendi, que me ensinaram assim, eu, eu aprendi assim/

Don: Quem ensinou você?

Edilson: Eu num sei, talvez outos colegas, talvez comentários, né? Viado pra a gente sempre foi uma fonte de renda, uma fonte, um jogo de interesse.

Don: An-rã, an-rã.

Edilson: Desde pequeno que eu aprendi isso. Num sei se eu aprendi por mim próprio, mais sempre que alguns viados se interessava por mim, eu também tenho/queria ganhar alguma coisa.

E: I always li/liked money, it's because . . . one is poor . . . don't get me wrong . . . without education . . . viados for us are . . . a source of income.

D: Yeah.

E: Always, since I was little I knew, who taught me, that I learned that/

D: Who taught you?

E: I don't know, maybe friends, maybe I just heard comments, you know? A viado for us was always a source of income, a source, a scheme.

D: Uh-huh, uh-huh.

E: I learned this when I was a kid. I don't know if I just picked it up on my own, but whenever any viados were interested in me, I also had/ wanted to get something out of it.[8]

Don: An-rã. Então sempre quando
você transou com um, um viado,
você recebeu algum/

Edilson: Eu sempre recebi alguma coisa.

Don: Algum dinheiro, ou qual/

Edilson: É, alguma coisa, sempre
procurando fazer um tipo de
amizade pa poder ganhar uma
camisa, um relógio . . . [uma calça.

Don: [É verdade?

Edilson: É, sempre querendo exigir
um presente—não exigindo, mas
. . . sabendo pedir, né?

D: Uh-huh. So whenever you had sex
with a, a viado, you got something/

E: I always got something.

D: Some money or what/

E: Yeah, something, [I was] always
trying to make some kind of
friendship to be able to get a shirt,
a watch . . . [a pair of pants.

D: [Really?

E: Yeah, always wanting to demand a
present—not demand, but . . .
knowing how to ask, you know?

It is not merely coincidental that Edilson, knowing this, later formed attachments only to travestis.

The second, related reason why it would not do justice to travestis to see their relationships with their boyfriends simply in terms of their being exploited or deluded (or both) is that travestis are not unaware of the power they exert over boyzinhos and, later, their boyfriends, by virtue of the goods and money that they bestow on them. The coercive nature of the gift was pointed out to me by Keila on many occasions. She maintained that travestis give in order to dominate their boyfriends. At first, I was surprised at this assertion. But when I objected to its stark Machiavellian undertones and suggested that many travestis might give out of affection, Keila—who at this point was, of course, herself deeply involved in supporting Tiane and giving him some new present virtually every day—was dismissive:

Keila: Não, não é não. Porque com
todos eles com quem eu converso,
eles dizem assim: "Ah eu gosto de
dar dinheiro, porque aí eu humilho
ele, eu posso mandar nele." Então,
é uma coisa pra se sentir bem, de se
sentir poderoso sobre uma certa
pessoa.

Don: Verdade?

Keila: É.

Don: Os travestis falam assim,
[abertamente?

Keila: [Falam isso, "Se você"/abertamente: "Se você usou o meu dinheiro, então você deve obrigação a

K: No, it's not that. Because with
everyone I talk to, they say this:
"Ah I like to give money [to my
boyfriend] because then I can
humiliate him, I can order him
around." So it's something we do
to feel good, to feel powerful in
relation to another person.

D: Really?

K: Yeah.

D: Travestis say that [openly?

K: [They say it, "If
you"/openly: "If you used my money,
then you owe me, me who supports

mim, eu que sustento você, seu gigolô barato." As bichas dizem mais ou menos desse jeito. Então pronto.

E eles acostumam-se com esses termos que as bichas vão chamando, e pronto, não ligam mesmo. O problema todo é esse, todo travesti gosta disso, todos eles.

Don: Verdade? Porque a Tina por exemplo, eu sempre/ela dava muitas coisas a seus namorados.

Keila: Então ela só consegue homens assim. Aí os homens, por ela dar esse dinheiro mesmo, bastante, muito dinheiro que ela ganha, como ela ganha, eles têm um certo respeito, e um certo temor dela. Eles não fazem nada que ela não gosta na presença dela, embora eles façam às escondidas.

Então é isso que o travesti quer: que o homem pratique alguma coisa errada, mas que pratique longe dos olhos, que ele jamais saiba, que ele jamais veja. Entendeu?

Então pra isso que eles gostam de sustentar, porque o homem imagina o seguinte: "Puxa, se eu perder, eu 'sujar'"—como geralmente é falado na gíria—"eu vou perder, então eu não vou sujar."

Como o Tiane vive agora comigo: ele tem roupas boas, ele tem todas as coisas que ele precisa, entendeu? Então, ele jamais vai pensar em sujar comigo—se ele sujar comigo ele vai perder—ele vai voltar pra Rita Lee. Rita Lee vai dar o quê a ele?

you, you cheap gigolo." The bichas say things more or less like that. Like that.

And they [the boyfriends] get used to getting spoken to like that, and they don't mind. This is what it's all about, all travestis like that, all of them.

D: Really? Because Tina, for example, I always/she always gave lots of things to her lovers.

K: That's because it's the only way she can get men. And so the men, because she gives them this money, lots of money that she earns, 'cause she earns lots of money, they have a certain respect and a certain fear of her. They're not gonna do anything that she doesn't like in her presence, even if they do things when she isn't around.

And this is what a travesti wants: that her boyfriend does things wrong [here Keila is talking about having affairs with women, for example], but that he does them far away from her eyes, so that she'll never know, never see. You understand?

And that's why travestis like to support their boyfriends, because the man will think like this: "Sheez, if I lose this, if I 'dirty'"— as it's generally called in slang— "I'll lose it all, so I won't dirty" [i.e., betray or cheat the travesti].

Like Tiane lives with me right now: he has nice clothes, he has everything he needs, you know? So he'll never think of betraying or cheating me—if he "dirties" me, he'll lose it all—he'll go back to Rita Lee. Rita Lee will give him what?

Don: Nada.

Keila: Nada. Então pronto. Ele vai achar que não vai encontrar mais uma pessoa como eu pra ficar com ele, porque ele tinha Marília, Marília morreu, ficou eu, agora ele não vai encontrar uma outra pessoa. Então ele não quer isso. É por esse motivo de ele se sentir assim, um pouco receoso de nos perder, eles ficam submissos à gente. A gente lá pode dominar eles um pouco, pode falar mais alto que ele, pode dar um ordem e eles tem que aceitar.

Don: [laughs]

Keila: É. O problema todo é esse. Porque a gente gosta de/por a gente ser uma classe muito humilhada na rua, muito . . . é . . . vítima de muitos preconceitos na rua, a gente tem que ter uma pessoa sempre pra a gente se montar em cima dela. E a gente procura botar em quem? Nos casos da gente. Como a gente pode montar em cima deles? Sustentando eles, dando dinheiro a eles, para que a gente possa dominá-los, pelo menos dizer assim: "Na rua eles podem me criticar, mas em casa, pelo menos, tem uma que eu mando nele, ele faz o que eu quero, na hora que eu quero."

D: Nothing.

K: Nothing. So that's it. He'll think that he will never meet another person like me to be with him, because he had Marília, Marília died, then it was me, now he'll never meet another person. So he won't want [to lose everything]. This is the motive—for him to feel like that, a little afraid to lose us, they become submissive to us. We can dominate them a little, we can talk louder than them, give orders and they have to listen.

D: [laughs]

K: Yeah. That's what it's all about. Because we like/since we're a group that gets really humiliated on the street, really . . . we're . . . the victims of a lot of prejudices on the street, we need to have a person who we can always straddle and be on top of. And we try to be on top of who? Our boyfriends. How can we be on top of them? Supporting them, giving them money, so that we can dominate them, at least be able to say this: "On the street they can criticize me, but at home, at least, I have someone to boss around, he does what I want, when I want."

Keila draws attention to an important dimension of travesti-boyfriend relations that would be missed if one examined them only from the point of view of an outsider observing the flow of cash and presents from travestis to the men with whom they live. As Michelle did in her dispute with Treze about men, Keila foregrounds the respect and even fear that travestis feel their boyfriends will have for them, because the boyfriends understand how much they will lose if they "dirty" their relationship with the travesti. Keila also draws an explicit connection between boyfriends and a travesti's professional life as a prostitute, pointing out that travestis' interactions on the street have a significant bearing on the type of relationship they wish to maintain at home with their boyfriends.

I suspect that in highlighting domination as starkly as she does here, Keila is enunciating an insight afforded by her relative age and maturity (she is in her early thirties). I am uncertain whether travestis in their late teens, for example, explicitly see themselves as dominating the boyfriend they support in the manner Keila describes. I also suspect that the majority of newly "impassioned" travestis, no matter what their age, do not interpret their giving in terms of domination. My guess is that they see their giving as being motivated primarily by being impassioned and wanting to "please" the object of that passion. As a relationship wears on, however, the subtext of dependency and domination that Keila foregrounds may become increasingly apparent. One older travesti regularly announces publicly to her boyfriend of many years, "I support you, I can humiliate you" (*Eu te sustento, eu te humilho*). And the awareness that giving implies power is never totally absent, even in the case of young travestis; during conflicts, even adolescents will remind their boyfriends that they give them things. In a fight with her boyfriend that had the whole house on São Francisco Street awake at 3 A.M., nineteen-year-old Erica screamed, "I took you off the street, sleeping in the gutter—you hear?! You're a beggar!" (*Eu peguei você na rua, dormindo no relento, tá?! Você é mendingo!*).

In addition to not shying away from reminding their boyfriends that they are dependent on them, travestis know that they can stop giving whenever they want, and they do stop supporting their boyfriends when they tire of them or when their boyfriends betray them in some way (such as by having an affair with another travesti). Dismissing a boyfriend is not entirely without problems, however. One of the biggest risks for travestis within the framework in which they establish and maintain intimate relationships is that a boyfriend who is sent packing may not go. Having grown accustomed to a life of relative comfort and extreme ease, he may resist the travesti's attempts to dislodge him, and it is not uncommon for boyfriends in this situation to either rob the travesti of everything she owns one night when she is out working (some boyfriends go so far as to haul off refrigerators) or begin threatening and harassing her. "If I can't be with you, no one will," seems to be something that these soon-to-be-ex-boyfriends fairly often announce to their travesti girlfriends who tell them to get out.

A travesti deals with this threat in one of four ways: (1) she threatens the boyfriend right back, telling him she is not afraid of him and will stab him if he tries anything; (2) she makes sure that she has already established a relationship with another (bigger, stronger, meaner) man and hence can count on his support to eject the old boyfriend who refuses to go; (3) she skips town—an option that tends to hinge on how many

Mabel preparing dinner for herself and her boyfriend

belongings she has and whether she wants to leave them; or (4) she acquiesces to the boyfriend's threats and continues to live with him until she can either meet someone new or skip town (one travesti told me that she would have to go to Italy to escape her boyfriend, because she was certain that he would follow after her "like a dog" if she moved anywhere in Brazil). This latter option results in relationships that are clearly oppressive and abusive, and I know several travestis in Salvador who remain with their boyfriends only because they are afraid of them. Relationships like this are not common, however, and when they do occur, they are generally the subject of much discussion among other travestis, who regard them with concern and distaste. Most travestis who find themselves in a conflict with an ex-boyfriend choose the second or third option, and young travestis, especially, who have very few possessions and rent their rooms by the week, will leave town at a moment's notice because of a dispute with a rejected boyfriend. Nineteen-year-old Stefani's boyfriend Ulysses, for example, hit her one evening during a fight they were having over a rumor that Stefani had done a vício with a boyzinho earlier in the day when he was away. In a rage, he left the room they shared in the basement of the house on São Francisco Street. The next morning, when he returned to change his clothes and eat his breakfast, Ulysses found the room empty, and Stefani gone.

Boyfriends and Sex

Travestis win their boyfriends over with money and material goods, and if we take Keila's arguments about domination seriously and grant that travestis may construe their giving as a way of dominating their boyfriends (even if it may not always work out that way in practice), then it becomes somewhat clearer what they get out of a relationship that otherwise might appear rather empty and one-sided. But even if we do acknowledge the needs that Keila articulates to dominate and feel that one at least has control of one's home, the question remains of how a travesti's boyfriend makes her "feel like a woman." If a travesti, in order to feel like a woman, has to acquire the proper dress, attributes, and relationship with a man, what are the dynamics of the relationship that helps a travesti realize her ambition to feel like a woman—what exactly does her man have to do to make her feel *mulheríssima?*

The first thing he has to do is look like a man. Travestis are drawn to men who are classically masculine in their appearance. When I asked various travestis what an ideal man was for them, many responded as Banana does here, by listing a number of stereotypically masculine physical traits that they found attractive:

Banana: Gosto de homem novo.
Don: An-rã.
Banana: Bonito.
Don: An rã.
Banana: Pernudo, carnudo, bundão.

Don: É?
Banana: Pernão [laughs].
Don: É, eu também [laughs].
Banana: Ah, necão [claps hands together], né?
Don: É.
Banana: A neca boa.
Don: É.
Banana: Né? A aparência bonita, feio eu não gosto, de feia só basta eu [laughs].

B: I like young men.
D: Uh-huh.
B: Handsome.
D: Uh-huh.
B: With big legs, big muscles, a big behind.
D: Really?
B: Huge legs [laughs].
D: Yeah, me too [laughs]
B: Ah, a big dick [claps hands together], right?
D: Yeah.
B: A nice dick.
D: Yeah.
B: Right? A handsome appearance, I don't like ugly men, me being ugly is enough [laughs].

After such a list, or even instead of it, travestis talking about men would immediately bring up another criterion—how men behaved in bed. Angélica told me:

Angélica: Eu gosto assim, o tipo do home assim, retado. Que tem mulé.
Don. É.
Angélica: Que fode tabaco de mulé.
Don: An-rã.
Angélica: Tudo.
Don: Sim.
Angélica: Eu gosto de home assim, num gosto de home feminado, gosto de home assim.
Don. É.
Angélica: Às veze eu brigo cum ele assim, mas também, reconheço que ele é home, né? Eu deixo pra lá. Eu só gosto de home assim.

A: I like that, the type of man who is, like, macho. Who has a woman.
D: Right.
A: Who fucks the cunt of a woman.
D: Uh-huh.
A: All that.
D: Yeah.
A: I like that kind of man, I don't like effeminate men, I like that kind of man.
D: Right.
A: Sometimes I fight with him [her boyfriend, because he is always chasing after women], but then I recognize that he is a man, you know? [So] I leave it be. I only like men like that.

Tina told me something similar, making explicit what Angélica only implies here—namely, that a man is someone who always assumes the penetrative role in sexual encounters:

Tina: O que eu acho do homem é que ele/ele ser homem mesmo, entendeu como é? Ele ser homem

T: What I think of men is that they/they are really men, you know? They're really men, you know?

mesmo, entendeu como é? Aí é que
importa. Ser/ele ser um homem.
Não é ele ser um homem e na
Hora H ser uma mulher. Um
homem tem que ser um homem
mesmo.

Don: O que é isso?

Tina: O quê?

Don: Ser um homem mesmo.

Tina: Ser um homem mesmo?

Don: Sim.

Tina: É ele não usar certos tipos
de sexo, meu filho. Porque tem
homem que é homem mesmo que
faz o que? Chega no outro canto,
dá o cu. Esse é homem? Isso não
é homem não. Isso é viado.

Don: É.

Tina: Porque um homem tem que ser
um homem mesmo tem que ser
homem. Tanto na mulher como
no viado na cama, que ele tem que
ser homem, entendeu como é?
Porque não pode, não pode. Isso
não pode.

That's what's important. To be/for
him to be a man. Not for him to
be a man then at the Moment of
Truth turn into a woman. A man
has to be a real man.

D: What's that?

T: What?

D: To be a real man.

T: To be a real man?

D: Yeah.

T: It's for him not to use certain types
of sex, boy. Because there are men
who are real men and what do they
do? Go to bed with some other
person, give their ass. This is a man?
This is no man. This is a viado.

D: Yeah.

T: Because a man has to be a real
man, has to be a man. No matter
whether he's in bed with a woman
or a viado, he has to be a man, you
know? Because he can't [suddenly
want to give his ass], he can't. This
he can't.

Erica says something similar, explicitly ruling out a man who "gives
his ass" from all consideration as a boyfriend:

Erica: Eu gosto de comer. Eu nunca
tive homem que me desse o cu, entendeu? Se por acaso ele me der eu
vou achar uma coisa estranha, né,
ficar com homem que dá cu dentro
de casa, né?

Don: É.

Erica: Eu vou achar uma coisa estranha, né? Porque ó—eu posso
também comer, e no outro dia botar pra fora também, né? Eu vou
achar uma coisa estranha, né? Um
homem que dá cu dentro de casa é
viado, né?

Don: É, é.

Erica: Como hoje em dia não existe
mais homens mesmo. Tudo dá o

E: I like to penetrate. I've never had a
boyfriend who gave me his ass,
you know? If by chance he did, I'd
find it strange, you know, being
with a man who gave his ass in the
house?

D: Yeah.

E: I'd find it strange, you know? Because, look—I can penetrate him,
but the next day I'd probably put
him out. I would find it strange,
you know? A man who gives his ass
in the house is a viado, right?

D: Yeah, yeah.

E: These days, men don't exist anymore. They all give their ass. They

cu. Tudo pega na pica. É difícil hoje em dia. Eu fui fazer um boy zinho mesmo essa semana, um boyzinho. Peguei na neca dele, ele aparpou logo a minha. Já pensou? Como não existe mais homens. Tudo gosta de pica.

all grab your prick. It's difficult these days. I did a boyzinho this week—a total boyzinho. I touched his prick and right away he groped for mine. Can you imagine? There's no more men. They all like prick.

Mabel, in her answer to my question about men, repeated many of the same themes that travestis like Angélica, Tina, and Erica developed when I interviewed them. She also suggested why travestis are so appalled at the thought of having a boyfriend who "gives his ass."

Mabel: Que ele tá comigo, ele tá me/ele tá fazendo sexo comigo, eu tô sendo, pra ele passiva, ele tá sendo ativo pra mim. Tá entendendo? Ele num tá sendo pra mim passivo, e a gente o ativo—pelo contrário. Eu num gosto de ter homem pa morar comigo que seja bicha, seja maricona não. Prefiro homem galinha com mulher, tá entendendo, do que ter/ser badalado por bicha. Que a pior coisa é cê ter um homem badalado por viado.

Don: Verdade?

Mabel: É.

Don: Por quê?

Mabel: Porque é, porque uma chega. "A, aquele homem foi meu, eu fiz aquilo com aquele homem, eu botei na bundinha dele, ele fez uma pa mim, uma gulosa, ele bateu uma punhetinha pra mim. Saiu com a outra, fez aquela mesma coisa."

E o homem galinha, ele é aquele homem galinha que ele não dá a bunda, que ele não faz chupeta pa ninguém, que ele não bate punheta, não pega no pênis de ninguém. É aquele galinha que vai, cê vira, virou pra ele, tá pondo, POU, tá gozando, "Inté, tchau."

M: That when he is with me, he's/ when he's having sex with me, I'm being passive for him and he's active for me. You understand? He's not being passive for me, and me active—on the contrary. I don't like to have the man living with me be a bicha or a maricona. I prefer a womanizer, you know, than to have/to a man who is chased after by bichas. The worst thing is to have a man who is chased after by viados.

D: Really?

M: Yeah.

D: Why?

M: Because some [bicha] will come to you and [say]: "That man was mine, I did that with that man, I stuck it in his little bunda, he sucked my dick, he jerked me off. He went with another [bicha], did the same thing."

And a man who chases after women, he's the kind of man who won't give his bunda, he won't suck anyone's penis, he won't jerk anyone off, won't touch anyone's penis. [What I want] is a womanizer who goes [to bed with you], you turn, turn [your back to him], he puts it in, POW, cums, "Later on, bye."

The concern expressed here by Mabel that a man who "gives his ass" will give it to any bicha who wants it also emerged in a discussion between Angélica, me, and Boca Louca about the kind of man a travesti wants:

Angélica: Mas pa ter homem, ela quer ter homem machudo, pra ela/fuder ela, né?
Don: Para e, para que ela/
Boca L: se sinta mulher.
Angélica: Porque, se vo/se, ê, você morar com um homem e você comer o cu, você toma nojo dele.
Boca L: É.
Don: É. Verdade?
Boca L: Que ali ele é viado, ele pode dar o cu a outro também.
Angélica: É.

A: But to have a man, she [a travesti] wants to have a butch man, to her/to fuck her, you know?
D: To, for her to/
BL: feel like a woman.
A: Because if you/if you live with a man, and you penetrate his ass, you'll feel disgust towards him.
BL: Right.
D: Yeah. Really?
BL: Because then he's a viado, and he can give his ass to other people too.
A: Yeah.

All these responses indicate that travestis are extremely preoccupied with the sexual behavior of the men they take as their boyfriends. A male's status as a man, it would appear, is crucially dependent on what he does in bed. Even if he is in bed with a viado (that is, a travesti or some other homosexual), a man is someone who will always assume the penetrative role, and not suddenly "turn into a woman" at the "Moment of Truth." This understanding of "men" is shared by every travesti in Salvador. Even bullied, unlucky Treze shares it: though her partner, like those of other travestis, is biologically male, she doesn't refer to him as a "man." On the contrary, in her talk to me and Keila and Michelle, she makes it clear that he is not a man at all but a viado, like herself and all the other travestis.

Within the understandings of gender that travestis draw on to interpret and create their relationships, males are thus not naturally and self-evidently men. Manhood is the result of particular interests and particular acts. And one of the defining attributes of being an *homem*, being a man, in the gender system that the travestis invoke is that a male classified as a man will not be interested in another male's penis. A man, in this interpretive framework, will happily penetrate another male's anus. But he will not touch or express any desire for a penis. For him to do so would be tantamount to relinquishing his status as a man. The sexual act freighted with the most significance here is to *dar o cu*, as it is called in Brazilian Portuguese—to "give the ass," to allow penetration. That act is transformative, like the wave of a magic wand; it changes a male from a man into a *viado*, a homosexual—a person who shares a sexuality with *travestis*.

The disturbing nature of this transformation for *travestis* arises from the fact that they are uninterested in males who share their own sexual desire. This is one of the profound differences between *travestis* and the people whom *travestis* refer to as *os gays* or *as bichas gay* (gay males). Whereas gay relationships are understood to be based on sameness (both partners in a relationship desire males), *travesti*-boyfriend relationships, in order to function and exist at all, must be founded on deep and dividing *difference*: Here, one partner will desire males and the other will desire females. This configuration of desire is not merely a Brazilian version of the insistence of North American and European male-to-female transsexuals that the relationships they maintain with men are definitionally heterosexual even before they undergo sex-reassignment surgery, because they feel themselves to be women. As has already been made clear, *travestis* do not define themselves as women, and hence they do not define their relationships with their boyfriends as heterosexual. To the extent that they would apply such terminology at all to their relationships, they would say that they are homosexual, but their boyfriends are heterosexual. Or, as Keila's ex-boyfriend Edilson put it succinctly when I asked him to define his own sexuality, "I'm heterosexual, I won't feel love for another heterosexual, because to do that [i.e., for two males to be able to feel love], one of the two has to be gay . . . Between a heterosexual and a gay there can exist a kind of sincere love" (*Eu sou heterosexual, eu num vou sentir amor por outro heterosexual também porque aí, um dos dois tem que ser gay . . . Agora entre um heterosexual e um gay pode existir o tipo de amor sincero*).

Edilson articulates the basis of the gender system with which *travestis* and their boyfriends understand and coordinate their relationships. In this system, a heterosexual male—that is, a male who desires the "opposite sex"—is definitionally a man, and a homosexual male—that is, a male who desires the "same sex"—is definitionally, the "opposite sex" in relation to a "man." "Between a heterosexual and a gay there can exist a kind of sincere love," Edilson says, a statement that can make sense only from the point of view of a system that perceives such love as generated from two completely different natures and perspectives. Furthermore, it can make sense only from within a matrix that conceptualizes desire as meaningful only in relation to difference. The underlying assumption that gives this matrix form and makes it sensible is that it configures *all* desire as heterosexual desire. Homosexual desire in the sense of desire between two males *as men* (or between two females as women) is not recognized here, or is recognized only as an aberration, a farce; it is regarded as vaguely repellent by many travestis (who find gay male pornography, for example, offensive and "disgusting" [*nojento*] because images of two stereotypically macho men engaging in intercourse make no sense to them). Not only is desire meaningful only in relation to difference, it is also what *produces* that difference—a male is a man *because* he desires a woman; a travesti can "feel like a woman" *to the extent that* she desires a man and is desired in return by him. It is this relationship between desire and the production of difference that excludes viados from consideration as partners for travestis. It takes a man to make a travesti feel like a woman. A viado would short-circuit the conceptual system and make a travesti feel like—what? (The answer: a lesbian.) [9]

What all this means is that the gendered status of males is not given, but must be produced through the appropriate desires, which are manifested through the appropriate practices. And the single most significant of these practices is sexual behavior. The bed is the arena where some males make themselves into "men," by penetrating their partner, and other males make themselves into "women," by allowing themselves to be penetrated by those men. It is thus in bed where gender is truly established. But it is also in bed that the risk for gender slippage is most acute. It is there that one experiences, as Tina so poignantly put it, Hora H—the Moment of Truth. Edilson, as the boyfriend of a travesti, was aware of this: he told me that he has never, in all his fifteen years of sex with various travestis, touched a travesti's penis or allowed a travesti to penetrate him. He believes that "if I did that type of thing, I'd stop being a man, right?" (*se eu for ficar fazendo esse tipo de coisa, eu vou deixar de ser homem, né?*) In order to prevent such a fate, Edilson explained, "I have to control myself, right?" (*Aí, tenho que me dominar, né?*).

Edilson has had two long-term relationships with travestis, one that lasted for six years and one, with Keila, that lasted for seven. One of the main reasons for the longevity of those relationships was precisely his ability to "control himself." Because when it comes to the sexual behavior of boyfriends, travestis have eyes as sharp as hawks', and they are alert to any lapse of self-control. While they enjoy penetrating other males and do so regularly while they are working, or when a boyzinho they have called into their room makes it clear that he is willing to "give his ass," almost no travesti will tolerate a male who is interested in her penis *dentro de casa*—at home. As Erica explained, "I'd find it strange, you know, being with a man who gave his ass in the house." Adriana was even more decided. She told me that the only reason her current boyfriend was still *dentro de casa* was because "he's penetrating me" (*ele tá me comendo*). If he had wanted Adriana to penetrate him, she would have already sent him away: "I'd look at his face and I'd keep seeing that he isn't a man. I'd see that he is a viado just like us, and I'd think, 'I'm having sex with, supporting, giving food to, all that—a viado?' No."

Other travestis also feel so strongly about not wanting men who "give their ass in the house" that they will expel any boyfriend who begins to do so. The reasons they give for ridding themselves of such a male are several.

First, they will, as they say, "lose respect" (perder respeito) for their boyfriend. Keila explained to me that one of the reasons for having a boyfriend was to have "a masculine presence" that one can respect, because it is "a little superior to you—even if you are the master of the situation, and pay all the bills." From being held in high esteem as a man, a male who expresses interest in the travesti's penis becomes nothing more than um viado igual a gente—"a viado just like us." And this change in gendered status is accompanied by a plunge in respect. I have heard many travestis express what they would feel about such males in very strong affective terms, including nojo (disgust, as Angélica puts it) and vergonha (shame). One travesti told me that a man who expressed an interest in her penis would, in her estimation, be reduzido a nada—reduced to nothing. This reduction to "nothing" will be expressed in the way the travesti addresses her boyfriend. Many travestis told me that they were certain they would begin publicly humiliating their boyfriend the moment he allowed them to penetrate him. They would jogar na cara dele—throw it in his face— that he was a maricona, a debauched faggot. "The whole house will know the day my boyfriend gives me his ass," Erica told me. "I already call him maricona, even though he isn't one—imagine what I would call him if he really did give me his ass!"

Second, if a boyfriend whom she thought was a man turns out to be a viado just like herself, a travesti will wonder why she should support him. Why should she be out on the streets working to support someone who desires the same thing (sex with men) as she does? What is preventing that person from working the streets as well? Treze took this thought to its logical conclusion and acted on it: she put her partner in a dress and took him along to work.

Third, travestis strongly believe that boyfriends who begin to allow themselves to be penetrated will never again want to penetrate. Travestis are unanimous in agreeing that they would never decline a boyfriend's offer to be penetrated. "Quem é que dispensa um cu?" they all say— "Who would pass up an ass?" Banana even told me that she has requested her past boyfriends to give her their ass: "Vá painho, deixa mainha comer teu cu" (Come on Daddy, let Mommy penetrate your ass), she urged them. But this request was a kind of test. Because the concern is that a boyfriend who begins to *dar*, to "give," will become so smitten with the joys of anal penetration that he will never want to return to his old ways. And while travestis can happily penetrate their boyfriends for several weeks or months or, in exceptional cases, even years, they will eventually *enjoar*—a word that all travestis use when talking about this situation, and that means "grow tired of," "get sick of"—this sexual behavior. "It would be like eating chicken every day," one travesti told me with an expression of distaste. (It is both interesting and significant that the reverse situation—that is, the desired state of affairs in which the boyfriend only ever penetrates the travesti—is never spoken about in this way. No one ever suggested that they would *enjoar* of only ever being penetrated by their boyfriend, and whenever I suggested that I would find such behavior tiresomely repetitive, they looked at me with curiosity and surprise, then waved my objections aside, saying "Ah, that's because you're a gay.")

The belief that boyfriends who begin to "give" won't be able to stop giving is tied to the idea, expressed by both Mabel and Angélica, that a male who begins to *dar* will engage in a frenzy of anal promiscuity and seek out travestis everywhere to penetrate him.[10] One travesti said she wouldn't dare bring clients to her room if her boyfriend were interested in "giving," because the boyfriend would probably want to have sex with the client.

Travestis also suspect that a male who begins to "give" has always really wanted to "give" all along, which means that he has probably been "giving" to other travestis in secret. And the gravest and most bitter humiliation that a travesti can face, as Mabel makes clear, is that her boyfriend has "given" to other travestis but not to her. The extreme mortification a travesti feels upon hearing such news is not due to the fact that the boyfriend has been unfaithful. On the contrary, one of the expectations that travestis have of their boyfriends as men—as both Mabel and Angélica indicate—is that the boyfriends will be sexually promiscuous with women. Travestis are fully aware that some of the money they give to their boyfriends gets spent entertaining girlfriends. The disgrace centers entirely on the fact that the travesti has been deceived—she has been supporting someone who she thought was a man but who suddenly turns out to be not a man at all but a viado, just like her; a person who "gives his ass on the street," just like her. Fernanda Farias de Albuquerque calls this "a pior das traições"—the worst of treasons (Albuquerque and Janelli 1995:74–75; see also Fry 1995:204–5). The extreme power of this "treason" seems to be derived from the gender configuration that travestis draw on and elaborate: the revelation that one's boyfriend is not a man also implies that one is not as much of a woman as one would like to believe.

A final reason why travestis will end relationships with males who allow themselves to be penetrated is that they feel as though the boyfriend, by "giving his ass," has desperately played the last card in his hand to try to hold on to a travesti who is on her way out. Erica expressed this understanding when she told me one night on the street that one of her most recent boyfriends, a young man universally referred to and addressed as Negão—Big Black Man—had "given his ass" to her early on in their brief relationship. She pondered this for some time, and came to the conclusion that he did it in order to try to prolong the relationship that he somehow sensed was doomed. Erica, who is black herself, said that she didn't like black men. "I don't even like to do them as vícios," she told me. "I only have sex with blacks on the street for money. But I don't like blacks. And I was together with that black guy. I don't know where my head was when I got together with Negão." She continued:

Erica: É maricona também, Negão.
Don: É?
Erica: É maricona, querido. Dá cu e tudo. Ficar com maricona ainda mais negro. Acho que foi por isso que ele me dava a bunda.

E: He's a maricona too, Negão.
D: Really?
E: He's a maricona, love. Gives ass and everything. I should be with a maricona—one who is black to boot? I think that's why he gave me his behind.

Keila also elaborated this thought, asserting that any boyfriend who "gives his ass" always does so with *segundas intenções*—a hidden agenda. She told me many times that boyfriends who suddenly begin to *dar* do so because they realize they are losing their travesti girlfriend:

Men, because they have a head that is more . . . mistaken (*errada*) than a travesti's, will think that a travesti will only be happy when things are going his [the travesti's] way—which, the majority of times, is true—and so he'll think what?: "I have a travesti and I have everything he gives me—everything I want he gives me. But we're not 100 percent OK sexually. So sooner or later I'm gonna lose the travesti. So what do I do? To not lose the travesti? I'm gonna try to do something for him, that I can, that it's possible for me to do, so that I'll succeed in being with him always. So that I won't lose my comfort, the advantages (*minha mordomia*) that I have."

And so what does he do? To try to make the travesti dependent on him? He goes to bed with the travesti and inverts the roles (*inverte os papéis*), lets the travesti penetrate him (*deixa que o travesti coma ele*), sucks the travesti['s penis]. And sure—at that exact moment, that month, for the days to follow, the travesti, because it's a new thing, because it's a new experience—because every travesti is curious—will like the new arrangement. But there will come a certain moment when the travesti will get sick of it (*vai enjoar daquilo*). And then he [the boyfriend] won't have another chance to win over the travesti again, because he already did the last thing that he had left to do (*a última coisa que eles tinha que fazer*).

As soon as the boyfriend starts misunderstanding the situation (*perde a noção da coisa*) and starts thinking that by being passive in bed he'll be able to dominate the travesti more than he could when he was active—as soon as he thinks he can secure the travesti through sex—he's roundly mistaken, because that way he'll end up falling out of the picture completely (*porque aí acaba desmoronando de vez*). A travesti doesn't get attached to anyone for sex, because a travesti doesn't need a boyfriend to cum (*O travesti não vai se prender a ninguém por sexo, porque o travesti não precisa de homem em casa pra gozar*).

What emerges very clearly from the ways in which travestis talk about and interact with their boyfriends is that relationships between them are structured along a very strictly upheld schema. Brazilian Portuguese is felicitous here, because the verbs it uses to denote socioeconomic relationships of giving and consuming are *dar* (give) and *comer* (eat—this is the verb used by Treze, for example, when she declares to Michelle, Keila, and me that no man is going to "eat," that is, consume, what is hers). These exact same verbs are used to denote the sexual practices of being penetrated (*dar*/give) and penetrating (*comer*/eat). Thus, a male who penetrates another person (male or female) is said to *comer* "eat" that person, and that person is said to "give" to the male who is penetrating him or her.

The schema along which travesti-boyfriend relationships are structured is one in which travestis should "give," in both the economic and the sexual sense, and boyfriends should "eat," in the sense of both consumption and sexual penetration. The boundary between giving and eating is very heavily patrolled and upheld by travestis, and any boyfriend who "starts misunderstanding the situation," as Keila so slyly expresses it, and attempts to "invert the roles" does so at the cost of his relationship with his travesti girlfriend.[11]

In both the economic and the sexual sense, the controlling agent here is the "giver," because she can, at any moment, decide to cut off the flow of goods and services that she supplies to the "eater." She may not always be successful in achieving this, and travestis' predilection for tough, strong, macho men can result in their having to leave town to escape them; in the worse cases, they can find themselves entangled in an oppressive and abusive relationship. In the vast majority of cases, however, travestis can and do sever relationships with boyfriends that they wish to be rid of.

If one examines travesti-boyfriend relations in terms of the normative gender expectations that exist in Brazil, what one sees very clearly is that boyfriends, for all their masculine props, are feminized. Rather than working and supporting their spouse, as Brazilian males are normatively exhorted to do, the boyfriends of travestis are supported by their spouses. They are economically dependent on them, living in their rooms, eating food bought with their money, and wearing clothes purchased by them. Furthermore, it is the boyfriends who are expected to (and often do) stay at home while their spouses are out making a living. Once when I was walking home with Tina after a night on the streets, before I realized the extent to which travestis support their boyfriends, I asked her if her boyfriend worked. She looked at me incredulously and laughed out loud. "No," she told me, "he's laying in my room, watching television, waiting for me to come home from work." And Keila's ex-boyfriend Edilson complained to me that whereas the boyfriends and husbands of women "sleep away from home, have other women, hang out with other men and everything," travestis want "to have a man in the house, always at their disposal (o todo tempo à disponibilidade)."[12] In addition, in contrast to the majority of heterosexual relationships in Brazil, where it appears that it is the woman who runs the greatest risk of being abandoned, in travesti-boyfriend relationships the one who runs this risk is the "man." Both the travesti and her boyfriend are aware that the travesti can up and go anytime she wants to, leaving the boyfriend (unless he has managed to rob her before she leaves) with nothing.

It is perhaps because boyfriends are so undisguisedly feminized in relation to travestis (and travestis, hence, so clearly masculinized in relation to their boyfriends) that many travestis regularly employ a number of pronouncements and practices that encourage misrecognition of this fact. It is the case very frequently, for example, that a travesti will publicly proclaim that her boyfriend has not allowed her to do something or go somewhere or wear some particular article of revealing clothing. Erica once told me, with a proud smile on her face, that because of her boyfriend's objections "I can't wear short skirts, I can't wear off-the-shoulder blouses because they show my breasts, I can't go to any parties, he won't let me go to the beach . . ." Even more dramatically, Chica spent the entire week of Carnival 1995 inside the house on São Francisco Street. She couldn't go out, she told everybody who wondered: "O bofe não deixa" (The man won't allow it).

I was dumbfounded at announcements like these, because I knew that travestis like Erica and Chica were economically supporting the men who were issuing such restrictive edicts. What did they mean, their boyfriends wouldn't allow them to do something they wanted to do?

It was Keila who, in her usual incisive way, cut to the heart of the matter for me. Travestis, she told me, love for boyfriends to order them

around, because then they can *se sentir amapô*—feel like a woman. Travestis think that men should dominate women, Keila explained, "so how
are they going to feel like a woman? With a man dominating her." A travesti broadcasts this domination to other travestis, so that they will envy
her for having a boyfriend who cares enough about her to order her
around and make pronouncements about her clothing and behavior.

But even infinitely perceptive Keila did not identify the misrecognition involved in the sexual relationships between travestis and their boyfriends. One of the main reasons travestis insist that their boyfriends
restrict themselves to the role of penetrator, Keila explained to me, is
that travestis are so dominating in every other dimension of the relationship that they enjoy relinquishing their dominance when they are in
bed. Sex is the one context in which boyfriends *really* dominate travestis,
Keila said.

Considering the way travestis police the sexual conduct of their boyfriends, however, it would perhaps be more reasonable to interpret sex
between a boyfriend and a travesti not as a case where the travesti relin-
quishes her dominance but, on the contrary, as a case where the travesti
resolutely and absolutely *exerts* her dominance, even in bed. Especially in
bed. Rather than constituting an exception to the rule of travesti control
of boyfriends, sexual behavior in bed is an enactment of the rule; indeed,
it is a concentration of it.

One important practical outcome of this exertion of power in bed is
that the majority of travestis do not normally have orgasms when they
have sex with their boyfriends. Sex with a boyfriend consists, for the
most part, of the travesti sucking the boyfriend's penis and of her boyfriend penetrating her, most often from behind, with the travesti on all
fours or lying on her stomach on the bed. If the boyfriend touches the
travesti at all, he will caress her breasts and perhaps kiss her. But no contact with her penis will occur. Several travestis I know wear panties
whenever they have sex with their boyfriends or sleep next to them, so
that the boyfriend will not be confronted with the fact that the travesti
has a penis. One travesti told me that she had been living with her boyfriend almost two years and the only way he could possibly have seen
her penis was if he peeked under her panties at night while she slept.

Whatever else travestis may get out of their boyfriends, then, it is not
sexual fulfillment.[13] As Mabel explained in her description of what kind
of man she wants, sex with a boyfriend involves him "go[ing to bed with
you], you turn, turn [your back to him], he puts it in, pow, cums, 'Later
on, bye.'" And as Keila stated explicitly, "A travesti doesn't get attached
to anyone for sex, because a travesti doesn't need a boyfriend to cum."
The point of having a boyfriend, instead, is for him to help a travesti feel

like a woman, by looking like a man and most of all by upholding the sexual behavior of a man in bed. Boyfriends of travestis do little else than that because that is all they are supposed to do. And as long as they continue looking like men and being men, boyfriends can remain relatively secure and travestis can remain happy (until the time, of course, when they find somebody else who does it better). That these rigid expectations and demands result in relationships in which travestis get very little sexual fulfillment is, for them, beside the point. They do not want boyfriends for sexual pleasure. They don't get sex from their men—what they get, instead, is gender. Sexual pleasure is something that travestis obtain elsewhere; from their boyzinhos, their vícios, and the clients they meet on the street at night.

Four

The Pleasure of
Prostitution

Late one night at about 2 A.M., I was on my way back to my room on São Francisco Street after having spent the evening with travestis who were working the streets at a point of travesti prostitution near the center of the city. On the way home, I decided to pass by another street on which travestis stand, to see who might be there that evening. When I arrived, I saw that the street was deserted except for Erica, the young black travesti who lived in the room next to mine. The street that evening had been *uó* (horrible), Erica told me when I inquired. Even though she had been working for over two hours, she had still not done a single *programa*—that is, she had still not had a single customer. Bored with gazing out onto the street, trying to attract the attention of drivers in the cars passing by, Erica sat down on a step with me, and we began to chat. I asked her about the new boyfriend that she had recently installed in her room. Oh, she adored him, she told me. She adored him. And he was totally devoted to her. In words that could have been uttered by virtually any other travesti talking about her boyfriend, Erica told me about hers:

Erica: Ele é um homem que/ele é um homem que não fica com viado. Ele não fica com viado nenhum. Ele disse "Inha, enquanto eu tiver com você, eu vou respeitar você para sempre. Nunca vou lhe trair." Não sabendo ele que eu traio ele pencas. Cada boy gostoso que eu pego na rua . . .

Don: [laughs]

Erica: Eu vou/Eu vou dizer, aqui na pista, aparece cada boy gostoso que a gente não resiste.

E: He's a man who/he's a man who doesn't hang out with viados. He doesn't hang out with any viados. He said, "Mommy, when I'm with you, I'm gonna respect you forever. I'll never cheat on you." And him not knowing that I cheat on him all the time. So many sexy boys that I get hold of on the street . . .

D: [laughs]

E: I'll/I'll tell you, here on the street, so many sexy boys walk by that one can't resist.

Don: Nao, claro que não.

D: No, of course not.

Erica: Nao resiste nao querido, mas não resiste mesmo.

E: Can't resist, love, can't resist at all.

Don: Lógico.

D: Of course.

Erica: Cada boy gostoso com neca desse tamanho . . . ah . . . Adoro homem branco. Coisa mais/adoro homem branco, adoro Don, ai.

E: So many boys with dicks this big . . . ah . . . I adore white men. The most/I adore white men, I adore them Don, ai.

Don: É?

D: Really?

Erica: Adoro homem branco. Essa semana mesmo, saí com um branco, que a neca/a neca era desse tamanho-ô [Erica touches the forefinger and middle fingers of her right hand to the crook of her left arm], a grossura [Erica cups the fingers of one hand into a wide circle]. Lindo, lindo, um boyzinho aí, que escândalo.

E: I adore white men. Just this week, I went with a white guy who had a dick/his dick was this big—look [Erica touches the forefinger and middle fingers of her right hand to the crook of her left arm], and the thickness [Erica cups the fingers of one hand into a wide circle]. Pretty, pretty, he was a boyzinho, a scandal [i.e., fantastically beautiful].

Don: É.

D: Huh.

Erica: Branco. A minha neca endurece logo Don, me dá uma (   ) inha.

E: White. My dick gets hard in a second, Don, they give me a little (   ).

Don: Não, mas essa coisa de só transar com uma pessoa, eu não acredito. Não acredito mesmo.

D: Yeah, this thing that one should only have sex with one person [i.e., that one should remain faithful to one's boyfriend], I don't believe in it. I really don't.

Erica: Olhe a gente/o negócio do dinheiro—a gente não transa só por dinheiro não. A gente/a gente tá na rua. A gente não se interessa por aquele cara, entendeu? Vai pra aqui só por causa de dinheiro? Não, não é querido. Eu faço meu vício. Faço mesmo. Né amor?

E: Look, we/this thing about money—we don't just have sex for money. We/we're here on the street. What, we're not gonna be interested in some [beautiful] man who walks by? We're here just for money? No, no way, love. I do my vícios. I really do. You know, love?

In this short conversation, Erica glides effortlessly from a discussion of her boyfriend to talking about the pleasure she obtains from standing out on the street prostituting herself. Prostitution and activities associated with it (such as robbing clients) are the main or exclusive source of income for the vast majority of travestis in Salvador. Travestis work several specific streets in and around the city, and many of them also frequent a local pornographic cinema—where they roam the aisles wondering loudly if the men watching the movies with names like *Noites quentes de mulheres perversas* (Hot nights of the perverse women) "wanna cum" *(quer gozar)*. They perform their "programs" *(programas)* in cars, on backstreets, in secluded areas of the beach, in hotel rooms, in the aisles of the pornographic cinema or in its restrooms, and in the rooms where they live. If they are enterprising, they may cross the Atlantic and spend several months or years in Italy, prostituting themselves on the streets of Milan or Rome, saving up money that will provide them, and their mothers, with security in their old age.

The most striking differences between most existing accounts of prostitution and the prostitution practiced by travestis in Salvador is the extent to which travestis continually regale one another with exuberant descriptions of the sexual encounters they enjoyed with the men they met on the street while working. Although travestis obviously do not enjoy sex every time they have it or with every client, whenever they talk about thrilling or fulfilling or incredibly fun sex, their partner is always either a client or a *vício*. Sometimes, if the *vício* is especially attractive, is known to have an especially large penis, and/or is known to be especially versatile in bed, the travesti will even pay *him*.

Travesti prostitution is thus not only a source of income but also, as Erica emphasizes, a source of pleasurable and reaffirming experiences. It is therefore thought about and practiced in ways that differ markedly from the prostitution described in most reports and studies. Rather than seeing the prostitution they practice as a degrading form of sexual exploitation, travestis regard it as work, much like any other job—except that their work on the street makes them their own boss, and it provides them with access to more money than they could ever dream of earning through salaried employment. Furthermore, prostitution provides travestis with one of the few arenas open to them in Brazilian society for receiving compliments and accolades. Prostitution makes individual travestis feel sexy and attractive. It is one of the only contexts they have in which they can experience themselves as tantalizing objects of desire and develop a sense of personal worth, self-confidence, and self-esteem.

Falling into the Life

Travestis commonly refer to their entrance into prostitution with the phrase *cair na vida*—"fall into the life." This expression is a wry acknowledgment of the fact that street prostitution is regarded as one of the lowliest occupations an individual can perform, and it also reflects the fact that throughout Brazil, prostitution is called *a vida*—"the life." Most travestis in Salvador "fell into the life" with the advice and help of older and more experienced travestis. Luciana told me that at age sixteen, she had been working in a beauty shop for two years, doing manicures, pedicures, and waxing. She was already taking hormones, and she had many friends who were homosexual. Some travestis she knew told her, "Come with us and work, you'll like it." "And," she said, "I went and worked—and I liked it." When Magdala was seventeen, a travesti friend urged her, "'Bicha, come on, take a little walk around the street at night, it doesn't cost anything.' And so I did," she told me. Cintia began prostituting herself at age thirteen while she was still living at home, at the encouragement of her young travesti friend Catita. Elisabeth was twelve when she asked a travesti friend to take her to the *pista* (the street). "She took me," Elisabeth told me, "and I've never left it since." Lia Hollywood started at age seventeen, after she was fired from her job as an "office boy" in a bank because she sometimes arrived at work wearing makeup. At the time, she was sharing a room with several other bichas in the center of Salvador. "Oh, my God," Lia recounted that she said to herself after she was fired, "how am I going to pay my share of the room?" A travesti friend of hers had a suggestion: "Take a little walk in a dress. You never know, maybe you'll earn some money." This travesti lent Lia a dress. She put it on and took the first "little walk" of her fifteen-year career as a prostitute.

Not all travestis come of age in cities where there is a developed market for travesti prostitution, however. Traditionally in Brazil, and in many rural areas throughout the country to this day, males have not entertained the concept of homosexual prostitution. On the contrary, like Edilson and the boyzinhos discussed in the previous chapter, men used to believe—and many men still do believe—that it is the viado, the homosexual, who should pay *them* for sex. When travestis live in places where that idea is prevalent, it often doesn't occur to them that prostitution might be a possibility—until the day they are unexpectedly given money for sex by a man who for some reason feels compelled to pay.

This is what happened to Keila. She did her first programa as a prostitute without even being aware of it. Keila was fourteen years old at the time; she had already left home and had just begun working as a domestic servant in a small boardinghouse in the town of Teresina, the backwater capital of the northeastern state of Piauí. Every night after work, Keila put on some makeup, rubbed conditioner into her hair to make it hang and look longer, dressed up in crepe blouses and wide, silky trousers, grabbed a handbag, and went off to the town square, to join the group of local bichas who congregated there. These bichas, all looking like taller or thinner or stouter or older versions of Keila, spent much of the evening in the square, socializing with one another and flirting with the men who happened by.

One evening, Juraci, an older bicha friend, suggested to Keila that they leave the square and walk over to an open-air arts and crafts center in the middle of the city, which housed several bars and functioned as an evening gathering place for men. While they were walking through the center, "um certo senhor, um senhor gordo"—an older, fat man—began looking at, and then following, Keila and her friend. They left the center and made their way back to the square. The man followed them. Seeing that he was more interested in Keila than herself, Juraci told Keila that she was going to "take a little walk," and she left Keila alone on a bench in the square, with the man hovering nearby.

The man approached Keila, and the two began talking. After a bit of small talk about whether Keila liked the arts and crafts center, the man announced to her, "'Look, my car is parked over there in that block. It's a blue Fusca, with such and such a license plate number. You wanna go?' I said, 'I'll go,'" Keila told me. She added as an aside, "Just for you to see how inhibited they [i.e., men] were [at that time, in that city]—they would never allow you to walk together with them from one place to another. He had to go first, and then after a certain time, I would follow after him and we would meet." She continued:

> I gave him enough time to walk a couple of blocks, then I went to meet up with him. Got there, he was already in his car, a blue Fusca. And him: "Get in," opened the door, and I got in. He had already laid back the passenger seat so that it was completely reclined [so that nobody would perceive Keila in the car], and I lay down, with him sitting. He was talking to me, "Ah, let's go for a little ride" (vamos dar uma saidinha).
>
> I said, "What do you mean, a little ride?"—I was wanting to tell the man that I didn't have any money to pay him, and so I didn't want to go. And so me: "Go where?"
>
> And he said, "No, we're just gonna take a little spin" (uma voltinha só).
> And I said, "OK, if it's just a little spin, then let's go."
> So he started up the car and we left, me lying down on the seat. He went around the whole city. We went to a motel really far away, the Pôr do Sol [Sunset]. Talking the whole time. He said, "You work? You get paid poorly?" (Você ganha pouco?) Me: "Yeah." "How much do you earn?" I said, "I earn 1,500 cruzeiros." "A month?" I said, "Yeah."

Brazil has changed its currency so many times over the past few decades that even Brazilians have lost track of what their different currencies were called and what they have been worth. Not having any conception of how much the amount of money she was talking about added up to in terms of the most recent currency released in Brazil (in 1994), I interrupted Keila at this point to ask her how much fifteen hundred cruzeiros might be.

"I have no idea," she told me. But whatever its monetary value, she

said, it was 70 percent of a *salário mínimo*—a minimum salary, that is, what
the majority of Brazilians engaged in wage labor earn in a month. So if
the minimum salary today is one hundred reais (about one hundred dollars), she explained, it would be like seventy reais.

> And so we got to this motel. I had never been in a motel until that exact
> moment. And when we got there, I thought that it was a house. I thought
> it was his house. I had been lying down on the seat, too, so I didn't see any
> sign. And I was surprised: "How come you brought me to this house?" Him:
> "No, this isn't a house, this is a motel. We're gonna spend the night here."
>
> I said, "But how am I gonna spend the night with you here, sir? (*Como
> eu vou passar a noite com o senhor aqui?*) I shouldn't, I have to be at work early
> in the morning."
>
> "Don't worry, I'll take you back to your house, when we've spent some
> time here."
>
> And so we stayed.
>
> I already knew that we were gong to have sex in the room, of course. I
> wasn't an innocent ingenue (*Eu não era nem ingênuo nem nada*). And so I had
> sex with him, without agreeing on anything [i.e., on any price that Keila
> might have to pay], without saying anything. I said, "Good," thinking to
> myself, "I don't have any money, but this old man isn't going to want me
> to pay him, imagine. I'm going to have sex with him because I'm gay (*eu
> sou gay*), I like having sex with men." And at that time, when I was really
> young, I was really attracted to older men. I had a fixation for older men.
> These days I don't anymore, well, just a little, but not like I did when I was
> fourteen, fifteen.
>
> And so, we had sex. Me and this man. I sucked him and he just pene-
> trated me, of course, he didn't touch me, my penis, nothing. He just
> wanted me to be passive, and I was, from when I entered to when I left.
>
> And when we finished, he slept, and I slept too.
>
> And he—when it was seven in the morning, he was very honest, be-
> cause I was sleeping, I was sleeping really hard, and he woke me up at
> seven, no, at six in the morning. He went, "Oh, boy, wake up, we're leav-
> ing now." He called on the phone, asked for the bill, he guy came to the
> room with it, he paid it, and we got into the car, and we left. He inclined
> the seat back again, put a towel on top of me, and we left.

Keila then told of how the man offered to bring her to the boardinghouse in which she was living and working, but she was afraid that the
woman who owned the boardinghouse would spy her getting out of the
car and begin asking questions. She asked instead to be let off near
the square where the man had picked her up.

As she was getting out of the car,

> He put his hand in his wallet and gave me five hundred cruzeiros and said,
> "Take this and buy yourself a snack." I looked at that note and I fell into a

panic, because I had never seen a note of five hundred cruzeiros—I mean, I'd seen one, but in other people's hands. In my own hands, I'd never seen one.

I interrupted Keila to ask her why she had never held a five-hundred-cruzeiro bill, if she was already working. She told me that all this occurred before she had received her first month's salary. And still confused about the amount of money she was talking about, I asked her how much five hundred cruzeiros might be in the currency being circulated in 1995. She explained:

It's as if—look, I was earning three five-hundred-cruzeiro bills a month. He gave me one, so two more would have made my whole monthly salary, you see? I needed to work a whole month to earn three five-hundred cruzeiro bills, and he gave me one after just one programa that I did with him. I was in such shock (*Eu fiquei tão abismado*) that I didn't even manage to say good-bye to him. He started the car and left.

Keila then entered the boardinghouse to find the owner waiting for her "with a face this big," she laughed, spreading out her arms. "Why are you coming to work?" the woman asked her angrily. "I had to make breakfast here myself—how am I gonna be able to not fire you?"

I said, "Look, if the Mrs. doesn't want me to work here anymore, just pay me what is owned me and I'll leave." I thought that with those five hundred cruzeiros I had in my hand, that the world was at my feet, and I didn't want anything else, you know? But boy was I wrong (*Ledo engano meu*), because after a while, I saw that it wasn't like that at all.
And she said, "What do you mean by this arrogance?"
"Because Ma'am, I work here in your house, and I spend a whole month working for three five-hundred-cruzeiro bills, being humiliated, working all day long, without any breaks, I don't even get Sundays off, and I'm working here in your house to earn less than a minimum salary. I went with a man last night and he gave me a five-hundred-cruzeiro bill." And I showed it to her. "I went with a man last night and we went to a motel"—'cause by now I knew what a motel was, all that. "And he gave me this money."
She was shocked: "What's that?! You robbed him!"
I said, "I didn't rob him. He gave it to me. The man that I left with last night, from Pedro II Square, we went to the Sunset motel, he gave me this five-hundred-cruzeiro bill. And so, Dona Quitéria, I don't think I need to work for the Mrs. anymore. He gave me this money that I have in my hand, and I'm leaving."
She was very sensible (*sensata*). She said, "OK, you want your money [that she owed Keila], I'll give it to you. I don't want you to go. And this is an illusion. You're not going to manage to survive on those 500 cruzeiros plus the 750 that I will give you"—because I had worked there for fifteen days, so she had to give me 750 cruzeiros.

So she gave me 750, and I had 1,250 cruzeiros. With that money, I rented a room, paid the month's rent. The rest of it I spent on stupid things—I was really young, I didn't understand enough to buy myself things I wanted to eat chocolates, buy snacks, sandwiches, I invited my friends to eat things with me, to go to the movies with me—all those things. I know that in less than a week, I'd spent all the money.

With her money gone, Keila took the step that seemed most logical to her: she enlisted the company of Azeitona, a bicha friend with whom she had traveled from her hometown to Teresina, and the two of them started strolling around the town square at night, looking for more men who would pay for sex. Unfortunately for them both, no such men appeared. "We met men who would say, 'I'll penetrate you, if you want, and you can suck my dick, but I won't pay,'" Keila told me. She and Azeitona would often go with those men anyway, because she was there to have sex in any case. "But I kept hoping that as the month wore on, or at least before I needed to pay the next month's rent, that that same man, or some man like him, would appear."

In the end, Keila and Azeitona had to go back to salaried employment, because they were earning nothing as prostitutes. The situation continued in this way until many months later, when the owner of the small cafeteria in which Keila and another bicha friend were working decided she had to close down the cafeteria. This woman told Keila and her friend Bruna that they ought to go to Recife, to try to earn some money there. "In Recife," the woman told them, "bichas stand on the corners and earn a living that way." Keila and Bruna didn't believe her. But she insisted, saying that she knew some travestis who lived there: "There bichas have houses, furnished apartments—all bought with money they earned on the street." "Well, in that case," Keila said to Bruna after thinking about it, "let's go to Recife." And they did.

Keila has been earning her living as a prostitute ever since.

The Work of Prostitution

Travestis consider the prostitution they perform as work, and they see themselves as professionals. Although they normally refer to themselves as *prostitutas* (prostitutes) and will sometimes jokingly call themselves and one another *putas* (whores), in certain formal contexts, such as an interview with a journalist, some travestis refer to themselves as *profissionais do sexo*—sex professionals.[1] Travestis use the word *prostituição* to name their profession, but in their everyday talk to one another they more commonly speak of *trabalho* (work) or *batalha* (battle), a common Brazilian slang term for work. They call the men who buy their sexual services *clientes* (clients) and *fregueses* (customers), among other, less neutral names. They extend the work terminology even to the clothing they wear on the street: most travestis have a favorite outfit that they know attracts clients and that they enjoy wearing to work, and they refer to it as their *farda* (uniform). I once heard a travesti who was swishing her clothes around in a large metal basin joke to another, "I'm washing my uniform so that I can enter into service tomorrow" (*Tou lavando minha farda pra amanhã entrar no serviço*).

Like travestis themselves—who began emerging in large numbers in Brazil only in the 1970s, with the arrival of female hormones and later with the discovery of silicone—travesti prostitution of the kind practiced today does not have a long history. It began in the large southern cities of Rio de Janeiro and São Paulo and eventually spread to other parts of the country. Martinha told me that when she first began prostituting herself as a travesti, the whole idea was to get the client to believe that one was a woman. Because silicone was not yet available, many travestis wore Styrofoam padding in order to enhance the girth of their hips and buttocks (this padding is called *pirelli*, in playful reference to the Italian tire manufacturer). They also placed Modess sanitary napkins over their genitals and smeared these with lipstick, in order to be able to tell the client who picked them up that they were menstruating and therefore were available only for anal intercourse.

It took many years—and the abolition, in the mid-1980s, of the oppressive military regime that had ruled Brazil for over twenty years—for travesti prostitution to flourish. The military regime had made it extremely difficult for travestis to appear openly on the street in female clothing—males who did so risked being arrested and subjected to prolonged humiliation and torture, such as being made to sit on a billy club as police paddy wagons sped over potholed roads. Although violent police repression continues today, sometimes in the form of organized campaigns directed as "cleaning up" the cities in which travestis work, travestis are no longer arrested simply for appearing on a city street in female attire. And while travestis must still regularly confront unscrupulous policemen who harass, rob, beat, and even shoot them, they have secured the freedom to stand on street corners at night. This is largely due to what Keila calls travesti "persistence" (*persistência*). Enumerating common police actions against travestis, Keila told me many times that "the police can throw rocks, they can break arms, they can pull out nails, they can cut hair, they can let loose their dogs, they can pack travestis into their paddy wagons and drive them out of town. They can do all that and those same travestis will be back on the street, with their arms bandaged and with whatever is left of their nail stubs painted red, the very next night."

To judge from the accounts I heard from various travestis, what seems to have happened in the late 1970s and 1980s is that travestis began to "invert the roles," as one travesti put it, and began charging—instead of paying—men who approached them for sex. They could do this partly because they themselves were becoming, thanks to hormones and silicone, more attractive and desirable, and partly because they fashioned themselves after female prostitutes. Martinha told me that to those men who balked at paying for sex with a viado, she and others retorted, "You're the one who's gonna penetrate me, I'm the one who will be the woman, you're the man. You pay female prostitutes, and so you can pay me" (*Você é que vai me comer, eu que vou ser a mulher, você vai ser o homem. Você paga uma prostituta, você pode muito bem me pagar*).

Through this kind of reasoning, and because of the increasingly open establishment of specifically travesti points of prostitution as Brazil began to experience a general liberalization—sexual and otherwise—after decades of military rule, travesti prostitution became an established phenomenon in many of the country's major cities by the mid-1980s, and travestis in these cities began to be able to earn their living exclusively through sex work.

These days, there are a number of ways for travestis to advertise their services. In Salvador, any travesti with access to a telephone can either open or be part of what is misleadingly and grandiosely called an *agência*, an agency. One is considered by other travestis to have an agency if one places a short ad under "Masseur/Masseuse" in the classified section of local newspapers. The code word for travestis in this context is *boneca*—doll—and none of the ads I have seen do much more than announce the availability of "dolls": "Isabela e suas bonecas femininas" (Isabela and her feminine dolls) or "Boneca bem bonita, sex" (Very pretty doll, sexy), followed by the telephone number to call, are typical in the genre.

Although some individuals make themselves available in this way for shorter or longer periods of time, most travestis in Salvador dislike working through "agencies," even if the money they receive for their services is usually higher than it would be on the street. One main reason for this dislike is that travestis do not first see the client they are called on to work with, and hence they have no idea what to expect when they arrive at the agreed-upon meeting place. They also object to having to give a cut of their money (usually half) to the owner of the telephone (if the telephone is not their own, which in the vast majority of cases it is not). Finally, travestis dislike working through "agencies" because the relative formality of the situation (telephone numbers being known, others being aware of where one is) implies a degree of surveillance and control that makes it difficult for the travesti to rob her client should she want to.

The vast majority of travestis, then, even those who occasionally make themselves available to one or more "agencies," work the street—referred to in Portuguese as *a rua* (the street) or *a pista* (the track or runway). In Salvador, there are three main areas in which travestis have *pistas*. Two of them are in the center of town, one just outside the Historic Center on a street called Rua da Ajuda, and one about a fifteen-minute walk towards the central square, Campo Grande, in an area of town known as the Aflitos.[2] The third area—the most popular—is a twenty-to-forty-minute bus ride from the center of town to a busy highway along the beach that passes by the middle-class suburb of Pituba.

In addition to these three main areas of travesti street prostitution, a few travestis "battle" along the road in front of the beach in Barra, another middle-class suburb closer to the center of town, and several of the travestis who live on São Francisco Street never leave there—they simply sit or stand in the doorway of the house in which they live, attracting their customers from among the men who walk by on the street, often on their way to or from work.

These different areas of Salvador attract different kinds of clients. The highway running by Pituba attracts more middle-class men in cars than do the narrow streets and alleys around Ajuda Street or São Francisco Street, where the clients tend to be poorer and on foot. Travestis are very familiar with the sexual and economic topography of their city. They work different parts of the city depending partly on how far from their rooms they feel like traveling and how much money they want or need to earn, and partly on the state of their relationships with other travestis who work in particular areas of town.

In the hierarchy of areas of prostitution that exists among travestis, Pituba ranks highest, and on any given night there will be at least ten and perhaps as many as twenty or twenty-five travestis standing along the highway and the nearby streets in that part of town. Aflitos comes next, and a good night will find between seven and fifteen travestis standing on the corners. Ajuda is rather low on the list because the men there tend to have less money, but it is attractive to travestis who live nearby, and there is a steady core of five to eight travestis who work there most nights. São Francisco Street is worked all day long, from early morning to the wee hours, by travestis who live there. Finally, the narrow road along which travestis stand in Barra has a strip of bars and restaurants on one side, which leaves travestis too exposed to too many different kinds of people (many of whom have been drinking) for their liking. It is also

At work on the *pista*

known primarily as a point of female prostitution, which makes it unattractive to most travestis, since they know that many of the men who stop for them will be expecting a woman (at the other points of prostitution where travestis work, the majority of men who stop know they are stopping for a travesti). The few travestis who work Barra tend to live relatively isolated from, and not have much contact with, the travestis who work the other areas of the city. Treze and her partner who dresses in female clothing, for example, often work Barra together.

In addition to the street points of prostitution, there is also the pornographic cinema, the Pax. I learned very early in my stay with travestis that when a travesti says she has "been to the cinema," she does not mean she has just seen the latest Hollywood release. (In addition to universally referring to the Pax as simply *o cinema*, travestis also call it *o colégio*— "school"—because, since it closes at 8 P.M., they work it during the day. Hence, a travesti on her way to the cinema will sometimes announce to everybody that she is "off to school.") The Pax is popular, and up to fifteen or even twenty travestis at a time can congregate there and troll the aisles in search of clients. The cinema can support this volume of travestis because it is enormous—with thirteen hundred seats, it is one of the biggest cinemas in Salvador. And although it is never full, I estimate that at any one time, there will be one to two hundred men slouching down and smoking in the sticky seats, masturbating to 1970s heterosexual pornographic films with titles like *Ânus veludo* (Velvet anus) and *As máquinas do orgasmo* (The orgasm machines).

The Pax has low status among travestis, largely because the men who go there are *penosos*—poor and stingy. The most that the majority of men are willing to pay travestis for their services (which for the most part involve the travesti leaning over the man's crotch and performing a quick *chupadinha*, or blow job, as he sits concentrating on the movie) is the equivalent of three to five dollars. In addition, the Pax is frequented by homosexual males who go there to have sex with other males. They will happily masturbate or perform fellatio on other males for free—something which irritates travestis, who are there to earn money. But the reason so many travestis frequent the Pax despite this aggravating competition from homosexual males and the embarrassingly low pay they receive is partly because there they are completely freed from the harassment and violence that working on the street exposes them to, and partly because with a bit of luck, a travesti can perform quite a few *chupadinhas* and may even manage one or two *transas* (acts of penetrative sex) in a toilet stall during the two to four hours she will stay there. I once overheard a travesti react with anger when she heard another travesti disparaging those who worked in the Pax. "I don't work there because it

Baby working the Pax

is so *penoso*," the first travesti announced dismissively. "In that 'poor' cinema," the other travesti informed her in an annoyed tone of voice, "you can come away with forty or fifty reais on a good day. I don't go there every day," she continued, "but I go when the street isn't giving" (*quando a rua não tá dando*).

The Programa

The service that travestis sell is call *o programa*—the program, the act of sex. A programa begins the moment a travesti's lips touch a man's penis in the Pax or, when she is working the street, the moment she gets into a man's car, enters her room with a man, or instructs a man on foot to follow her as she begins to walk in the direction of a backstreet or a hotel. From this moment, the travesti considers that she has earned her money, and if for some reason the man changes his mind and decides he doesn't want to have sex, she will still demand full payment. During one rainy night when Banana and I were huddled in the doorway on São Francisco Street, I remarked that I felt sorry for the travestis who were working in Pituba that night, because there was little protection against the rain there. Banana disagreed—she liked to work Pituba when it rained, she said, because the men driving by couldn't see clearly, and they tended to stop for the first travesti they saw standing on the street. This was to her advantage; she would hop in the car and not get out again until the man paid her for a programa and/or until she robbed him.

The programa with a client ends, usually, when the man ejaculates. The amount of time that travestis are willing to allow for this varies according to how attracted they are to the client, what the client has agreed to pay, what sort of mood the travesti is in, and what sort of sexual act is being performed (a travesti will have much less patience with a man who is paying five reais for a blow job than with one who is paying sixty to penetrate her). Generally, travestis allow about five to ten minutes for fellatio on the street or on the beach, twenty to thirty minutes for sex in a client's car or in one of the cheap fleabag hotels around Ajuda Street, and up to an hour or more in one of the more expensive motels around Pituba. If the client simply cannot ejaculate within this time limit (something that in fact only rarely happens), the travesti will terminate the programa and demand her money. If the client protests, she will offer to continue, but on the condition that he pay her more money. If he refuses, she will get dressed, rob him, and leave.

Although travestis readily tell journalists and anyone else who wonders that they have fixed prices for their programas, in practice the price varies dramatically from client to client. The price of a programa will be raised or lowered depending on three factors: what the travesti judges the client can pay, how desperately she needs to earn some money, and how attracted she is to the client. A man in an expensive car will routinely be asked to pay more than a man approaching a travesti on foot. And a travesti who owes her rent money the following day and who has been unable to earn any decent money (or rob anyone) during a night's work will readily do what travestis refer to as *varejões* (sg. *varejão*), which means "bargains"—that is, they will perform programas at a discount, simply to earn some money.

Bargains are also sometimes given to clients who have little money but to whom the travesti feels attracted. Often, the attraction a travesti feels towards a client has little to do with his appearance. Travestis regularly pointed out to me men whom they found desirable who were not stereotypically attractive by any stretch of the imagination. Sometimes they were in their late forties or older, overweight, poorly dressed, etc. One man living near São Francisco Street with whom several travestis regularly did vícios (had sex for free) was a man they all called "o Vampiro" (the Vampire), because he had only two rotting teeth in his gums. But what he and the other men to whom travestis were attracted did possess was a large penis.

The attraction of a large penis is something that travestis talk about continually in their conversations with one another, and hardly an hour goes by in travesti company without someone touching her right forefinger and middle finger just below the crook of her left arm to indicate *uma pica desse tamanho*—a dick this big—that some client or vício possessed. But the incident that brought this attraction home to me most forcefully occurred one evening as I stood by the side of the road chatting with Rita Lee and Elisa, an attractive travesti in her early twenties. As we were talking, a drunken, unshaven, nearly toothless man in his late fifties, wearing tattered shorts and a soiled shirt, tottered up behind us and stood unabashedly staring at Elisa. The man was so drunk that he could only produce vague, mostly unintelligible utterances. But he was clearly taken with Elisa, and he kept muttering that she was "bonita" (beautiful) and "gostosa" (sexy). From where she was standing, about three meters away from him, Elisa looked over her shoulder and barked, "Thirty reais." The man said nothing in reply; he just kept swaying and muttering how beautiful she was.

At this point Elisa told him, "Vai" (Go away), but he remained. She then went up to him, repeated "Thirty reais," and asked him if he had thirty reais to pay for a programa. He slurred that he had no money, but he did have, on the other hand, an enormous penis. Elisa made a noise of disgust and walked back to me and Rita Lee, ordering the man to go away before she started charging him just to look at her. She began talking to us, keeping one eye peeled on the street again. The man, in the meantime, had stumbled off and settled a few meters farther away, against a wall behind a telephone pole. Sheltered in this way from the gaze of people passing by in cars, he reached into his dirty shorts and pulled out his penis.

I was alerted to this because I heard Elisa suddenly gasp. "Ô meu Deus" (Oh my God), she cried, and put her hand to her open mouth. She called Rita Lee to see what the man was holding in his hand, and Rita Lee rushed over and gasped as well—with good reason: the drunken man's flaccid penis was the size of a large Italian salami.

Rita Lee and Elisa burst into laughter, reaching out to support one another as they doubled over in amusement. This incident happened early on during my stay with the travestis, and I stood next to them thinking that they were laughing *at* the man, at how ridiculous he was to think that Elisa would be interested in him just because he had an unusually large penis. But I was wrong. Rita Lee said to Elisa, "That's the kind you like, isn't it?" and they summoned the man to move closer to them. He shuffled up, and they began feeling and squeezing his penis like housewives trying to determine the ripeness of a squash. Suddenly Elisa announced to Rita Lee, "É meu programa" (He's my programa), and she took the man by the shoulders and herded him off down the street, telling him now that her price was two reais (!) and that they could go to her room on São Francisco Street to have sex.

One of the reasons travestis fluctuate their prices so dramatically between different clients is that in the end, it really makes little difference what price they quoted prior to the programa. No matter what price a travesti agrees to before a programa begins, by the time it finishes, the price will have inflated, and the travesti will almost invariably demand more from her client. A difference between the prostitution practiced by travestis in Brazil and prostitution in many other parts of the world is that clients pay travestis *after* sex, not before. The only time a travesti demands money before sex is when the programa is to be performed on an isolated, dark beach, where travestis know—often from bitter experience—that the client can suddenly run off into the darkness and never be found.[3]

Being paid after sex would, at first glance, seem to put the travesti at a disadvantage, since it allows a client the possibility of fooling the travesti into thinking that he has more money than he really does. In fact, this only happens extremely rarely. If a travesti has some reason to doubt that a man has money, she will ask to see it before she agrees to do a programa with him. But she will not demand payment until the programa is finished. One of the rare times a travesti may end up with little or no money from a client is when the pulls a drunken man into her room, on a weekend night or during Carnival, thinking that he may have more money hidden on him than he claims. The travesti may have sex with the man just to be able to rifle through his clothing while he is preoccupied trying to penetrate her. Surprisingly often, a travesti finds more money in this way (many of them seem to have a sixth sense about such matters). But sometimes she realizes, to her colossal annoyance, that the drunk was telling the truth when he told her he had no money. I have seen drunken men being lured into rooms by travestis who beckon with the suaveness of sirens, and seen those same men being literally hurled back out onto the street ten minutes later by the same sirens, now metamorphosed into maddened Furies, with only a few reais in their hands.

Waiting until after the programa is finished to collect her money gives a travesti two advantages. The first is that the man, now sexually satisfied, will be less likely to resist when the travesti inflates her price. Another one of the understandings of bodily processes that travestis in Salvador seem to share is the belief that ejaculating spends one's *força*, one's vigor, and leaves a person both psychologically and physically disinclined to fight. Hence, travestis pounce when they believe their client is feeling weak and satisfied, thinking that he will only be interested in leaving the scene in order to "enjoy his orgasm" (*curtir a nice dele*), as one travesti put it to me.

The second advantage that payment after sex provides travestis is the opportunity to claim that the client did something during the programa that hiked up the price. In the initial negotiations between a travesti and her client, what is normally specified by the travesti is the price of a programa. For example, a man who pulls up in a car at Pituba and asks a travesti, "How much?" might get the response "Vinte no carro, quarenta no hotel"—the equivalent of twenty dollars for sex in the car, forty dollars for sex in a hotel. Note that the exact type of sex to be practiced for this price is left strategically unstated in this reply. This creates an ambiguity that travestis can later use to their advantage. It leaves the exact conditions of the programa vague, allowing the client to believe he understands what he has agreed to pay for. At the end of the encounter, however, the travesti will direct the client's attention to the "fine print" of the original agreement. And that fine print always contains a surprise for him.

Robbing Clients

What often happens when payment is being handed over is that the travesti will first demand more money, and then, even if the client agrees and gives it to her, she will often rob him anyway. As Tina, who was renowned in Salvador for her brazen assaults on clients, once told me, "If a man opens up his wallet for me, Don, and pays me fifty [reais], and he has more than that, he's gonna give me all of it" (*Se o homem abrir a carteira pra mim Don e me pagar cinqüenta, e ele tiver mais do que aquele, ele vai me dar tudo*).

And during the interview that Keila and I conducted with nineteen-year-old Cintia, she recounted an incident that is typical of the way travestis conclude their programas with their clients:

> Last Thursday, yeah, it was last Thursday, I went with this man, you know, he stopped for me, but he stopped far away from where I was standing, so I didn't even go up to him. So he drove around the block and stopped right in front of me, and he said "How much?" and I said, "It's twenty in the car and forty in a hotel." He opened the door and said "Get in, but I'm in a hurry, so we're going to do it quick (*a gente vai dar uma pressinha*)." I said "Great." And so he took me to the Jardim [dos Namorados, which is a huge parking lot just off the highway where the travestis stand in Pituba. At night this lot is sometimes filled with over a hundred cars parked side by side, each one with its windows rolled up and dripping with steam, and each one bouncing and jerking and shaking from the actions of the couples copulating inside].
>
> When we got to the Jardim dos Namorados, there in Pituba, it was full, and so he said, let's go to the Air Club, so I went with him to the Air Club.
>
> There in a really dark parking place, near the gas station. And I went with him there, when we got there, this man kissed and hugged like crazy (*esse homem fez o pior romance*). But he was a man (*um homem homem*), he wasn't a maricona [i.e., he penetrated Cintia and did nothing with her penis]. And so he said, "You were so good with me," and he gave me thirty reais [i.e., ten more than Cintia had asked for].
>
> Only, I saw that he was really soft (*mole*) [giggles], and so I said to myself "I'm gonna rob him." And so, when he stopped the car [to let Cintia off at the spot where he had picked her up], I said "No, give me more money." Him: "I don't have any more." "Give me more." "I don't have any," "Give me more," "I don't have any"—I took his car key and yanked it out of the ignition.
>
> Right then Rafane [Cintia's friend, another travesti] arrived, and it was a real fight—this man wouldn't give up no matter what (*esse homem não quis deitar de jeito nenhum*) [laughs]. Me inside, Rafane at the door took him in a stranglehold and I went through his pockets—the man was hitting me, I was hitting him, he was hitting me, I was hitting him, Rafane said "Let's leave this creep (*este peste*). Get out of his car." So Rafane let him go, and I got out. And he was pointing at me "I'm gonna get you, I'm gonna get you," and we ran away.
>
> He disappeared, but a bit later, when I was standing at the gas station, we saw him driving around, and Rafane: "He only saw your blonde hair," and while he was driving around looking for us, we got a ride back into town.

Like Cintia, the overwhelming majority of travestis in Salvador regularly rob their clients (and only their clients, despite the widespread belief that travestis assault anyone they set eyes on). This happens in one of several ways. The most common way, not attempted here by Cintia, is by pickpocketing. Pickpocketing—known variously in travesti slang as *azuelar, dar a Elza, dar uma churriada, beijar* ("kiss"), or *dar uma dedadinha* ("insert a little finger")—can occur with truly magical speed as a travesti stands massaging a potential client's penis while negotiating a sexual encounter on the street. I have seen one particularly skillful travesti remove a potential client's wallet, count the money, take most of it, replace a tiny amount of money plus the man's identity card, and put the wallet back in his pocket in a matter of seconds. She managed this by keeping him distracted by squeezing his penis with one hand (and removing his wallet from his back pocket with the other), then turning her back to him to vibrate her bottom against his crotch (while examining the contents of the wallet), then hopping back around to continue massaging his crotch with one hand (and replacing the wallet with the other). A travesti who pickpockets a man in this way will usually send him on his way after she has slipped the wallet back into his pocket, saying she can't do a programa with him because she is "busy." However, upon examining the contents of a potential client's wallet if she has discovered that he has a great deal of money, she will often remove some of it, but not enough for him to immediately be able to perceive that he has been robbed. She will then replace his wallet in his back pocket and try to get him to do a programa. When the time comes for the client to pay and he discovers that he doesn't have enough money, the travesti will accuse him of trying to cheat her, and she will become aggressive—usually ending up walking away from the scene with all the client's money, plus his watch or anything else of value that he might be carrying.

Pickpocketing also commonly occurs while a travesti performs oral sex on a client in his car. Here the trick is to get the client to lower his trousers so that they are on the floor, then for the travesti to position herself across his lap in such a way that her body, and especially her hair—which she will repeatedly fluff up and toss in the direction of his face—will obscure the client's view of what the travesti is doing with her hands while her mouth is busy performing other services. Similar pickpocketing occurs during other forms of sex, in hotel rooms, in the travesti's own room, or on the beach. Generally speaking, wherever a client lowers his trousers or removes his clothing (travestis know that many men keep their money in their shoes, so those are often removed and examined at some point during a sexual encounter), a travesti will attempt to extract money.

A second way to rob clients is to directly assault them (*azuelar, grudar* or *tomar no grito, pegar na tora, dar o gogó*). This can occur if the travesti judges, as Cintia did, that the client is *mole* (soft). Usually the travesti has also determined that her client doesn't have a weapon, or, alternatively, she has already located a weapon in his car or clothing and has taken it herself. When the travesti is reasonably sure that she can overpower her client, she will do as Cintia's friend Rafane did—grab his shirt at the neck and press him up against a wall or his car door, demanding money.

In assaulting their clients, some travestis may employ knives or razors or small, sharp nail scissors. One especially inventive travesti in Salvador sometimes used a syringe that she filled with tomato juice and pressed against the necks of her clients, telling them that the red fluid inside was HIV-infected blood. No travesti in Salvador uses guns to assault clients, largely because they know that armed assaults are regarded by police and the courts as much graver than assaults with other weapons, and that if they are caught in possession of a firearm, the consequences would be serious indeed.

Travestis frequently cooperate with one another in assaulting clients, in a system known as *fazer a portinha* (literally, "do the car door"). This is what Rafane did together with Cintia. Travestis "do the car door" when a client, after sex, drives a travesti back to the place where he picked her up (all travestis insist on this). Sometimes a travesti will alert others that she intends to rob the man upon return, either by discreetly making a "come here" gesture with the fingers of one hand as she enters the client's car and settles into the passenger seat, or by quickly shouting to another travesti in travesti argot, "Cuenda a portinha mona quando eu voltar" (Do the door, mona, when I come back). When the travesti returns with the client after the programa and he stops to let her out, she will do what Cintia did: yank the car key from the ignition and make her demands. At this point, one or more travestis will come to their colleague's assistance and position themselves in front of the door on the driver's side, thereby blocking the client's exit and adding a further degree of menace to the situation. If the client gives the travesti more money, his key will be returned and he will be allowed to drive away. If he resists, as Cintia's client did, he will be openly struggled with and robbed.

The third means of extracting more money from a client is one that travestis refer to as *fazer um rebucête, dar um show,* or *dar um escândalo*—make a show or a scandal. A scandal consists of a travesti publicly attempting to shame a client into compliance with her demands for more money. Scandals will be made if pickpocketing has been unsuccessful, if direct assault is for some reason impossible, if the client has discovered that the travesti has robbed or attempted to rob him and becomes aggressive, or if the client has no money or valuables left but has been discovered to have an automatic-teller bankcard or a checkbook. (Travestis will accompany clients to bank teller machines and wait for them to withdraw money. They also accept checks for their services).[4] In any of these cases, a travesti may decide to make a scandal.

A scandal consists of loud, abusive cries at the client that he is a *maricona safada* or *maricona desgraçada* (a "disgusting faggot" or "disgraceful faggot") who has engaged the services of a travesti and afterwards is refusing to pay the agreed-upon price. The key lexical item here, one that features prominently in all scandals, is *maricona*—a word that contains the culturally weighty assertion that the referent is a homosexual who enjoys being anally penetrated. Regardless of whether the travesti in fact penetrated the client, she will announce that she has "eaten [i.e., penetrated] the ass" (*comi o cu*) of the client, and she will expand on and embellish this announcement with details of how the client "sucked [her] dick" (*chupou meu pau*) and how he wanted to be called by female names during sex. Extended scandals frequently also involve the travesti removing or threatening to remove all her clothing as she stands halfway inside or beside the client's car (if she has left the car to make a scandal, she will have also taken the car key or the client's identity card with her) or just outside the hotel room where she has had sex with him.[5]

Travestis are all well aware that they scare clients away when they rob them. Banana told me that a client will often "go with us [older travestis] a few times, then a new travesti appears and they go with her. And when the new travesti robs him, he comes back to us. And when he comes back to us, we rob him too. And so it goes." In the end, Banana continued, clients will stop going to travestis altogether. She lamented to me that she has no regular clients at all anymore, because she robbed them all so many times that they are afraid of her.

Whenever the street goes through extended periods of being *uó* (bad) or *morta* (dead), travestis, finding themselves spending entire evenings working in vain to attract clients, will begin complaining loudly to one another that men have stopped going to travestis because they know they will be robbed. And they begin lecturing one another that if travestis only worked *na moral*—honestly, without robbing—then there would be so many happy clients seeking out travestis that no one would ever have to rob. Ironically, it is precisely in the midst of such times and such bouts of lecturing that robberies increase, because when the volume of clients decreases, each travesti will feel that any client she manages to attract may be her only one that evening—and so he will be squeezed for everything he is worth. The same dynamic occurs whenever policemen decide to harass travestis and try to drive them away from their various points of prostitution. The only effect this has is to compel travestis to rob their clients using increasingly violent means, since they need to earn money and they are unsure of when they will find another client.

Travestis themselves express surprise that men keep coming back to them despite being robbed. They are all agreed that every man who has ever done a programa with a travesti has in all likelihood been robbed—they've all been *passado e repassado*, hashed and rehashed (as Adriana liked to put it), by travestis. I asked several travestis why they thought that men kept coming back to them, despite the fact that they could virtually count on being robbed. "That's the Great Unknown (*a incógnita da questão*)," Keila answered, and offered the hypothesis that they liked travestis too much to be able to stay away. She mentioned the example of one man who regularly went with travestis: "I'm not even going to ask you what you charge," this man apparently tells travestis, "because no matter what we agree on, you'll still take everything I have."

Travestis frequently comment to one another that many men "like to be robbed' (*gostam de ser roubados*). And while one can readily recognize the self-serving message carried by such a statement, it is also, in many cases, difficult to disagree with it. It is hard to interpret the actions of some men as anything other than playing with fire. It is not unusual for travestis to return from Pituba, which is near a bingo hall, with the equivalent of one hundred dollars or more that they have stolen from a single client. (If a travesti robs a client of a large sum of money, she will immediately hop into a taxi, head home, and stay away from the area where the robbery took place for several days, in order to avoid having to confront the irate client and perhaps the police.) In late 1996, a travesti robbed a *velhinho*—a little old man—at knifepoint of the equivalent of fifteen hundred dollars when he entered her room on São Francisco Street to do a programa with her. And Pastinha's biggest coup to date occurred several years ago when she invited a client into her room and slipped six Rohypnol tablets into a bottle of beer she offered him. She did this because she had heard from other travestis (who had all already robbed the man) that he tended to walk around carrying lots of money. When the man passed out, Pastinha reached into his pockets and extracted forty-one thousand cruzeiros, the equivalent at the time of about four thousand dollars. Knowing that the client would not take kindly to being robbed of so much money, she cleared out her room and caught a bus to a town in another state, where she remained for several months, until all the money was spent.

That many men carry substantial amounts of money on them when they approach travestis would seem to indicate that at least some of them find some sort of excitement in purposely exposing themselves to the risk of losing it all. And travestis are more than happy to play that game, indulging this particular pleasure to its fullest by giving a client a vigorous, and sometimes violent, run for his money.

The Clients of Travestis

But who are these men who seek out travestis for sex? That, too, is in a sense "the Great Unknown." Seen from a distance, the males who pay travestis for sex are Brazilians of all ages, races, and social classes.[6] I spent virtually every night of my time in Salvador in the company of travestis working different parts of the city, taking note of the men who pulled up in cars or went off with travestis into dark alleys or cheap hotel rooms. In the end, I was unable to discern any one type of man who could be considered the "average" client. Clients range from about thirteen to sixty years old (the majority being between about seventeen and forty-five); they are white, black, and everything in between; they can be extremely poor, extremely wealthy, or anything in between.

During the entire time I spent in Salvador, I was unable to speak to any client of travestis. One of the reasons for this was practical—when a male approaches a travesti on the street, they engage in a brief conversation, then she either hops in his car and gets driven off, or the two of them begin walking in the direction of a hotel or a deserted street. After the programa, the male on foot goes his way and the travesti goes hers. The client who has picked up the travesti in his car will drop her off back at the point where he picked her up, then he will speed off. For me to have attempted to approach a client at either of these times (something I never even considered doing) would have been viewed by travestis as a gross interference in their professional activities, an action that could easily have frightened off clients. Also, I am reasonably certain that the males themselves would not have responded particularly warmly to a foreign man running after them wanting to ask them questions about the sex they had just paid to have with a transgendered prostitute. Keila is fond of saying that if a survey were taken of all Brazilian men, it would conclude that not a single one of them has ever had sex with a travesti, since no one would ever admit to doing so.

Because I had no access to the clients themselves, all I could do to try to figure out why they go to travestis is ask the travestis. They, of course, have thought about this a lot, and they give two main reasons why clients seek them out.

The first is that travestis are "different." "Most clients have women at home, you know?" Elisabeth explained to me. "So they go with travestis because they want something different (*outra coisa diferente*), you know?"

Cintia told me something similar: "I think that men, they already know, they have lots of women, they already know women, so they want something different, something new," she said. "'Cause men don't just content themselves with one person, you know, not with one kind of sex. These days they want to know about all kinds of sex, you know?"

What is "different" and "new" about a travesti is that she has the appearance of a woman but the genitalia of a man. Magdala explained that this was why she thought men were drawn to travestis:

> I think that what clients like about us is to see the appearance of a woman . . . with the penis of a man. It's like seeing a woman—more than a woman, you know? Because a travesti has these two sides, we can satisfy a man actively and passively—I think it's about that. The beauty of a travesti is that on the street corner, you see a woman. But you take off the clothes, you're going to see that it isn't a woman. So there's a penis that will satisfy some things and then there's other things too, you know?

Lia Hollywood reasoned that men wanted this penis in order to "desenvolver a parte mulher dele"—develop their feminine side. She also offered the intriguing proposition that some men may seek out a travesti's penis as a means of rebellion against the moral strictures of Brazilian society.

> That kind of thing, "Don't do that 'cause it's wrong. God will punish you. It's a sin"—I think that men resist that, and they seek us out when they're looking for something that might be, like/I had a case where a married man went with me and said, "Today I'm gonna give you my ass." I said, "Why, love?" [He answered:] "I had a fight with my wife. I want to do something really . . . horrible." Imagine that. To want to give your ass because you had a fight with your wife. It's a way, maybe it's a way to give vent to something. Let loose the rage he was feeling because he fought with his wife.

Martinha thought that many of the men who seek out travestis "have homosexual tendencies," but they don't approach other men because they don't have the courage to do so. This fear of approaching other men for sex was the second main reason given by travestis for why men seek them out. Adriana told me that one of her recent clients had told her, "'I only have the courage to go with you, who have the face of a woman, rather than to put a man with a beard in my car. Because you are all really feminine and you have the thing that we're looking for'—What's that?" Adriana asked me rhetorically. "Dick. They want dick."

When I asked Luciana why she thought that men went with travestis, she answered that it was out of shame:

Well, I think it's because . . . they're all promiscuous (*viciosos*), right? . . . But I think it's because . . . It's like the man who goes with a travesti . . . he'll never go with another guy, you know, because . . . he's ashamed to pick up another guy, you know? He feels like a man, he's married . . . he's ashamed to pick up a guy on the street, so . . . he picks up a travesti, who has the appearance of a woman, who dresses like a woman, but . . . who doesn't stop being a man. A travesti will have the same behavior as a man (*vai ter a mesma attitude que um homem*) and he [the client] will get satisfied. I think it's more or less like that, you know? They are ashamed to go with a guy. I've heard lots of them talking, you know, I've said "Why don't you go with a guy?" and they say "Me?! I don't want to do anything with a guy!"

Keila interrupted Luciana here to add, "Except that they give us their asses, but if you ask them 'Why don't you go with a guy, why are you going with a travesti?' they'll say 'No, I don't get turned on by guys, I get turned on by women, and you look like a woman.' A lie. We know that what they like is our male side, our female side can fuck itself (*o lado mulher vá se foder*). All they want is dick."

These varying responses about why males seek out travestis assert two facts about clients on which all travestis are agreed. First, the overwhelming majority of clients seem to self-identify as heterosexual and maintain relationships with women. Second, a very large number of them want to be anally penetrated by the travesti.

In their talk to one another and to anyone else who wonders, travestis maintain that most of the men who approach them for sex are interested in "giving" to the travesti. Most travestis complain, as Erica did in the last chapter when talking about a boyzinho who started grabbing for her penis as soon as she got him alone, that "there are no men anymore." Banana told me that out of a hundred clients, only ten will be men who want to penetrate the travesti. "It didn't used to be like that," she reflected. "When I first started whoring (*no começo da putaria da minha vida*), there were more men than mariconas. Earlier in my . . . artistic career, right?" Banana laughed, "there were more men. Nowadays it's the reverse, they all want to 'give.' Even the boyzinhos. These days they all want to suck, 'give'—in the past it wasn't like this." In a conversation with Martinha about how there are no men anymore, Keila recounted to me how "[i]n Zé Mocoto's house [a house across the street from Keila where the owner, Zé Mocoto—alias the nearly sixty-year-old travesti Angélica—rents out rooms to prostitutes for three reais a programa], we used to do fifteen programas, ten programas, all the men putting it into us [*mentendo na gente*—i.e., penetrating the travestis]. We'd go into the bathroom to wash out the sperm of ten, of eight men, because we didn't have time to go to the bathroom between clients, they came one after the other, just to penetrate us. Today, they come with their asses wide open, wanting to give." "And they want big dicks, too, thick ones," Martinha chimed in, "because their asses are so wide open. They're like tunnels." Another travesti added the tart suggestion that whereas previously, travestis who put the most silicone into their bundas made the most money, these days, a sure way for a travesti to make a fortune would be to inject five liters of silicone into her penis.

It is difficult to know to what extent this travesti consensus that the majority of males who seek them out for sex "nowadays" want to be penetrated is the reflection of some empirical reality and to what extent it is an element of travesti folklore. In order to get some idea of this, in mid-1995, Keila and I informally charted the programas done over a one-month period by five travestis we knew well, asking them once a week to recall the programas they'd done during the previous week and to specify what sexual activities were performed. We gathered information on a total of 138 programas.

Sexual service performed by travesti	Number of programas	Percentage of total
Dar (be penetrated by client)	72	52%
Chupar (perform fellatio)	26	19%
Comer e dar (penetrate and be penetrated by the client)	25	18%
Comer (penetrate the client)	12	9%
Bater punheta (masturbate the client)	3	2%
Total	138	100%

These numbers reflect what the travestis we spoke to remembered, and any sample like this will be influenced by the sexual preferences of the individual travestis—some of whom greatly enjoy penetrating and some of whom prefer to "give." Even if we acknowledge the highly imperfect nature of this little sample, however, it is still somewhat surprising in light of travestis' claims that the travestis remember so many men paying either to penetrate them or to have the travesti perform fellatio on them. Those two services together constitute 71 percent of the sexual acts performed. It is far from insignificant that 27 percent of the men in this sample sought out travestis to be penetrated by them. But those men would seem not to constitute the majority that travestis habitually claim they do.

The Brazilian anthropologist Hélio Silva, in his book *Travesti: A invenção do feminino* (Travesti: The invention of the feminine), expresses doubt at travesti claims that the majority of their clients pay to be penetrated, even though he admits that he has no empirical data on which to base such doubts. Rather than consider such claims as statements of fact, however, Silva interprets them as "a kind of guerrilla warfare against macho men, married men, family men, 'squares' ('*caretões*'), all those who under the cover of good behavior can slip, under protection, into practices that are not compatible with their public images" (1993:99). I think that this interpretation is a plausible account of the *effect* that travesti claims about clients may produce when they appear, as they sometimes do, in newspaper and magazine articles about travestis. Were the general public to believe that travestis normally penetrate their clients (and this is something that most Brazilians seem not to be aware of, despite those journalistic reports), it would not only blur popular understandings of what travestis are and what they do in bed, it would also make it impossible for a "man" discovered in the company of a travesti to claim that he was not a viado himself. However, to the extent that Silva is claiming that travestis consciously understand their assertions that the majority of their clients want to be penetrated as calculated proclamations of war, his explanation seems rather contrived.

My own suspicion is that travestis claim that most of their clients want to be penetrated because, regardless of their actual frequency, those are the experiences that are most salient for them. They stand out more starkly in their memories. One of the reasons for this is that all travestis first began penetrating when they "fell into the life." I know of no travesti who penetrated a male before she became a prostitute. Penetration is something that travestis learn to do through being paid to do it on the street. And experiences like those probably forge an enduring association between prostitution and penetration. In addition, travestis often find such experiences exceptionally pleasurable: whenever a travesti ejaculates during sex with a client, it is almost invariably while she is penetrating him. One of the reasons Magdala suggested for travestis' wanting their boyfriends to always "eat" them was "so that we can feel that kind of pleasure that the man on the street feels when we are 'eating' him. We enjoy doing that, and so we want our boyfriends to feel that, the same pleasure (*o mesmo prazer*)."

But the third reason why acts of penetration carried out by a travesti are more salient to her is that even though travestis greatly enjoy penetrating, they also seem to find the act, when they reflect on it later, a bit discombobulating.[7] During discussions about contexts in which travestis felt more like a woman or more like a man, I specifically asked several travestis what they felt like when they were penetrating clients. Mabel's answer was short and sweet. "Like a man," she told me. And the man she was penetrating she felt to be "like a woman." Banana was more expansive. She explained:

> I look at myself in the mirror, it's a strange thing, Don. It's a strange thing, we look in the mirror, our hair swinging back and forth, with breasts, our breasts swinging back and forth and us penetrating the man . . . I think to myself: this is an atrocity (*uma safadeza*). Sometimes I think: what an atrocity, I'm here to serve as a woman, and this man wants me to serve as a man for him. This is a disgrace (*uma descaração*)—in my thoughts, I think that here inside. But I don't say anything to him, no. I say it later, you know, when I'm about to . . . rob them. Then I say it.

"What do you say?" I asked Banana.

"Have shame, man, you pig (*seu descarado*). You come here—for me you were a man, I'm here to 'give' like a woman, you come and 'give' more than a *puta* [a female prostitute], more than me. I want my money, more money. To 'eat' costs more than to 'give,' you know, Don. The price goes up."

Keila spelled out the problem in detail. When the travesti is penetrating a client,

Keila: Eles dizem "Ah eu sou gostosa! Diga que eu sou gostosa. Vá, coma meu rabo, diga que tá fodendo um cu. Diga que tá comendo meu cu, diga que você tá gostando, diga, diga, vá, diga, cê não tá gostando? Você não gosta de comer uma bunda?" Aí começa com essas coisas todas.

Don: Mais elas . . . as mariconas mesmo falam/

Keila: "Gostosa."

Don: "Gostosa"?

Keila: Falam, falam.

Don: "Gostoso" não.

Keila: Não. "Gostosa." É "gostosa." Ela tá se sentindo mulher enquanto eu tou comendo ela. Então, ela tem

K: They say, "Ah, I'm *gostosa* ["delicious and sexy" with the feminine grammatical ending -*a*]! Say I'm *gostosa*. Go on, eat my behind, say you're fucking an ass. Say you're penetrating my ass, say you like it, say it, say it, come on, say it, you're not liking it? You don't like to penetrate a behind?" And that's how it all starts.

D: But they . . . the mariconas themselves say/

K: "Gostosa."

D: "Gostosa"?

K: They say it, they say it.

D: Not "gostoso" ["delicious and sexy" with the masculine grammatical ending -*o*].

K: No. "Gostosa." It's "gostosa." She [the client] is feeling like a woman when I'm penetrating her. So she's

Banana relaxing during a break from work

que se sentir mulher, ela tem que usar o termo feminino. Elas dizem.

Don: É comum?

Keila: Comum, muito comum. Todos os que dão, que são . . . gostam de dão, com frequência, eles acabam

feeling like a woman and so she's using the feminine term. They say that.

D: Is that common?

K: It's common, really common. All the ones who give [i.e., get penetrated], who are . . . who like to

adotando este termo "gostosa," "boa." Outro termo feminino muito usado é . . . é . . . como elas dizem? Mandam a gente chamar elas de mulher. Elas inventam nomes fictícios: "Bote nome em mim, me batize." Essas coisas das mariconas são ridículas!

Don: [laughs] Não sabia.
Keila: São horríveis, é um horror.
Don: Mas então, as mesmas mariconas que falam assim devem falar que você é "gostoso."

Keila: É, e ela se auto-identifica mulher, e fica agindo como se eu fosse homem. Enquanto ela está dizendo que ela é gostosa, ela vai me chamar de "Gostosão, meu macho, que pau gostoso que você tem, enfie todo no meu rabo que eu quero me sentir mais mulher ainda." Elas falam todas essas coisas. Tem maricona ridícula. É horrível.

Tem muitas que não, que dá o seu cuzinho numa boa, lá assim deitado, dá, bate uma punhetinha, goza e pronto, como a que tem aos sábados e aos domingos.

Mais tem muitos, não, que são chatos, e eles inventam essas histórias e quer que a gente fale que eles são "gostosa." E não dá pra concatenar, um homem chamando ele por/com termos femininos, de "gostosa." Fica uma coisa tão desconexa. Se você já não tá concentrado pra fazer sexo com aquela pessoa, e você, a partir desse momento vai tratar ele como se fosse

give a lot, they end up adopting this term "gostosa," and "boa" ["pretty," with the feminine grammatical ending; the masculine equivalent is *bom*]. Another feminine term they use a lot is . . . is . . . what do they say? Tell us to call them like women. They invent fictitious names [and say]: "Give me a [female] name, baptize me." These things that mariconas do are ridiculous!

D: [laughs] I didn't know.
K: They're horrible, it's a horror.
D: But that means that the same mariconas who talk like that should say that you are "gostoso" [with the masculine grammatical ending].
K: Yeah, she self-identifies as a woman, and acts as if I were a man. While she's saying that she is *gostosa*, she'll call me "You big sexy brute, my man, what a delicious dick you have, put it all the way in my behind so that I can feel even more like a woman." They say things like that. There are mariconas who are ridiculous. It's horrible.

There are lots who aren't, who give their little ass with no sweat, just lying there, they give, jerking themselves off, they cum and that's it, like the [regular clients] I have on Saturdays and Sundays.

But there are lots who don't, who are a real drag, and they invent these stories and want us to say that they are "gostosa." And it makes no sense—calling a man by/with feminine terms, "gostosa." It becomes something so disconnected. As if you're not already concentrating to have sex with that person—and from this moment on

uma mulher? Aí, acaba tesão, acaba o caralho de aza todo.

É horrível. Você já tá ali porque é um homem. De repente, o homem vira uma mulher pra você, quer que você chama ele com nome feminino, com termos femininos, pronto. O tesão vai pra casa do caralho. É horrível.

you're supposed to treat him as if he were a woman? That's it, your erection will disappear right there.

It's horrible. You're there because he is a man. Suddenly, the man turns into a woman on you, wants you to call him by a feminine name, with feminine terms, and all that. Your erection will fly out the window. It's horrible.

Keila recounts experiences here that I later came to understand were shared by all travestis. I heard numerous stories about clients who wanted to be called "Gretchen" or "Baby Consuelo" or "Fabiana," who wanted to be called *bonita* (the feminine form of "pretty") and *gostosa* by travestis, and who even dressed in panties, bras, and other female lingerie while being penetrated. These stories occur far too frequently in travestis' conversations with one another to be dismissed as fabrications; and to idealize them as being some kind of strategic "guerrilla warfare" waged by travestis against macho men obscures the fact that such experiences disturb travestis. The words they use to describe the way they feel about them—Banana's "strange" (*estranho*), "an atrocity" (*uma safadeza*); Keila's "horrible" (*horrível*), "ridiculous" (*ridículo*)—indicate that for travestis, they are far from always unambiguous or positive.

The discomfort that these kinds of experiences can provoke in travestis appears to be a result of the way in which penetrative sex is thought about. As I argued when discussing the relationships that travestis maintain with their boyfriends, what one does in bed has immediate and lasting consequences for the way one is perceived (and the way one can perceive oneself) as a gendered being. If one penetrates, in this particular configuration of sexuality and gender, one is a "man." If one expresses interest in the penis of a male, and especially if one "gives"—allows oneself to be penetrated by a male—then one is no longer a man. In the language used by travestis, one is a "viado" or a "woman." It is thus in bed, through sexuality, that gender gets worked out. And it is in bed where travestis are most vigilant with their boyfriends, on the lookout for any indication that their "man" might really be a "woman."

The window of opportunity for gender slippage that penetrative sex opens is exuberantly exploited by many of the clients who pay travestis for sex. Those males take full advantage of the fact that penetration can change their gender. Some of them even elaborate this idea to its logical conclusion, asking to be "baptized" with a feminine name, wanting to be called by feminine terms, and putting on feminine articles of clothing. In other words, what those clients do in these brief encounters is more or less precisely what travestis spend their lifetimes doing—"feeling like women." There is a correspondence between a client's behavior in bed and a travesti's behavior in *life* that is absolutely striking. And travestis speak about this behavior in exactly the same manner as it is spoken about by Brazilians at large. When Keila expresses dismay at the client who "turns into a woman on you, wants you to call him by a feminine name, with feminine terms, and all that," she sounds like the *vox populi Brasiliani* opining on travestis.

Although no travesti ever suggested it to me, I would guess that one of the reasons they remember clients who want to be penetrated, and one of the reasons they find the more elaborate encounters of that kind to be so strange and horrible, is because they glimpse something of themselves in the behavior and desires of their clients. They see someone who is male wanting to be treated *como se fosse mulher*—as if he were a woman. And, influenced by a lifetime of derogatory messages about such behavior, they find themselves instinctively experiencing that desire in another person as "ridiculous." They also directly experience the transient and highly contextual nature of gender in the system in which they operate—during the act of penetrating a client, travestis can "suddenly," as Keila emphasizes, find *themselves* transformed from a woman into a "big sexy brute." Who could ever forget that?

Prostitution in Italy

In addition to prostituting themselves on the streets of Salvador and other cities throughout Brazil, a large number of travestis leave the country to spend time working in Italy. Italy is to travestis what El Dorado was to the Spanish conquistadores of the New World. It is the land of fabled riches to which one travels in order to make one's fortune and return with enough money to realize one's dreams.

The travesti migration to Europe in search of fortune dates back to the late 1970s, when Brazilian travestis began traveling en masse to Paris, working in the areas around Pigalle and especially in the Bois de Boulogne at night. When it began around 1978, the travesti presence in Paris was small; one of the pioneers remembers that for several years towards the end of the 1970s, there were no more than fifty Brazilian travestis in Paris (*Fatos e Fotos*, 4 November 1984). Those travestis were earning as much as a thousand dollars a week—a fantastic sum for most people, but a truly unimaginable amount of money for anyone coming from a country where the average minimum salary was the equivalent of about seventy dollars *a month*.

As the travesti grapevine back home in Brazil began to vibrate with the news of wealth to be made in Paris, increasing numbers made their way across the Atlantic. At the height of the migration, in the early 1980s, journalists estimated that there were between one and two thousand Brazilian travestis living and working as prostitutes in Paris. The market began to become saturated, and this gave rise to violent disputes between travestis, and between travestis and French female prostitutes, over the right to stand on a particular stretch of sidewalk. Travestis gained increasing visibility and notoriety, and Parisian newspapers began carrying regular sensationalistic and indignant reports about them. At one point, tour operators even began driving tourist buses through the Bois de Boulogne at night so that visitors to Paris could catch a glimpse of the city's exotic new attraction.

Partly as a reaction to this notoriety and visibility, the French government imposed visa restrictions on Brazilians in 1982, making it mandatory for all Brazilians entering France to have an entry visa. (Among travestis, this is the only thing that François Mitterrand is associated with, and the mention of that name provokes immediate grunts of distaste from any travesti who has ever heard it.) At the same time as these visa restrictions began to be enforced, police started arresting and deporting travestis. It took several years for these actions to have much real effect, and in 1984 a travesti could still tell a reporter from the Brazilian newspaper *Folha de São Paulo* (9 October 1984), "There are a lot of Brazilian travestis working in Paris. This is one of the best markets in Europe. Despite the police, it's still worth trying one's luck here. For every travesti they deport, ten more arrive the next day."

By the late 1980s, however, France had become closed to travestis and the center of travesti prostitution had shifted to Italy. Italy is today what France was in the early 1980s. Each day, scores of travestis leave Brazil with round-trip tickets to Brussels or Frankfurt or Vienna, but their final destination is Rome or Milan or Genoa. And what the travesti quoted in the *Folha de São Paulo* reported for France in the early 1980s goes double for Italy in the late 1990s—for every travesti that gets deported, I would guess that at least twenty more arrive the next day. Fernanda Farias de Albuquerque describes the influx of Brazilian travestis into Italy as "a virtual invasion" (Albuquerque and Janelli 1995:117).

Brazilian citizens do not need a visa to enter Italy as tourists, but travestis believe, presumably with good reason, that they will be deported if they attempt to enter the country openly. Therefore, they always travel to some other European city where they are fairly certain they can enter without difficulty. Crossing an international border with a passport bearing a male name, however, is always stressful for a travesti with breasts, plucked eyebrows, long hair, and a conspicuously ample, silicone-filled bunda. Most travestis making this journey attempt to pass as men, wearing long pants, no makeup, a man's shirt, and a baseball cap, into which they stuff their hair. Other travestis think that such a disguise will only make them look suspicious. The day Chica arrived back in Salvador after having spent several months in Italy, she recounted her first experience of going through a passport control in Vienna for me and several travestis who had gathered to listen:

Chica: Eu rezei muito, digo "Com fé em Deus, Nossa Senhora, não vai ter babado." Aí fui bicha. Na hora de dar os passaporte . . . O babado é a hora de dar os passaporte. Tu sabe, né?

C: I prayed a lot, said "With faith in God and the Virgin Mother, there won't be any screwups." And I got into the queue, bicha. When the time came to give the passports . . . The worst part is when you give them your passport. You know, right?

Don: Sim.

D: Yeah.

Chica: Tem umas cabine, assim, né?

C: There's these cubicles, like, right?

Don: Sim, sim.

D: Yeah, yeah.

Chica: Aí todo mundo em pé, você/você acompanha—tu sabe dessas coisa. Aí pá pá pá pá pá. Ninguém é de ninguém naquela hora. Não pode ficar cochichando nem não. Você fica sério na sua fila.

C: And everyone standing, you/you follow—you know about this. And pa pa pa pa pa [sounds of passports being stamped and people going past the passport control]. It's every man for himself. You can't stand there whispering to anybody. You have to stand there quiet in your queue.

Piupiu: Cada um é cada um.

P: It's everyone for himself.

Chica: Aí fica, espera sua hora. Aí vem . . .

C: And you're there, waiting your turn . . .

Piupiu: Ave Maria.

P: *Ave Maria.*

Chica: Ali seu cu tá assim Piupiu [Chica makes a ring with her thumb and forefinger the size of a dime]. Aí se você botar um linha, um cordão, um barbante, parte!

C: Your sphincter is like this, Piupiu [Chica makes a ring with her thumb and forefinger the size of a dime]. [Your sphincter is so tight with fear that] if you put a thread, a string, a cord in it, it would cut it in two!

Piupiu: Acredito. [Ficar preso, lá.

Chica: └Naquele hora é
babado. Aí meu Deus do céu. E eu
de mulher. Não tinha como ir de
homem. Minha amiga disse "Chica
não vá de homem, que é mais
ridículo ainda, parece como qualquer traficante. Vá do jeito que
você é."

Eu peguei prendi minhas tran-
ças, botei um blaiser chique, minha
calça jeans. Agora, não fui depra-
vada. Um blaiser, uma camisa por
dentro, assim, bem chique, né?

Aí nisso o homem só: "Olhar
seu passaporte aí." Aí eu passei
primeiro do que ela. E a vez dela:
"Vai indo na frente Chica, pelo
amor de Deus, vai na frente que tu
nunca veio. E qualquer coisa"—ela
foi nessa fila, eu fui nessa—"qualquer coisa, se você não souber
falar, eu já digo que você veio fazer
compras." Aí também não precisou.
Na hora ela deu o passaporte dela,
o homem carimbou, aí passou.
Quando chegou do outro lado,
ela olhou pra mim, disse, "Pronto
querida, bem dizer você já está
na Italia, né? Que já passou aí?"

P: I believe it. ['Cause you can get
                  arrested right there.

C: └That moment is the
worst. My God in heaven. And me
as a woman. I couldn't go as a man.
My friend said, "Chica, don't go as
a man 'cause it'll be even more
ridiculous, you'll look like some
common drug smuggler. Go like
you are."

I tied my braids back in a pony-
tail, put on a chic blazer, my jeans.
Now I didn't go looking depraved.
A blazer, a shirt tucked in like this,
real chic, right?

And the man only: "Let me see
your passport." So I passed through
before her [Chica's friend Marcela,
who was accompanying her]. And
she was saying the whole time:
"You go first Chica, for the love of
God, go first since you've never
done this before. And if something
happens"—she was in that queue
and I was in this one—"if something happens and you don't know
what to say, I'll say that you're
coming here to do some shopping." But it wasn't necessary.
When she gave her passport, the
man took it, stamped it, and she
passed through. When she got to
the other side, she looked at me
and said, "Well, love, we can say
that you're practically in Italy now,
right? Now that you've passed
through this!"

Once Chica and Marcela were in Austria, they made a beeline for
Italy, entering the country locked securely away in a train compartment
that a friendly conductor had offered them in exchange for sex. All travestis enter Italy clandestinely like this, but few meet up with friendly
train conductors. Many find themselves having to elude border posts by

climbing over mountains and hills. And some enter the country hiding in the sleeping compartment of a trucker—who usually helps the travesti, again, in exchange for sex.

Because the road to Italy is so complicated, most travestis traveling to Europe for the first time will try to do as Chica did and go with someone who has been there before. Luciana, for example, went with a travesti friend popularly known in Salvador as Simone Concreto (because the numerous liters of silicone in her body have turned it hard as concrete). Simone had worked in Paris, and when she was deported she returned to Europe and started working in Italy. Luciana went with Simone because Simone knew the ropes about how to enter Italy, where to go, and what to do once one got there. But even so, this first experience of getting to Italy was, Luciana said, "horrible":

> I didn't know how to say anything in Italian . . . and I went to Lisbon, we got there, me and Simone, we entered Europe through Lisbon. We "battled" [worked] in Lisbon one or two days, then we went to Spain. We "battled" in Spain, I think it was one or two days too, then we went to Barcelona. We only stayed one day in Barcelona—it was impossible to "battle," the police were bothering everyone, the police were disturbing, so we didn't "battle," we just slept in a hotel and in the morning we left. We passed Junqueira, which is the border between Spain and France, you know, and then we had to cross all of France to get to Italy, right?
>
> We got to this big parking place where there were a lot of trucks, right, where all these truckers were stopped to fix their papers, their documents for customs. And there we met a trucker who would take us both across the border—there were two truckers, friends, from the same company. Simone went with one and I went with the other one.
>
> When we started getting close to the border, I said I was sleepy [laughs]. And I go in the back, in the little sleeping compartment. And I throw myself on the bed and throw a mountain of blankets on top of me, and I stay there all quiet. They don't usually check trucks, so the trucker will go into the border station and come out again, and he'll pass across the border.
>
> Only this time Simone's truck passed through, and mine did too, but then he stopped at some company to fix some papers or something, to resolve something, and it took forever. And by the time we got to the place where Simone and me had arranged to meet each other, she had already left. She waited and waited for me and saw that I wasn't coming, and so she got a lift to go to Italy. She couldn't wait for too long because if the cops caught her hitchhiking along the road, they would have taken her right to the plane [to be deported]. She left me alone on the highway, not knowing how to say anything, not knowing anything. I didn't even have any money. The only thing I had in my address book was the name of a hotel in Milan. I was desperate—started to cry and everything. I didn't

know whether to go back, or to go on forward—not knowing how to say anything . . .

And I said, no, I won't go back, you know, 'cause that's fucked (*uó*). I'm gonna go forward. So I hitchhiked, a truck stopped, they took me . . . to Nice. I got to Nice and got another lift who took me across the border and let me off in Milan. Six o'clock at night, he let me off on an overpass on the outskirts of Milan. And me not knowing anything . . .

So a car stopped, with two guys, you know, asking me where I wanted to go, and I said   I showed them the name of the hotel, 'cause I couldn't speak Italian, right? So I showed them the name of the hotel, and they said OK we'll take you. So we go to the hotel, but there wasn't anybody left— the police had closed it, cleaned it out, and there wasn't a single travesti. I got desperate, with those two guys in the car, not knowing what to do, you know? And so I laid all my cards on the table for them, I said that I was Brazilian (*brasileira*) and I wanted to know where the other Brazilians who worked around here were . . . And they took me to the place where they worked, which was [Avenue] Melchiorre Gioia they took me there. And there I met Ximena [a travesti Luciana knew from Brazil]. I met Ximena, and she was staying in the same hotel as Simone. She said she would take me there. So I got out of their car—I didn't do anything with them—I got out, talked to her, she got a taxi, took me to the hotel, we got there and there was Simone sleeping away on the bed. I said, "Bicha you"—I said, "You bitch (*você descarada*), you left me on that highway, not knowing how to say anything . . ."

The reason travestis go to Italy today is the same reason they went to France in the late 1970s—to make money. All travestis tell one another that they can make fabulous money in Italy, far more than they could ever dream of making anywhere in Brazil. And this seems to be true: although travestis are understandably reluctant to discuss with anyone exactly how much they make in Italy, most of them who spend any time there return with enough money to buy a house or an apartment, and maybe a car. One travesti I know well told me in confidence that during the three months she spent in an Italian city in 1995, she made enough money to be able to return to Brazil with sixteen thousand U.S. dollars protected by a condom and ensconced in her rectum. If one adds to that her living costs while in Italy (rent, food, etc.), the clothing, jewelry, and accessories she bought there, and the cost of her plane ticket to and from Europe, it seems probable that in only three months, this travesti made around thirty thousand dollars.

Travestis who go to Italy *need* to earn lots of money, because when they arrive there, the majority of them are already heavily in debt. Most travestis do not have enough money to purchase a plane ticket to Europe (which in 1996 cost just over one thousand dollars from Salvador) and to get from their port of entry to Italy (usually about five hundred dollars). What has happened, therefore, is that a number of travestis who have been traveling back and forth between Salvador and Italy for several years and who have access to capital have set themselves up as moneylenders. They lend a travesti the money she needs to get to Europe, and once there the travesti pays back the loan—plus interest. The catch, of course, is that the interest is high: 400 percent in 1996. The travestis who everyone knew loaned money in this way were loaning two thousand dollars and demanding eight thousand in return.

For individual travestis, this system offers both advantages and disadvantages. The advantage is that one can be assured of at least getting to Europe and, barring some major mishap with the Italian border police, into Italy. Sometimes the moneylender will even accompany the travesti to Europe. Once there, the borrower will be able to rely on the contacts of the travesti who has lent the money, and she will rapidly be integrated into the circle of Brazilian travestis with ties to that particular moneylender.

The disadvantages are that the borrower will be under continual surveillance by these travestis and under pressure to make money in order to be able to pay back the loan. In addition, because she often will be sharing a room with travestis similarly in debt, the risk that she will be robbed by another travesti is high, as is the risk that the moneylending travesti will charge her very high prices for room, board, and the right to use a certain area of sidewalk. Moneylending travestis who function as *cafetinas* (madams) in Italy also arbitrarily impose high "fines" (*multas*) on the travestis living in rooms they control, demanding that a travesti pay one or two hundred dollars if she has left the communal bathroom dirty or fought with another travesti living in the same house, for example (this same thing happens in Brazil—especially in Rio de Janeiro and São Paulo, where the system of *cafetinagem* is much more developed than it is in Salvador). Under circumstances like these, a travesti risks finding herself in a position of virtual slavery—she must work every night until sunrise to pay off a debt that only continues to increase. (Fernanda Farias de Albuquerque ended up in an Italian prison because she stabbed her *cafetina* to death during a dispute over money; see Albuquerque and Janelli 1995:133–34.) In addition, in the event that one is deported from Italy (something that has happened at least once, and often as many as three times, to most of the travestis I know in Salvador who have gone to Italy), the debt to the moneylender still needs to be paid—and this usually involves borrowing even *more* money, in order to get back to Italy and start all over again.

Life in Italy generally seems to be extremely hard. Travestis who have been there say that they practically work themselves to death out on the streets every night from sunset to sunrise. This is a schedule that travestis from Salvador—where work hours at night are usually between about 7 P.M. to midnight, or 2 A.M. at the latest—are unaccustomed to and dislike intensely. They need to work this hard, however, partly to save up the money they went there to earn in the first place, and partly to pay off the debts they continually accumulate while they are there. One characteristic of travestis working in Italy seems to be that they are atrociously ungenerous towards one another. Chica recounted how horrified she was at the extent to which travestis cheated and robbed one another and charged excessive sums of money for the smallest favors. "Bichas from my part of Brazil, from my city, my friends, who have been to my house, who I have lent clothes to," she said, "I could call them up and say 'Mona, the street where I'm 'battling' is horrible, let me come over to where you work, for one night, just to make some money, I'm not even eating lately,' and they would say 'Five hundred dollars, Chica. You want to come here, you pay me five hundred dollars.'"

Two other specific dimensions of life in Italy are problematic and can lead to a travesti's ruin. Elisabeth, who has spent a total of about three years in Italy, spelled these out to be: "If you're an intelligent travesti, you can go to Italy and become rich. But if you're a stupid travesti, you'll come back poorer than you were when you left. Because there are two things that you can never get involved with in Italy: men and drugs."

The latter problem is serious because the most popular drug among travestis in Italy, according to Elisabeth and other travestis with whom I have spoken, is heroin—which is, of course, ruinously addictive. Although heroin does exist in Salvador, it is uncommon and expensive. Until late 1995, when crack began appearing in the city, the hardest drug circulating in the milieux in which travestis live was cocaine. Over the years, however, a number of drugs that do not exist anymore have come and gone among travestis. The most powerful (and dangerous) of these was a drug called Algafam. Algafam was, travestis tell me, a horse tranquilizer. It was sold on the street in the form of a big yellow pill; one washed off the yellow color in order to get at the white pill underneath. The user then crushed the pill, added water, and filtered it into a syringe though a piece of cotton or, more commonly, through a cigarette butt. It was then injected into a vein. If one grain of the pill entered the syringe and was injected into the body, a huge abscess would develop. Several travestis who regularly used this drug in the mid-1980s (it disappeared from the streets about 1987) have large discolored patches on their arms and legs as a result of such abscesses.

Generally speaking, the mid- to late 1980s seem to have been a period when drugs were much more widespread among travestis than they are today. Banana and her boyfriend of the time were always doing Algafam, she told me, but she stopped when he died of an overdose and she realized that she would be the next to go. Mabel was so seriously hooked on cocaine and crack in São Paulo at the end of the 1980s that she ended up serving an almost three-year prison sentence for assault. Rita Lee always tried to keep her legs covered, even at night, because of the scars that years of Algafam abuse in the 1980s had inflicted on them. Stories circulate among travestis about well-known individuals who ended up dying of overdoses or in utter poverty because of their drug addictions. Chispita, the legendary travesti who began injecting hormones at age eight, was killed when, stoned on some drug at age thirteen, she misjudged the velocity of traffic and tried to cross the highway in Pituba.

By the mid-1990s, the majority of travestis in Salvador were not heavy drug users. These days, many travestis smoke marijuana one or more times a day; some of them snort cocaine whenever they have the money to buy it; some, like Banana, regularly take Rohypnol as a stimulant; and I once saw a travesti take a plastic bottle of glue off two street children who were sitting with her on the street at night and sniff from it. But only a few are rumored to use heroin (significantly, two of the four travestis I heard such rumors about had spent many years in Italy, and the other two had spent considerable amounts of time in São Paulo, where heroin is reportedly much more widespread than it is in Salvador). And although a number of travestis were selling crack in 1996 to supplement their incomes, only about five of them (none of whom sold it) were rumored to smoke it regularly.

On the other hand, many travestis do no drugs at all. Many of those who used drugs heavily in the 1980s, such as Mabel, don't even smoke marijuana. And other travestis, such as Keila, never began in the first place, because they saw what happened to their colleagues who became addicted. Elisabeth, who became addicted to heroin during one of her stays in Italy and ended up being deported, returning to Brazil with only the clothes on her back, told me, "if you get involved with drugs in Italy—or anywhere, in any country—you'll always, always end up in misery, with nothing left at all, you know?"

Heroin is a problem in Italy, however, because it apparently is much more readily available than it is in Brazil (Fernanda Farias de Albuquerque recounts how during her time in Italy, travestis didn't even have to buy it on the streets—heroin and cocaine were delivered to them in their rooms by travesti dealers; see Albuquerque and Janelli, 1995:117.) Also, since travestis in Italy earn so much money, they can afford heroin much more easily than they ever could in a place like Salvador. Many travestis start using heroin, they say, because of the cold. They suffer so much from standing out on the streets at night, wearing virtually nothing, that they need something to help them take their minds off the fact that they are freezing. Those who do not start shooting up in Italy often become dependent on alcohol, since they take to packing a bottle of whiskey with them at night to warm them up when they begin to shiver.

Aside from drugs, Elisabeth warns that one other thing should be avoided in Italy: men. Involvement with Italian men is extremely risky, because the kind of relationships that travestis promote with their boyfriends in Brazil—relationships based on the travesti "giving" and the man "eating"—can backfire horribly. When an Italian boyfriend reckons that the travesti has accumulated enough goods (television, stereo, jewelry, perhaps a car, etc.), he can denounce her to the police, have her deported (for working without a work permit), and disappear with or sell off all her belongings before she can return to Italy. This has happened to a number of travestis in Salvador, who suddenly found themselves being arrested on the street and deported without any warning. Upon her return from Italy, Chica recounted the story of a man who paid her for sex early on during her stay in Rome, then returned three days later saying that he was crazy about her and would do anything for her. She accepted his invitation to come to his house after she finished work, where, at six o'clock in the morning, she was treated to the most sumptuous breakfast she had ever experienced. All the while, the man kept imploring Chica to move in with him. But Chica is nobody's fool. "You know why," she told us. "Because they know that Brazilian travestis make lots of money. He wanted to see my money, mona, 'cause living in his house, he'd have to see it." When it became obvious to him that Chica's polite declinations of his invitation to come and live with him were serious, this man asked her for a loan of ten million lire. "They're rotten, Italian men," she concluded. "Don't trust any of them."

Despite all the risks that travestis expose themselves to when they go to Italy, the overwhelming consensus is that it is worth it. And the more travestis that go, the more others see that it is possible to go, and so they go too. Italy has become an ideal, a fixed point of reference for travestis in Salvador. As a European country, Italy is considered by travestis to be part of o primeiro mundo—the first world—whereas their own country is lamentably third world (one of the highest accolades that can be given an object, such as a wig, a dress, a pair of shoes, or a wristwatch, is to say that é uma coisa do primeiro mundo—"it's a first-world thing," meaning that it is elegant, European, and clearly not Brazilian). This patina of glamour is extended to travestis who have been to Italy; and those who have traveled between Italy and Salvador for many years and who are beautiful and haughty—and/or are known to own an apartment and possess some wealth—are widely referred to as *bichas européias* or *bichas ricas,* that is, European bichas or rich bichas (the terms are synonymous).

References to Italy are present even in the day-to-day lives of travestis who never have been there. Some of the most popular music among travestis is Italian pop performed by singers like Laura Pausini, Gianna Nannini, and Mafalda Minnozzi. Some travestis take pride in having learned the Italian lyrics to many of these songs. And they sometimes amuse themselves by talking about what they will do when they get to Italy, or how one says things in Italian. One lazy Sunday afternoon while Keila, Mabel, Rita Lee, Tânia, and Elisa were relaxing in the doorway of the house, chatting and keeping an eye open for any potential client who might happen by, Keila began using the Italian she has managed to pick up from Italian songs and from travestis who have returned from Italy.

Keila: *Mi piace, per favore.*[8]

K: *I like it, please.*

Mabel: Não fale comigo em italiano, *bella.*

M: Don't talk to me in Italian, *bella.*

Keila: *Io voglio um cappucceno, bella.*

K: *I want a cappuccino, bella.*

Mabel: *Vaffanculo.*

M: *Up yours.*

Keila: Só sabe falar isso.

K: That's all you know how to say.

Mabel: Isso mesmo. Eu vivi num prédio só de italianos em São Paulo. Só de italianos.

M: That's it. I lived in a building that only had Italians in it in São Paulo. Only Italians.

Elisa: As bichas falam italiano e eu cato tudo.

E: When the bichas speak Italian, I understand.

Mabel: Eu não cato tudo, tu vai catar tudo.

M: I don't understand, but you understand.

Elisa: Mas eu fico ouvindo o que elas estão dizendo, né?

E: But I sit listening to what they're saying, you know?

Mabel: Mas quando tá falando "maconha" cata.

M: And when they're talking about marijuana, then you understand.

Keila: Vocês tão falando besteiras. Porque se vocês forem pra Itália, quando eles começarem a falar vocês não vão entender nada. Que eles falam muito rápido. Ligeiro não entende nada.

K: You're both talking nonsense. Because if you go to Italy, when they start talking, you're not gonna understand anything. 'Cause they speak fast. If they speak fast you won't understand a thing.

Tânia: Falam rápido e a gente entende. A gente entende. Agora quando a gente fala eles não entende porra de nada.

T: When they speak fast we understand. We understand. But when we speak, they don't understand fuck all. [Tânia is the only one in this group who has actually been to Italy.]

Rita L: Vai entrar no carro e "Sali". Eu saio na hora [laughs].

RL: You're gonna get into a car and [they say] "Sali" ["get in", similar to *saia*, Portuguese for "get out"]. I'd get out right away [laughs].

Keila: Se ele quiser que você entre, ele diz "Sali."

K: If he wants you to get in, he'll say "Sali"

Mabel: *Sali fanculo.* Vou ficar aqui ( ) "Quero seu dinheiro, tua fria desgraçada."

M: *Sali up yours.* I'm gonna be there ( ) "I want your money, you cold son of a bitch" [Mabel is speaking to an imaginary client, robbing him; "cold" is a reference to the fact that Italy is known to be freezing in the winter].

Keila: Você fala assim/Eu que já arranho muitas palavras italiano, vou chegar lá e me perco? Porque, ô, eu sei ( ) palavras colher: *cuchialho*, garfo: *forqueta*, faca: *cotello*, tomate: *pomodora*, pimentão: *peperoni*, pimenta: *peperoncine*, cebola: chi/e cebola é *carota*/cenoura é *carota*, cebola é *chipolla* . . . que mais, pepino: *chicriolle*, salada é *salata*, arroz é *rizo*, feijão: *freijole*, qualquer tipo de spagetti é *massa*, *pasta*, carne é *bistecca*.

K: You say like this/I who already can say a lot of words in Italian, I'm gonna get there and lose my way? Because, look, I know ( ) words spoon: *cucchiaio*, fork: *forchetta*, knife: *coltello*, tomato: *pomodoro*, bell pepper: *peperoni*, chili pepper: *peperoncino*, onion: chi/and onion is *carota*/carrot is *carota*, onion is *cipolla* . . . what else, cucumber: *cetriolo*, salad is *insalata*, rice is *riso*, beans: *fagioli*, any kind of spaghetti is *massa*, *pasta*, meat is *bistecca*.

Rita L: Qualquer tipo de carne?

RL: Any kind of meat?

Keila: É. *Bistecca.*

K: Yeah. *Bistecca.*

Tânia: Bife de carne bem douradinho assim chamava . . . é/como é o nome . . . é *tortellini* . . . esqueci o nome . . .

T: A well-done steak was called . . . ah/what's it called . . . *tortellini* . . . I forgot what it's called . . .

Keila: Galinha é *pollo*/

K: Chicken is *pollo*/

Tânia: *Bistecca! Bistecca.* Dá uma *bistecca* aí.

T: *Bistecca! Bistecca.* Give me a *bistecca* here.

Keila: Bom dia é *buon giorno*.

K: Good day is *bon giorno*.

Rita L: Me dá um *bistecca* aí-o.

RL: Give me a *bistecca* here.

Tânia: *Bistecca*, bistequinha. A carne. Mal passada.

T: *Bistecca*, bistequinha [*bistecca* with Portuguese diminutive suffix]. Meat. Rare.

Elisa: Me dá uma *bistecca* com oro/ arrore [laughs].

E: Give me a *bistecca* with oro/arize [unsuccessful combination of the words for rice in Portuguese (*arroz*) and Italian (*riso*); she laughs at this].

Keila: *Io voglio* uma *bistecca* com *rizo* e *salada*.

K: *I want* a *bistecca* with *rice and salad.*

Going to Italy is the high point in the lives of most travestis in Salvador. It is what allows them to realize their dreams. Those dreams consist of, first of all, a house for their mother and, second, an apartment or a house for themselves. If a travesti's mother does not live in a house that she owns, the first thing a travesti will do with the money she has earned in Italy is buy her a house. And although I assume that there must be travestis who do not buy houses for their mothers with the money they bring back from Italy, I know of no travesti who has made money in Italy and not bought her mother a house if she didn't already own one. This is always their first purchase. In many cases, the travesti's father will still be alive and even still living with the mother, and many times the travestis say that they get along very well with their fathers. But the house they purchase upon returning from Italy is always, without exception, referred to as *a casa da minha mãe*—my mother's house.[9]

A travesti's second dream is to purchase either an apartment or a house for herself. In rare cases, a travesti will return from an extended trip to Italy with enough money to buy both her mother a house and herself an apartment or house. Much more often, however, the travesti will buy her mother a house and then return to Italy to accumulate money for her own apartment or house.

Once a travesti has an apartment, she can stop worrying about having to earn enough money to pay the exorbitant rents charged by the landlords who own the shabby cubicles in which travestis live. And if she has bought a house, she will often partition it into shabby cubicles and become a landlord herself, living primarily off the exorbitant rents that she will charge her tenants—who will often be principally travestis.

Prostitution for Money

Whenever journalists or television reporters ask travestis why they prostitute themselves, they usually explain that they are forced into prostitution because they cannot gain employment in any other sector. In Brazil, as in most countries, there are no laws prohibiting discrimination against individuals on the basis of appearance or sexual orientation, and throughout the country people are regularly fired from their jobs and denied access to educational programs simply because they are homosexual. For this reason, many homosexuals—both men and women—do their best to conceal their sexual orientation from all but their most intimate circle of friends. Individuals like travestis who are openly and unmistakably homosexual have little hope in the job market, and during the usually brief periods in their lives when they are engaged in salaried employment, they invariably work in jobs that are strongly marked as feminine—as domestic servants, as cooks in private residences or small restaurants, or as hairdressers or pedicurists in tiny beauty salons that are usually squeezed into the rooms in which they live. Because of the harsh and open discrimination they face in the job market, travestis explain to journalists who ask, they are forced to "fall into the life" in order to avoid starving.

This explanation is an incisive and crucial one. Any discussion of any dimension of travesti life must continually keep in mind that unless travestis can find a way to support themselves, they will inexorably starve to death. Travestis share this circumstance with the majority of people in Brazil, who can count on nothing from the government or any other organization should they find themselves unemployed and with no money.[10] But travestis are even worse off than most people on this count, because normally when people find themselves on the brink of destitution, they are at least able to count on receiving some aid, no matter how modest, from members of their family. Travestis, however, have either been expelled from their families or left them of their own accord, which means that the majority of them are unable to count on any aid of this kind. On the contrary, the cruelty with which many families treat their sons and siblings who become travestis is chilling. Pastinha told me that her deceased mother, whom Pastinha worshipped, was a fundamentalist Protestant who never accepted Pastinha's transformation into a travesti. She happily accepted the money that Pastinha sent or brought with her on her occasional brief visits to her childhood home, but she informed Pastinha coldly that if she contracted AIDS, she never wanted to see her again: "My mother said that if I got that sickness, she wouldn't let me enter her house, she would let me die on a bed in some hospital. She said she would be disgusted by me." Tina's mother sent her a letter a few years ago asking her never to visit the family home again, because Tina's father had announced that he would abandon his wife if she accepted a visit from her. Tina was so upset at this letter that she had a travesti who was literate write a letter back to her mother announcing that she had died.

Although Tina cut off all ties with her family upon receipt of the letter from her mother, many travestis seem to react to rejection by their families by trying to buy back some affective support. From very early on, whenever they can, they send money and gifts back to their families, which in practice almost invariably means their mothers. If they correspond with their families, they will often wait to send a letter until they can also enclose some money or send some gifts along with it. Whenever they visit home, they arrive bearing the most expensive gifts they can afford to buy. And if they go to Italy, their first priority, as I have already noted, is to buy a house for their mother.

It appears that despite their initial rejection, the families (especially

Rosana with her mother in the backyard of the house she bought for her

the mothers) of most travestis eventually come to accept them, and even welcome them back into their homes when they arrive on short visits. But few travestis delude themselves into thinking that this acceptance is unconditional. Most are aware that their families accept them only as long as they can provide them with financial support. The moment that support stops, the door to the family home is likely to shut tight. I witnessed this process with Rita Lee, the travesti who became extremely bitter towards Keila because she believed that Keila had stolen her boyfriend Tiane from her. Rita Lee's family lives in a suburb not far from the center of Salvador, and early on in my stay, I visited Rita Lee's family in her company several times. I also occasionally met Rita Lee's mother and sister when they visited her in her room on São Francisco Street. The family (with the exception of Rita Lee's stepfather, who always seemed to make himself scarce whenever Rita Lee appeared for a visit) struck me as having completely accepted Rita Lee. They seemed open and warm towards her, and her sister and mother even sometimes called her "Rita Lee" instead of her male name, "Tinho," when referring to her in conversations with me. What I did not fully appreciate at the time was that Rita Lee was earning enough money by working the streets and performing tasks for other travestis, such as cooking food and washing clothes, that she was able to regularly give some to her mother.

When, many months later, Rita Lee became sick with tuberculosis and then other illnesses related to AIDS, she was unable to work, and her income stopped. She was evicted from her room and began a nomadic existence, sleeping on the floor in the corners of the rooms of travestis who would let her stay with them. When she had exhausted this hospitality, she was forced to return to the home of her family. But they did not want her. Her mother and sister refused to take her in and care for her. In the end, her only alternative was the street or an AIDS hospice that travestis consider only if they know they are about to die. She went to the AIDS hospice and died there several weeks later.

The unidirectional flow of cash and goods from a travesti to her family is analogous to the unidirectional flow of cash and goods from a travesti to her boyfriend. In both cases, material goods are exchanged for affective recognition. What this means is that in order to feel desired by those individuals who mean something to them, travestis need to earn not just enough money to live on themselves, but enough to be able to support others as well. Furthermore, they must do this in a competitive context in which a sibling who gives his or her family more may eclipse or displace the acceptance that a travesti can expect from her family—or in which another travesti who earns more may snatch away a boyfriend from under one's nose.

In Salvador, it is impossible for a travesti to earn the kind of money she requires by working as a salaried employee. To the extent that travestis can get jobs at all, they will all be in the lowest-paying sectors of the Brazilian economy, often offering little more than one minimum salary a month (in 1996, this was the equivalent of $112). In addition, travestis are fully aware that the overwhelming majority of workplaces would put them into daily contact with people who would deride, laugh at, and humiliate them.

Prostitution, on the other hand, provides them with access to untold amounts of money. Although travestis do not necessarily earn money every night they work, after a busy night at a place like Pituba, a travesti can sometimes return home with the equivalent of eighty to a hundred dollars—that is to say, she can earn in one night what it would take her nearly a month to earn as a salaried laborer. And this doesn't even include what a travesti can bring home if she gets lucky enough to *pegar uma boa*—get hold of a lot of money through robbing a client.

So when travestis tell journalists that they are working as prostitutes because they have no other employment possibilities, they are articulating only part of the picture. A number of travestis I know quit their jobs when they realized they could earn more money as prostitutes. Keila quit hers the day she returned home clutching her five-hundred-cruzeiro bill. The first night Luciana prostituted herself, at age sixteen, she earned the equivalent of what she would have made in a week at the beauty shop where she was employed. She, too, quit work the next day. Elisabeth was taken to the *pista* at age twelve by a travesti she met while working as a domestic servant. The first night she prostituted herself, she earned *um dinheirão*—a large sum of money. "That was that," she told me. "From that day on, I've never wanted to work again." And Lia Hollywood, who was fired from her job at the bank because she wore makeup to work, told me that on the first night she put on a dress and prostituted herself, she earned more than the half-time monthly salary she had been receiving as an office boy. She never attempted to procure salaried employment again.

Money is thus a central reason why travestis prostitute themselves. They need to earn money partly to be able to eat and pay their rent, but also to be able to maintain affective relationships with their boyfriends and families. The inability to earn money is a devastating blow to a travesti in both material and emotional terms. I saw individual travestis sad on many occasions—such as when they heard news that their boyfriend had "given his ass" to another travesti, or when their mother did not respond to a letter that they had sent. But the only time I observed any of them fall into a state of lethargic, self-pitying depression was when they were not earning money on the street.

Prostitution for Pleasure

As important as it is, however, money is not the entire story of why travestis prostitute themselves. Whenever travestis talk with one another about their activities on the street, another dimension, aside from the purely monetary one, frequently gets foregrounded and elaborated: pleasure. Travestis derive pleasure from their work as prostitutes. They enjoy this work. It reinforces their self-esteem, and it provides them with sexual satisfaction.

This dimension of travesti prostitution runs directly counter to one of the most widely accepted truths about prostitution. Most accounts of prostitution, even those written or narrated by prostitutes themselves, either do not mention pleasure at all, or they mention it only in order to detail the practices that prostitutes say they adopt to avoid experiencing pleasure during sex with clients (e.g., Davis 1961; Day 1990; Gaspar 1985; O'Connell Davidson 1996; Winicke and Kinsie 1971). Some scholars go so far as to explicitly deny that prostitutes ever feel pleasure during encounters with clients. The position of those writers is that sex that is sold is sex that must necessarily be degraded and unpleasurable. Georg Simmel argued this long ago in his characterization of prostitution as the "nadir of human dignity" ([1907] 1990:337). Essentially repeating Simmel, Liv Finstad and Cecilie Høigård make the same argument when they state that "[t]o prostitute oneself is to give something of value for money, something that cannot be translated into the language of money without being destroyed" (1993:211). And Carole Pateman's blanket affirmation that "[t]here is no desire or satisfaction on the part of the prostitute" arises from her conviction that "prostitution is the use of a woman's body by a man for his own satisfaction," in an exchange in which "the prostitute is always at a singular disadvantage" (1988: 198, 208).

Assertions that prostitutes cannot possibly experience pleasure in their work must be heard in the context of widespread, ingrained public stereotypes that any woman who sells sex does so at least in part because she is sexually voracious. The counterclaim—that women sell sex because they are forced to, not because they want to—has been an understandable and necessary feminist response to those stereotypes. However, to the extent that this counterclaim assumes the status of unquestionable dogma and prevents us from hearing the voices of prostitutes who have other points of view, it impedes, rather than facilitates, our understanding of the lives of those individuals who sell sex.[11]

This goes for male prostitutes as well. Generally speaking, studies of male prostitutes do not go to the lengths that studies of female prostitutes do to argue that the prostitutes do not experience pleasure with their clients. Perhaps this argument is not needed in a cultural climate that makes it difficult for many people to imagine that sex between two males might be pleasurable for anybody. In this understanding of desire, the assumption—in stark contrast to dominant assumptions about female prostitution—would be that a male who sells sex to other men *must* be doing it out of necessity. This idea is frequently reinforced by what male prostitutes themselves say about their work. However, just as we should hear claims about female prostitutes in a cultural and political context, we should also examine the assertions of male prostitutes that they derive no pleasure from sex with clients in the context of the claims that many of them make that they are heterosexual. Within this framework, admission of pleasure with a male client would compromise their public identities and perhaps shake up their self-conceptions.

Travestis are different from the kinds of male prostitutes who have been written about in other studies (e.g., McNamara 1994; Perlongher 1987; West 1992) because they are openly and exuberantly homosexual. And they are different in that, in their conversations with one another and in their interviews with me, they habitually foreground the fact that they enjoy prostitution. Although travestis obviously do not always enjoy standing out on the street, and they don't enjoy sex with every client they encounter, they all emphasize the frisson they feel at being regarded as beautiful by men who pass on foot or in cars. And whenever they talk about especially fulfilling sex, their partner is always either a client or a vício—a boyzinho they take into their rooms or a man they meet on the street and find themselves attracted to because he is especially handsome, is known to be especially versatile in bed, and/or is known to have an especially large penis. Men who are aware that travestis do vícios and who are young and pretty or possess a large penis frequently stand across the street and flash at a travesti they desire, hoping to pique her interest enough for her agree to sex for free.

When I asked Elisabeth what she enjoyed about being a travesti, she answered that she liked "to dress as a woman, to feel like . . . like out on the street 'battling' atop a pair of high heels, to feel admired by men, you know?" Tina told me that what she liked most about being a travesti was "the night. When I go out. I get all dressed up and I go out at night and strike poses at everyone. That's what I like about being a travesti. Because people, people applaud and do all sorts of things with us. That's what I like."

Cintia said something similar when Keila and I were interviewing her.

Keila: A sua vida é isso, a su/Você vive na prostituição. Então o que é que você gosta dessa vida sua agora?

Cintia: Ah eu acho que eu devo gostar de tudo, né, porque . . . Tudo que vem eu devo gostar . . . eu tou com nessa vida.

Keila: Mas algumas coisas que você acha especiais mais . . . que tem nessa vida . . . ⌈acué, roupas . . .

Cintia: ⌊Acho acué, acué [laughs] . . . ficar bonita . . . é . . . é . . . desejar homens belíssimos, né? Acho bem isso. Ser elogiada . . . Um homem parar você, aí "Como você é bonita, entre no meu carro, fazer um programa comigo." Acho isso uma delícia.

K: Your life is this, your/You live through prostitution. So what is it that you like about this life now?

C: Ah, I guess I ought to like it all, right? because . . . Everything that comes I ought to like . . . I'm in this life.

K: But some things that you think are more special . . . about this life . . . ⌈money, clothes . . .

C: ⌊I think money, money [laughs] . . . being pretty . . . it's . . . it's . . . to desire really handsome men, you know? I like that. To be praised . . . A man stops for you, says "You are so pretty, get into my car, do a programa with me." I think that is delicious.

The same kind of response was offered by Mabel when I asked her when she most felt like a woman. She answered right away, "When I'm in bed with a man."

"Any man?" I asked.

"Yeah, it can be any man."

I persisted: "Even clients?"

"Sure," she said without batting an eye, "it can be a client. Sometimes when a client 'eats' me, I feel really fulfilled (*eu me sinto muito realizada*)."

Assertions like these that highlight the pleasure that travestis derive from being "admired," "praised," "applauded," and "fulfilled" by men on the street are continual in travesti talk about prostitution. When travestis return home from an evening on the streets, they often sit together and relax for a while in the street; or else several of them crowd into the room of a travesti who has a television—and maybe some marijuana or coke—and they lie on the mattress on the floor, talking and watching one of the violent American movies, often starring Jean-Claude Van Damme or Steven Seagal, that the Globo television network offers late every night. At times like these, travestis tell one another about what happened to them on the *pista* that evening. They talk about any police harassment that may have occurred, they laugh over descriptions of how they robbed clients, and they regale one another with tales of particularly "delicious" sexual encounters with clients.

While Tina was undergoing the silicone application that I witnessed, Xuxa—a travesti with dyed blonde hair who took her name from the television personality famous throughout Brazil largely because she had the good fortune to be born blonde and blue-eyed in a country where the majority of the population is dark—wandered into Tânia's room after returning from her evening's work. In the midst of a story by Tina about her recent trip to the dentist, which ended with Tina jumping up from the dentist's chair and dashing out of his office when she saw him approaching with a pair of dentists' pliers ("It's funny, isn't it," Tina reflected as Carlinhos inserted another needle in her bunda, "I have the courage to do this, and I didn't have the courage to get a tooth pulled . . ."), Xuxa suddenly announced to anybody who wanted to listen:

> Hoje o boy ficou passado comigo. O boy belíssimo. Me levou pro hotel, quando eu tirei a roupa, ele ficou assim viajando em meu corpo. "Você tem um corpo que nem todas mulheres têm. Vira." Quando eu virei, ele: "Ah, que cu é esse!" "Ave Maria meu filho não admire muito não senão vai muchar." Menina, o boy era tão escândalo que eu passei mais de duas horas no hotel.
>
> Tonight a boy was amazed by me. A boy who was so beautiful. He took me to a hotel, when I took off my clothes, he was like spacing out on my body. "You have a body that lots of women don't even have. Turn around." When I turned around, he says: "Ah, what an ass!" "*Ave Maria*, boy [I said], don't admire it so much or it'll dry up."[12] Girl, that boy was so brilliant that I was in that hotel with him for more than two hours.

Although the travestis present when Xuxa recounted this experience were at that moment too preoccupied with injecting silicone to pursue her story and follow it up with stories of their own, one travesti's tale of exciting sex on the street will often bring forth similar narratives from other travestis.

One afternoon while Keila, Carlinhos (the pumper), and I were sitting in Keila's room, the two travestis began telling each other about rewarding sexual experiences that they had had recently. Carlinhos told a long story of a fifteen-year-old boyzinho who was "lindo, lindo . . . um fenômeno" (phenomenally handsome) and whom she ended up penetrating when they had sex. This boyzinho became so enamored with Carlinhos that he wanted to leave his girlfriend and come live with her, something she couldn't even consider (since she had penetrated him). When Carlinhos had finished her story, Keila began a story of her own:

Keila: Ah minha filha, pois na Ajuda, tem um que passa, ele tem dois brinquinhos. A primeira vez que eu fui com ele—bicha, que maravilha. Ele me deitou assim de costas, aí foi, daqui do pescoço até o pé ele me lambendo, tudo. Não chupou meu cu. Fez só a roda, aqui com a língua. Aí desceu. Quando desceu eu disse asim "Vai na neca," mas não foi. Aí ele me deitou na frente. E eu com a menina presa, eu fiz a buceta. Aí ele "PÃ," daqui foi e veio. Aí desceu. Quando desceu já tava pronta. Aí, eu fiz só assim. E ele POF na boca.

Don: Ah!
Keila: Foi a conta certa. Não deu outra, querida.
Carlinhos: Tem homens mais descarados. Tem homens que eles pegam eles mesmos, botam a mão e puxam e tiram.

Keila: Não, mas o meu foi só/o meu já tava tão excitada, que eu fiz assim. Quando eu fix assim, ele puxou.
Carlinhos: Ficou louca.
Keila: Aí, foi só, não deu outra. Dei uma gozada na boca. Eu já não aguentava mais. Eu já tava só me excitando por ele ser tão bonito. Já tava tão excitada com ele lambendo minhas costas [laughs].
Don: [laughs]
Carlinhos: Já tava em tempo de gozar.

K: Ah girl, there on Ajuda [Street] there's one who walks by, he has two earrings.[13] The first time I went with him—bicha, what a marvel. He laid me down like this with my back up [and then] he licked me, from my neck to my feet—everything. He didn't lick my asshole. He just made little circles around it with his tongue. Then he went down. When he was going down, I thought "He's going to [suck] my dick," but he didn't. OK, then he turned me over on my front. I was holding the girl [i.e., her penis] between my legs, I was making a cunt. OK, he POW, moved his tongue back and forth [down the front of my body]. He went down lower. I was ready. OK, I opened my legs and he POF [popped my penis] in his mouth.

D: Ah!
K: It happened exactly like I wanted it to. It was perfect, love.
C: There are men with less shame than that. There are men who pull it [i.e., one's penis] out themselves, who put their hands in between your legs and pull it, and take it out.
K: No, but this guy/this one, I was already so excited that I went like this [i.e., opened her legs]. When I did that, he pulled it out.
C: You were crazy with excitement.
K: It was perfect. I came in his mouth. I couldn't hold it anymore. I was aroused—he was so beautiful. I was already totally aroused when he licked my back [laughs].

D: [laughs]
C: You were ready to cum.

Keila: Eu ia gozar aqui entre as pernas mas ele fez a delicadeza de abocanhar. Quando ele abocanhou eu disse "Eu já não aguento mais!" Aí ele: "Porra, agora você gozou—e eu?" Eu digo "Então você dá um tempinho, aí a gente goza de novo."

Carlinhos: Que babado, né?

Keila: "Não tem problema." Aí, eu fui no banheiro, me limpei e voltei. Quando voltei, já tava . . . querendo de novo [laughs]. Aí eu me deitei e a gente começou a se amar. Ele fez: "Então eu vou dar meu cuzinho pra você agora." Eu disse "Agora mesmo!" Pronto, foi maravilhoso. Ele me deu dois reais. ⌈O quarto era um, paguei um, fiquei com um.

Carlinhos: ⌊[laughs]

Keila: Tá ótimo querida. Pra mim foi ⌈maravilhoso. Essas coisas que acontece na vida da gente . . .

Carlinhos: ⌊Maravilhoso.

K: I was going to cum between my legs, but he had the delicacy and good taste to put my dick in his mouth. When he put it in his mouth I said "I can't hold it back anymore!" He [said]: "Shit, now you've cum—what about me?" I say "If you just wait a little while, we'll cum again."

C: How fun!

K: "There's no problem." OK, I went into the bathroom, cleaned myself up and came back. By the time I came back, I was already . . . wanting to do it again [laughs]. OK, I lay down and we started to make love. He said, "Well now I'm gonna give my little ass to you now." I said "Give it right now!" So we did it and it was marvelous. He gave me two reais. ⌈The room cost one and I kept one.

C: ⌊[laughs]

K: It was fantastic, love. For me, it was ⌈marvelous. These things that happen in our lives . . .

C: ⌊Marvelous.

That travestis can and do find regular fulfillment in the act of prostituting themselves means that they practice prostitution and incorporate it into their lives in a way that is very different from the prostitutes that have been described in other studies. In virtually all other studies, as I have noted, prostitution is depicted as being something that individuals do for money, not pleasure. Indeed, prostitution and pleasure are virtually antonyms.

While I hope I have made it very clear that money is a crucial element of travesti prostitution, it is not the only element, and an analysis of travesti prostitution that highlighted only economic remuneration would miss the crucial fact that the sexual marketplace provides travestis with one of the few arenas available to them in Brazilian society to receive what Elisabeth and Xuxa call "admiration," what Tina calls "applause," Cintia calls "praise," and Mabel refers to as "fulfillment." It is also one of the few contexts in which travestis can enjoy experiences like the one

Keila describes as "marvelous" and "fantastic." In any other social context in which they appear, travestis elicit consternation, dismay, harassment, and abuse. They are harshly discriminated against—sometimes security guards will not permit them to enter shopping centers, clerks in stores will refuse to wait on them, men and women on the street will widen their eyes and express open disgust at seeing them as they pass by. They are beaten by policemen, they are portrayed as drugged criminals in the press. Their families accept them to the extent that they keep giving them things. Even at home, many travestis are not completely unaware that their boyfriends are with them not out of love (recall Carlinhos's caution that "men can't love travestis"), but because they supply them with food, drugs, money, and a place to stay.

The only context in which anyone openly articulates admiration of travestis is when they are standing on the street prostituting themselves. Under cover of the night, hidden away in their cars, in back alleys, or in hotel rooms, men tell travestis like Cintia that they are "bonita." They compliment travestis like Xuxa on having "a body that lots of women don't even have." They lick travestis like Keila all over and offer them their "little ass."

This is not to say that prostitution is never degrading. Standing along streets and highways at night, travestis are fully exposed to the critical commentaries of motorists driving by, and to the violence of their throwing objects such as ashes, rocks, or even bottles out their car windows at unsuspecting travestis. It is also on the *pista* that travestis are the victims of police brutality. Adriana once told me in a weary voice that she sometimes hated the street at night.

> Because sometimes when you're on the street, people drive by and throw things, throw bottles. This wounds you inside (*Isso machuca a gente por dentro*), you understand? Because you feel like you're being treated like a crazy person. There are times when I stand there thinking, "My God in heaven, I'm here being treated like a clown." Because really, there are times when so many of them go by and laugh at you in the face that you feel like a clown. There are times when it makes you so angry, they look at your body and see you there, dressed as a woman, but they see you're not a woman, and they make fun of you (*eles tão tudo mangando*). And that makes you angry (*dá revolta*). There are times when that makes you so angry, angry like . . . because they mock you like that, you know? Instead of helping us, they . . . want to destroy us (*Em vez dele ajudar, não, eles . . . querem destruir-nos*).

Unlike other social contexts, however, where this kind of destructive mocking is the only response travestis receive from others, the *pista* is also the place where travestis can get compliments, recognition, amorous invitations, and, not least, financial rewards *for being travestis.* The sexual marketplace provides travestis with virtually the only context they have in which they can develop self-confidence and self-esteem. Whereas anyone else in Brazilian society can reap rewards and receive encouragement in various contexts and in various ways by virtue of being a man or being a woman, travestis have nowhere to turn but the *pista.* It is only there that they can transcend the insults and harassment they experience everywhere else they go. Without the *pista,* all that would remain for travestis to hear would be the jeers and the mocking. Without the *pista,* travestis would have little opportunity to ever see themselves as anything other than "clowns." Without the *pista,* the ill-intentioned desires of people to "destroy" travestis might well overwhelm travestis and succeed in doing precisely just that.

Five

Travesti Gendered Subjectivity

Cuenda
a mulher diferente
com peito e pau na frente

Gee look
A woman of a different kind
with tits and a dick, you're gonna find
—Leila, a travesti, joking with other travestis as she stands
on a street corner watching men drive by and ogle them

"I never understood whether the men in Milan were buying a woman with a dick or a man with breasts." So writes the travesti Fernanda Farias de Albuquerque about the time she spent in Italy, where the overwhelming majority of the men who paid her for sex did so only after they felt her to check the size of her penis (Albuquerque and Janelli 1995:112). Her bewilderment about what her clients thought they were buying raises a fundamental question about travestis: what are they? How exactly do they think about themselves in gendered terms, and how should we perceive them? Are they best understood as "women with dicks" or "men with breasts"—or are they, perhaps, something else?

In the preceding chapters, I have documented how travestis think about and arrange their lives in ways that invert, twist, double back on, and fold almost any configuration of gender that one might care to imagine. Travestis inject great quantities of industrial silicone into their bodies to give themselves feminine physical features, but they think that any male who claims to be a woman is suffering from a psychosis. They live with tough, muscular, macho males whom they treat like housewives. They stand out on the street at night wearing miniskirts and displaying their breasts, attracting males who want to be penetrated and be called female names by them. What, in the end, is the subjectivity of these complex, contradictory, and contrary individuals?

Chica's room

Constructive Essentialists

Travestis would not fit well into the debates that have raged within the humanities and social sciences about essentialism versus constructivism, because they are simultaneously both essentialists and constructivists; they are what we might call constructive essentialists. Travestis consider that males are males and females are females because of the genitals they possess. God made a person male or female. He may have sometimes erred and, as Luciana once put it, "when the moment came to make the cut, He pulled the skin out instead." But what He did can never be undone—one can never change the sex with which one was born. This is the essentialist dimension of travesti ideas about sex and gender.

The constructive part is this: even though God made a person irreversibly male or female by installing a particular set of genitalia, the different morphology of those genitalia allows for different gendered possibilities to be explored and occupied. Females get short-shrifted in this deal. Their genitals limit the gendered possibilities open to them and condemn them to being always and forever females. Females can never penetrate, they can only "give," travestis told me repeatedly. And whenever I objected to statements of that nature and pointed out that women could penetrate men or other women using dildos, fingers, or objects, they were dismissive: "Yeah, sure, a woman could stick a dildo or a finger or a cucumber or a carrot up a man's butt, or into a woman's cunt, but what is that? A dildo, a finger, a cucumber, and a carrot. It isn't a dick."

Male genitalia, on the other hand, facilitate a much wider range of activities—males can both penetrate and "give." This sexual flexibility allows them access to the entire spectrum of sexed and gendered behavior and subjectivities. So the idea that lies at the base of travesti understandings of sexuality, sex, and gender is that while females and males are ineluctably and essentially females and males because of the genitals they possess, the greater flexibility of male genitals permits males to construct themselves as feminine.

In this conceptualization, the defining attribute of women is that they have a *buceta* (pronounced boo-SEI-ta), a cunt. Most travestis find this part of the female anatomy repellent in the extreme. Although it is not exactly a common occurrence, all travestis can recount at least one experience of having been approached by a heterosexual couple wishing to do a programa with them. (Single women apparently never approach travestis for programas.) Most travestis will not accept these programas, and if they do, they make it clear that they will not perform sex with the woman. Some travestis, however, will accept such a programa, charging

an enormous price, and going with the intent to rob the couple of everything they have.

Tina is one travesti who accepted programas from male-female couples
so that she could rob them. She claimed that in order to be able to get at
a heterosexual couple's money, she sometimes went as far as "sucking
cunt" (chupar buceta). This is the ultimate gross-out for travestis, and Tina
sometimes delighted in trying to appall other travestis and me with detailed descriptions of bucetas that she had penetrated and sucked. Once,
in her room, Tina took it upon herself to inform me and two travestis
who were smoking a big joint with her that "cunts, even if they're washed
really well, have a smell like codfish (bacalhau). And there are cunts that
when you put your dick in them, they're like [here Tina made loud slurp-
ing noises]. Like they're gonna suck your dick up inside of them." Another time, when I was sitting in the doorway on São Francisco Street
with her and a few other travestis, Tina suddenly turned to me and
shouted, "Don, you ever sucked a buceta?" She and everyone else burst
into laughter, and she continued, "I've sucked one, Don, and it's horrible
(é uó). It's horrible, horrible, horrible, horrible, it's horrible, Don, it's horrible. All this slime. It's a really slimy thing (De instante instante baba. Ela é
negócio babento)." "É uó mona" (It's horrible, mona), Banana interjected
laughingly, adding that she once went with a man and a woman to do a
programa, but only to rob them.

This anatomical feature of women, as "horrible" as it is for travestis, is
at the same time what travestis understand to be the feature of a woman
that makes her attractive to men. During a long conversation about the
differences between female prostitutes and travestis, Keila explained to
me that the major difference was that whereas travestis preoccupied
themselves with their appearance to the extent that they had turned
prostitution into an art, women tended to go out onto the street looking
like they had just crawled out of bed in the morning, or like they were
on their way to some marketplace to buy beans.[1] Although Keila was ex-
aggerating, I had to agree with her point, and I commented that I was
surprised that the female prostitutes I had seen throughout Salvador
tended to look exceedingly ordinary—they often wore little or no
makeup, and the majority of them usually wore clothes no different from
the blouses and shorts that one saw on many women walking down city
streets during the day. These clothes did not even vaguely resemble the
kind of revealing, lingerie-style clothing favored by many travestis, especially those who work the highway at Pituba.

Keila explained that female prostitutes' lack of interest in their appearance was a main reason why men were often more attracted to travestis than to female prostitutes—"because a man likes to see something

exotic on the street, on the corners," she told me. "He already sees a woman at home, every day, and so he goes out on the street at night. And there he sees his woman on every corner, the same woman he has at home, he sees her standing on the street corners. But if he sees a different kind of woman, with exotic lacy clothes, with garter belts, with corsets, with hair all arranged, with a nicely made up face, of course he's gonna feel an attraction." I asked Keila why she thought that female prostitutes didn't perceive this and modify their appearance accordingly. She first replied that she thought women were "afraid" to dress up in exotic, revealing clothes because they feared that someone might laugh at them, or that some relative or friend would see them and realize that they worked as a prostitute—something which most women, she said, wanted to keep a secret.

But then Keila said this:

> O meu segundo pensamento é que as mulheres acham que porque elas têm uma buceta, o que os homens procuram na rua de noite é buceta, então elas não precisam de mais nada além da buceta para ficar na esquina. Porque todas as vezes que tem uma mulher discutindo com um travesti, ela fala assim: "Ah, eu sou rachada, eu tenho buceta, os homens vêm atrás de mim." Elas dizem assim. Elas acham que por elas terem uma vagina, e o homem precisar de uma vagina para se satisfazer sexualmente, elas não precisam de nada mais além daquilo, é só a buceta e pronto.

> My other thought is that it's because women think that because they have a buceta, and what men on the street at night are after is a buceta, they don't have to do anything else except have a buceta and stand on the street corner. Because whenever a travesti and a woman [here: a prostitute] get into a fight, she says, "Ah, I have a gash, I have a cunt, and men seek me out." They say that. They think that because they have a vagina, and because a man needs a vagina to satisfy himself sexually, they [i.e., the prostitutes] don't need anything else except that, just a cunt and nothing more.

While travestis will refute the value of a buceta in disputes of this kind with female prostitutes—shouting back, according to Keila, that even though they don't have a buceta they have more men coming after them than any woman could ever dream of—in private, travestis begrudgingly acknowledge the superiority of the buceta. Indeed, it is a pivot in the system of gender that travestis draw on and elaborate. In travesti conceptualizations of male sexuality and gender, a male is a "man" precisely because he desires a buceta. He may be intrigued by, or occasionally excited by—or, if he is provided with enough comfort and financial rewards, may eventually come to settle for—a travesti's cu, her ass; but his desire will be always and forever fundamentally directed towards a woman's buceta. A man's capacity for passion is linked to the buceta, and the buceta constitutes something of a dividing line between a "man" and a viado—a "man" desires it, a viado finds it *uó* (horrible).

The knowledge that all women effortlessly (and often gracelessly) possess the thing that all men want influences travestis' understandings of women, and it influences their perceptions of how women see them. There is a broad consensus among travestis in Salvador that women feel themselves to be superior to travestis. This sense of superiority is considered to be grounded in the fact that women know that no matter how hard travestis work at making themselves feminine and attractive to men, they will always lack the one characteristic that men desire most: a buceta.

Travestis often concede the superiority of women in terms of the attraction they exert on men. Such concessions can be heard, for example, in their discussions about passion, where travestis readily acknowledge that men become impassioned with women, not travestis. They also surface in conversations in which travestis declare they expect the worst from the men they desire. Recall the old travesti Angélica's comment, when discussing male passion, that men betray women: "They do it to women [i.e., men cheat on women], to them who have cunts they do it, you can imagine how they do it even more to viados." Chica, sitting on the doorstep on São Francisco Street and talking with several of us about her boyfriend, made a similar point. She had never revealed to her boyfriend how much money she made during the time she was in Italy, she said, because she knew that if he knew, he would try to get the money out of her, and then he would leave her. "He left a wife and four children in Recife to come here to Salvador—what, he's not gonna leave a viado?" Chica asked rhetorically. The assumption underlying comments like these is that men see travestis as inferior to women, and therefore more expendable and dispensable.

Travestis also tacitly acknowledge the superiority of women whenever they receive flattering comments from them. Elisabeth told me that she always feels good when a woman compliments her, because the compliment is coming from someone who was "born a woman." She explained, "There are women who see us on the street, anywhere, and say, 'Wow, how pretty, how feminine, you know, how pretty.' Once I was getting off a bus, right, in a black dress, real pretty, that I have, and a woman said, 'Wow, you're so elegant.' That made me feel beautiful (*belíssima*) that night. Even if I hadn't earned any money, I would have felt pretty."

Elisabeth's flushed reaction to such a compliment is meaningful only in the context of an understanding of women that sees them as having a privileged access to femininity. This understanding is rarely made explicit in travesti conversations with one another, but sometimes, especially in discussions about passing as a woman, it is more or less openly acknowledged. During a conversation between Keila and Carlinhos on the topic, Keila commented:

Keila: Porque por mais feminino que o viado se/E agora . . . agora, atualmente, quando as bichas sao muito bonitas . . . elas, dão muito mais pinta de que são travesti,

    por causa do, jeito, do gesto que

Carlinhos: por ser . . . é os trejeito que elas fazem, joga as mãos, cabelos . . .

Keila: fazem. Não precisa disso pra passar por mulher. Mulher é uma coisa natural, mulher é nature/é naturalidade. Não precisa você se . . . quebrar a mão, você jogar cabelo, porque isso não é coisa de mulher. Coisa de mulher é naturalidade. É, Maluma ontem falando assim: "Ai, eu entrei no . . . Bar Inverno e Verão na Pituba e passei batido como mulher. Todo mundo me olhou."

Eu disse, "Então, você não passou batido como mulher. Se você tivesse passado batido como mulher, ninguém ia lhe olhar." Lógi/"Se todo mundo lhe olhou você não passou como mulher."

Carlinhos: Verdade.

Keila: "Porque quando você passa como mulher, você age com naturalidade, você passa naturalmente, vai, faz o que tem que fazer, volta, sem que ninguém olha você. Ou se . . . pode se olhar, algum ou outro homem, e até pra paquerar, mas se todo mundo olha ao mesmo tempo, lógico que você não passou."

Carlinhos: É verdade.

K: Because however feminine a travesti is/And now . . . now, these days, when bichas are really pretty . . . they show much more that they are travestis

    because of the way they act, the gestures

C: by being . . . it's the gestures they make, swishing their wrists, their hair . . .

K: they make. You don't need to do that to pass as a woman. A woman is a natural thing, a woman is natural/is naturalness. You don't have to . . . swish your wrists, fling your hair around, this isn't something a woman does. Women act naturally. Yeah, yesterday Maluma was talking like: "Oh, I went into . . . the Winter and Summer Bar in Pituba and I totally passed as a woman. Everyone was looking at me."

I said, "Well in that case, you didn't pass as a woman. If you had totally passed as a woman, no one would have looked at you." Right? "If everyone looked at you then you didn't pass as a woman."

C: True.

K: "Because when you pass as a woman, you act with naturalness, you pass naturally, you go, do what you have to do, and then you come back, without anyone having noticed you. Or if . . . some people can look, a man or two, who maybe even will flirt with you, but if everyone is looking at you all at the same time, of course you didn't pass."

C: That's true.

The arguments about "naturalness" that Keila makes and Carlinhos agrees with are important dimensions of travesti subjectivity. Despite the fact that travestis use highly artificial means to attain the bodies they possess, they still esteem naturalness. The value they place on naturalness frequently surfaces in discussions about silicone, where travestis will publicly claim to have less silicone than everybody suspects or knows that they have. One afternoon, as a number of travestis were crowding around the doorstep on São Francisco Street, socializing and watching for clients, Cintia made such a claim:

Cintia: A que tem menos silicone aqui sou eu.
⌈ Eu tenho um litro e quatro
⌊ copos.
Chica: Você é um porquinho.
[Chica leaves]
Cintia: Uh? É o que Chica?
Rita L: Um litro e quatro copos, falta dois copos pra dois litros.
Cintia: [laughs] Um litro e quatro copos.
Rita L: Eu tenho dois e meio. Fora o meu rosto e do braço.
Elisa: Não parece. Parece que tem meio litro.

Rita L: É que eu já dei um a Michelle. Tenho que retocar.

Cintia: Um meio de cada lado, né?

Rita L: Um e meio de cada lado não. Um/um e meio mesmo. Não bicha. Um e meio dividido pros dois.

Cintia: Elisa tem cinco. Dois e meio cada lado.
Elisa: Nada disso.
Cintia: E é quanto?
Elisa: Três.
[Elisa leaves]

Ci: The one who has the least amount of silicone here is me.
⌈ I have one liter and four glasses.
Ch: You're as fat as a pig on silicone.
[Chica leaves]
Ci: What? What, Chica?
RL: One liter and four glasses is only two glasses away from two liters.
Ci: [laughs] One liter and four glasses.
RL: I have two and a half. Besides what I have in my forehead and arms.
E: You don't look like you have that much. You look like you have half a liter.

RL: That's because I gave some away to Michelle [this is a joke in reference to a travesti who doesn't have any silicone, but who everybody thinks ought to]. I need a touch-up.
Ci: You have a liter and a half in each side [of your buttocks], right?
RL: One and a half in each side, no. One/one and a half altogether. No, bicha. One and a half divided between the two [sides].
Ci: Elisa has five [liters]. Two and a half in each side.
E: Enough of that.
Ci: How much then?
E: Three.
[Elisa leaves]

Rita L: [to Cintia] Quando tá tu/tu fica chorando pros outros tu fica explorando dizendo que têm monte né?

Cintia: [laughs] Três eh? Mais que Piupiu/não, menos que Piupiu, né?

Rita L: Igualzinho a Piupiu.

[Keila arrives and sits down on the curb]

Keila: É o quê?

Cintia: Elisa tem quantos litros?

Keila: Três litros.

Cintia: E Piupiu?

Keila: Piupiu tem três litros também.

Cintia: Não é mais não Keila?

Keila: Uns três e meio.

Cintia: Eu como só tenho um litro.

Keila: Você tem o quê?

Cintia: Um litro.

Keila: Se manca,
    ⎡monstro de silicone. Olha,
    ⎢um litro.

Cintia: ⎣[laughing] Eu só tenho um.

Keila: Um litro?! Tu tem uns, não um.

Cintia: É só um mesmo.

Rita L: Ela pensa que a gente não conheceu ela.

Keila: É funil. Era funil, querida.

Rita L: Funilíssimo.

Keila: Funil. Funil não—família toda de funils. Essa aqui. A bunda dessa largura e as costas dessa largura.

Cintia: Êta.

Keila: Não era não.

Cintia: Eu já tinha quadril.

Keila: Tu era per⎡feita.

Rita L: ⎣Perfeita.

RL: [to Cintia] When you/you talk about other people you always say they have mountains [of silicone], you know?

Ci: [laughs] Three, ah? That's more than Piupiu/no, less than Piupiu, isn't it?

RL: The same as Piupiu.

[Keila arrives and sits down on the curb]

K: What's going on?

Ci: How many liters does Elisa have?

K: Three liters.

Ci: And Piupiu?

K: Piupiu has three liters too.

Ci: Isn't it more, Keila?

K: Three and a half.

Ci: And me who only has one liter.

K: You have what?

Ci: One liter.

K: Get out of here,
    ⎡you silicone-filled monster. Sure,
    ⎢one liter.

Ci: ⎣[laughing] I have only one.

K: One liter?! You have some, not one.

Ci: It's really only one.

RL: She thinks we didn't know her [when she arrived in Salvador].

K: You are a funnel. You were a funnel, dear. [Keila is saying that Cintia arrived in Salvador looking like a funnel—with broad, masculine shoulders that tapered down to nonexistent buttocks.]

RL: A big huge funnel.

K: Funnel. A funnel no—a whole bunch of funnels, one inside the other like this. A behind this size [extremely tiny], and shoulders this size [huge].

Ci: Yeah, right.

K: Like you weren't.

Ci: I already had hips.

K: You were per⎡fect. [sarcastic]

RL: ⎣Perfect.

Keila: Tinha quadril,
⌈cintura, culote, tudo.

Rita L: ⌊Oh já tinha quadril. Cuenda.

K: You had hips,
⌈a waist, a teardrop behind,
everything.

RL: ⌊Oh you already had hips. Sure.

Throughout this interaction, Cintia, Rita Lee, Keila, and the other travestis invoke and joke about shared notions of naturalness and artificiality. These notions exist in an uneasy and agitated relationship in travesti thought, and it is the tension between the desire for naturalness and the necessity for artifice that provides the background for the humor and the sarcasm that is elaborated here.

A basic understanding that all travestis share is that it is perfectly legitimate to do whatever it takes to improve one's appearance and become more beautiful. All the travestis speaking in this conversation have dramatically altered the way they look with the aid of hormones and silicone. It is not just Cintia who was once a masculine-looking "funnel"—they were all once "funnels." Now, however, through artificial means, they all have achieved at least viable approximations of "a waist, a teardrop behind, everything." This kind of transformation is expected, encouraged, and admired. Travestis discussing such transformations almost always cite Marcela, one of the best-known travestis in Salvador. Marcela started out *uó* (awful), everyone is agreed—one travesti told me with distaste that before Marcela went to Italy for the first time, she looked like a lesbian. After making money in Italy, however, Marcela had an operation on her nose to make it wafer thin, had two enormous silicone implants inserted into her chest, injected at least five liters of silicone into her hips and buttocks, and grew her hair down to her waist, thus transforming herself from an ugly duckling into a Swan Queen. Whenever she returns to Salvador from Italy—which she usually does each year during the Carnival season in January and February—Marcela dazzles everybody with her beauty, and she invariably wins whatever beauty contest for travestis she enters. Throughout the week of Carnival, she can be seen at various gay balls and discos, as well as in the gay areas of the Carnival space, parading around wearing little more than a minuscule bikini bottom and a few colored feathers in her hair.

But despite the admiration accorded travestis like Marcela, there is still a widespread conviction among travestis that individuals who do not require a great deal of artificial aid to become beautiful are even more impressive than those who do. Long, beautiful hair, for example, is much more admired if it is one's own, not a wig or the mass of synthetic-fiber hair extensions that the overwhelming majority of travestis weave into their hair. Similarly, wide hips and an impressive bunda achieved only

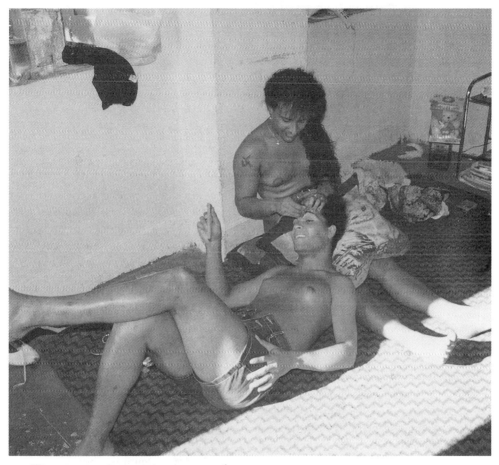

Tweezering eyebrows to become more feminine

through the ingestion of hormones are regarded with greater awe than the same forms achieved through the injection of silicone. This is the understanding that Cintia is invoking in her playful denials that she has more than one liter of silicone and in her claim that she "already had hips" when she arrived in Salvador, before she had injected any silicone. It is also the understanding that Brazil's most famous travesti, Roberta Close, draws on in her own repeated public denials of ever having had silicone injected into her body (a claim disputed by some, who say they know better—see, e.g., Albuquerque and Janelli 1995:150).

In conversations like the one initiated by Cintia, or like the one between Keila and Carlinhos about the "natural" femininity of women, travestis thus foreground the idea that "natural" forms and "natural" femininity are desirable. But they also suggest that such femininity is not readily available to most travestis. Travestis must employ artifice to achieve the appearance of naturalness. This state of affairs is ambivalent for travestis, for while they applaud individuals like Marcela who achieve feminine beauty through artifice, they regard as even more impressive individuals like Roberta Close who are (or who manage to convince others that they are) beautiful "naturally." This ambivalence ensures that travestis remain insecure about their appearance, and it makes them sensitive to accusations—especially from women—that they are merely defective copies of a natural femininity that they may approximate but never convincingly attain.

To defend themselves against such accusations, travestis have developed a number of ways of publicly denying that they desire the femininity women are born with. The most blatant of these denials take the form of assertions by travestis that they do not consider themselves to be women, they have no desire to be women, and they would never consider submitting to an operation that would provide them with the thing that, they are all agreed, men lust after. They don't need a buceta to attract men, they tell one another, and they shout back at prostitutes who deride them for not having one. They have other charms.

Travestis also deny that they want the "natural" femininity of women by denigrating women. Travestis sitting in the doorway on São Francisco Street engage in running commentaries on the bodies of all individuals who pass by. Men are appraised on the sexiness of their bunda and, always and most importantly, on the presumed or desired or known size of their penis. Women are evaluated according to other criteria. Travestis comment critically on the general appearance, hair, breasts, hips, and bunda of women, and they are all carefully judged according to how closely they approximate stereotypical ideals of feminine beauty. Although travestis will usually only deride a passing woman who falls short of those ideals in their whispered conversations with one another, if the woman should say or do anything that they interpret as a slight or a sign that she disapproves of travestis, then they will shout after her that she is ugly, that she has the hanging breasts of a dog, that she is as fat as a whale, that she should contact Ivo Pitanguy (Brazil's most famous plastic surgeon) for an appointment, and so on. Individual travestis can sometimes be severely dismissive of women: one travesti chuckled as she told me that she had heard that the travesti slang term for "woman," amapô, was a contraction of a mais podre—"the most rotten."

Most travestis in Salvador would probably not go so far as to assert that women are "rotten." But most would agree with Pastinha, who told me that she doesn't have many friendships with women because many women "treat travestis with falseness. They'll be friendly when they're talking to you, and behind your back they'll be wagging their tongues" (. . . *se dá cum os travestis na falsidade. Se dá cum você na frente agora, por detrás tá rumando a língua*). I repeatedly heard travestis say things similar to this, reminding one another that most women could not be trusted and that they would turn on travestis with the slightest provocation.

The reason for the falseness of women, travestis believe, is that women feel threatened by travestis. Female prostitutes are said to resent travestis because they attract clients who formerly would have gone to them. Women in general are said to dislike travestis because they fear that their husbands are attracted to them. Women feel that travestis threaten to "occupy their space" (*ocupam o espaço delas*), as one travesti expressed it.

Travestis agree that this is precisely what they do. Furthermore, they contend that they occupy that feminine space better than women do. Carlinhos once told me that travestis were more sensitive to the appearances and practices it takes to please men because whereas a travesti had passed through both "a masculine phase" (*uma fase masculina*) and a woman's "feminine phase" (*a fase feminina que é a delas*), "a woman is just a woman" (*a mulher só é mulher*). These kinds of repeated assertions by travestis that they are more perceptive and more attractive and generally better at most things than women constitute yet another way that travestis have developed to deny that they desire the "natural" femininity of women. Why settle for being "just a woman," travestis seem to reason, when one can be *mulheríssima*—more than a woman? It is in this light that one should understand Martinha's claims about how women live "a world of fantasy" whereas travestis confront reality, or Banana's dismissal of many women who populate her world as "shabby wrecks" (chapter 2). Many travestis regularly tell one another about women who approached them asking for advice about their clothes, hair, makeup, or shoes—or wanting to know more about silicone, because they admire travesti bodies so much that they are considering silicone injections themselves. Magdala told me that she thinks that travestis care for themselves (*se cuidam*) better than most women, and that this attention to their appearance made them more feminine (*mais feminino*) and more sensual (*mais sensual*) than many women.

The argument that travestis are better at femininity than women because they work at it harder was also expressed by Lia Hollywood. When she told me that in her opinion, travestis were more feminine than the majority of women, I asked her why she thought so. "Because travestis are striving for perfection," she answered. "And women already feel perfect. And so, they're never going to want to . . . develop beyond being women."

Keila once extended travesti superiority over women to encompass even anatomy. She commented that she thought travestis are better equipped anatomically than women for intercourse with men. She said that many women are afraid to have intercourse with men who are "well endowed" (*bem dotados*) because they have a "shallow uterus" (*o útero raso*). If a penis knocks against such a uterus, the woman will begin to feel pain and her uterus will get inflamed, which will result in bad abdominal cramps. Travestis don't have this problem at all. "A travesti doesn't have a uterus," Keila explained to me. "A travesti has a canal, a rectal canal, which is a thing that goes up, and so anything can enter it. A dick can enter it in that direction and the travesti won't feel anything. If there is any pain in the beginning, by the end it turns into pleasure."

Through ideas and talk such as this, travestis continually assert their superiority over women. But this talk is, again, articulated alongside other talk in which women are discussed as having access to a natural femininity, talk in which it is asserted that "God made man for woman," and talk that routinely concludes that "men" desire women, not travestis. Like travesti ideas about naturalness and artificiality, in which artificiality is admired but naturalness is revered, travesti ideas about women and travestis exist in a problematic, tense, and antagonistic relationship—one in which travestis are the reflections, but women are the mirrors.

Reminders of Maleness

The antagonistic logic of this relationship makes it impossible for travestis to grant that any travesti might legitimately lay claim to female subjectivity, because were she allowed to do so, she would immediately be seen to think of herself—as women are believed to do—as superior to travestis. To prevent any individual from ever being able to make such a claim, travestis have developed a number of practices—some subtle, some less so—designed to remind any travesti who may pretend otherwise that she is a male, not, ever, a woman.

The least subtle and most aggressive of these practices is to cut the hair of another travesti. Travestis all greatly value their hair. They spend a tremendous amount of time thinking about it, talking about it, and trying to grow it, and whenever they pass a mirror they always pause to inspect their hair, part it, and fluff it. They regularly dye their hair a variety of colors. Keila usually rings in the new year as a blonde, for example, letting her hair gradually return to its normal dark color as the months wear on and the roots grow out. Adriana once changed the color of her hair three times in as many days, unable to decide which color made her look more attractive. Travestis who manage to grow a thick mane of long, straight hair are envied by everyone else. Black travestis, whose hair is generally too brittle to be grown long, all weave long extensions made of synthetic fiber into their hair, and they spend hours discussing with one another what hair products are best for their type of hair. When I gave Roberta the photographs I had taken of her getting one and a half liters of silicone injected into her lower body, her first reaction upon seeing the pictures of her laid out naked on a bed with a number of thick needles protruding from her thighs and buttocks was "Wow, I see now that my hair looks really good." When Rosana was arrested and taken to jail, falsely accused by the police of having murdered Tina, one of the things that horrified other travestis most was that the prison officials cut off her hair. Chica once suggested to me that the reason why the travesti Roberta Close was more famous than other, more beautiful and talented travestis was "because she has hair."

Hair is one of the attributes that travestis cultivate to make them look more feminine. Like the ingestion of hormones and the injection of silicone, it is one of the dividing lines that travestis see between being a transformista—a male who just dresses up as a woman—and being a travesti, a male who lives "twenty-four hours a day" as a woman. Transformistas, travestis sniff, wear wigs. Travestis have hair. A travesti's relationship to her hair is the inverse of Samson's: whereas the scissors robbed the biblical hero of his masculinity, they divest travestis of their femininity. A few well-aimed snips are enough to transform a travesti from a beautiful woman to an ugly androgyne. All travestis know this, which is why cutting another travesti's hair is one of the most serious offenses one can commit against her. In mid-1996, Rosana forcibly cut Tina's hair because of a disagreement they had over money and men. By doing so, she set into motion a spiral of events that led to Tina's later breaking into her house with two armed men and practically scalping her, to the subsequent murder of Tina by a travesti sympathetic to Rosana, and to the arrest and imprisonment of Rosana for that crime.

Travestis also have other ways of stripping one another of their femininity to remind everyone that they are not women. One of those ways is to literally strip a person. Travestis sometimes engage in rough play, punching and wrestling with one another in the middle of São Francisco Street. Occasionally, this play goes so far as to involve several travestis holding another down on the ground and stripping off her dress and panties, then pushing the naked travesti into the middle of the street—thus unveiling the penis of the subdued travesti and forcing her to display it in public. This always occurs in the context of much laughter and roughhousing, but the message it conveys is similar to that of the cutting of hair: a travesti is not a woman. Stripped of artifice (hair, a dress), she is clearly and decidedly a male.

Another, more subtle way in which travestis remind one another that they are not women is through the forms of address and reference they use in their talk. Travestis regularly address one another with the feminine vocatives *menina* (girl), *mulher* (woman), and *minha filha* (my daughter). Travestis in their thirties and older also occasionally address each other with *mãe* (mother), a term that was used more during the 1980s than it is today. But even though these feminine terms are common, much more frequent in travesti talk are the address forms *viado*, *bicha*, and *mona*—words that can all be translated as "effeminate homosexual." And when referring to other travestis, words like *menina* or *mulher* are *never* used; the preferred term is *bicha*.

Not only are address and reference terms meaning "effeminate homosexual" continually employed in travesti talk, but those words often occur as responses to intimations by a travesti that somebody might think she is a woman. Hence, the pragmatic force of such words is to remind the addressee that she is most definitely not a woman. A typical occurrence of this kind happened one afternoon when Banana, Tina, and I were sitting on the doorstep on São Francisco Street. Banana was enjoying a cigar-sized joint; Tina was gazing into a tiny compact mirror, using a tweezers to pluck out the hairs on her upper lip and chin; and I was doing nothing, just sitting in the doorway holding my little tape recorder. At one point, the ash from the joint she was smoking fell onto Banana's lap. As she brushed it off her skirt, she discovered that one of her testicles had slipped away from its usual position against her perineum and was dangling outside her panties. "Yuck," she laughed as she stuffed it back in, "a bit of my cunt was slipping out and I wasn't even noticing" (*Vixe, a beirada do meu tabaco estava saindo e eu não tava vendo*). Tina, who was sitting with her back to Banana, looked archly over her shoulder and shot at her, "What bit of cunt, viado? It's a bit of your ball for sure that's slipping out. I never saw a piece of cunt with hanging wrinkled skin like that" (*Que beirada de tabaco viado? É beira de culhão na certa que tá saindo. Beira de tabaco, nunca vi tabaco ter péa [pelanca]*).

Something similar occurred on one of the *pistas* late one Friday night. At around midnight, a group of about five travestis who preferred working late suddenly appeared on the street. They gathered on a street corner together with several travestis who had been on the street for several hours, to catch up on gossip and to hear what the street was like that evening. The travestis were all in a good mood, and they joked and bantered with one another about their appearances, about the men driving by in cars, and about who had earned some money and who had not. As a car drove by and the driver shouted something derogatory out his window, Leila turned to the other travestis and said, in a loud voice full of mock surprise:

Leila: Menino, o que é homem vestido de mulher aqui?! Se manca negões! Esse negão aqui ó/Amanhã vou reunir todas pra um jogo de futebol amanhã no Pacaembu]. Olha He-Man!

L: Heavens, what is this men dressed as women here?! Get out of here you big black men! This big black man here/Tomorrow I'm gonna bring you all together to play soccer tomorrow in Pacaembu [a stadium in São Paulo]. Look, it's He-Man [an exaggeratedly muscular character in a popular television cartoon series]!

Pompom: Quem é He-man?!

P: Who's He-Man?!

Lalesca: [to Djanine] Quem é você negão?

La: [to Djanine] Who do you think you are, big black man?

Djanine: Oxe, não venha não recalcada.

D: My, don't start showing your envy.

Lalesca: Viu negão?

La: You hear, big black man?

Leila: [pointing at a travesti] Olhe, esse aqui é He-Man.

L: [pointing at a travesti] Look, this one here is He-Man.

Lalesca: É um monte de músculos acumulados.

La: That's a mountain of accumulated muscle.

Djanine: Aqui é carne querida.

D: This is flesh [i.e., not muscle], sweetheart.

Leila: [pointing to different travestis] Super-Homem, Batman, esse aqui é Rodark . . .

L: [pointing to different travestis] Superman, Batman, this one is Rodark [a monster character in the He-Man cartoons] . . .

Leila's mock astonishment that what she was seeing before her was a bunch of men dressed as women, her promise that she would bring together all the travestis present for a game of soccer the next day, and her merry designation of various travestis as hypermasculinized cartoon characters are all uttered in much the same spirit as Tina's acerbic observation to Banana that nobody could ever mistake the "hanging wrinkled skin" of her scrotum for a vagina. Leila's remarks provide the other travestis with an opportunity to make similar comments, and Lalesca in particular picks up on Leila's invitation to joke by aiming several barbs at Djanine, calling her a "big black man" who is "a mountain of accumulated muscle." As in the interaction between Tina and Banana, this kind of conversation between travestis has the effect of drawing their own and everyone else's attention to the fact that travestis are not women.

This kind of humor occurs regularly in travestis' conversations with one another, but it is risky humor, because no travesti will accept being called a man by somebody who she thinks says it to hurt her feelings. Should such comments be made with too much aggression or conviction, or by a travesti who is not on friendly terms with the addressee, they turn easily into fighting words. This is precisely what happened as the interaction between Leila and the other travestis on the street continued. As another car drove by and the young travesti Sheila comically flicked her hair extensions in its direction to express haughtiness, Lalesca suddenly broke the joking frame of the banter by exclaiming in a sharp, humorless tone:

1 **Lalesca**: Viado não joga isso não, que é nylon. Não é seu natural não.

La: Viado, don't throw that around, it's nylon. It's not your natural [hair].

2 **Sheila**: E a senhora, que não tem nem um na cabeça?

S: Says the lady who doesn't even have any hair on your head?

3 **Lalesca**: Que mona, eu boto uma coisa triste dessa viado? Parece um rasta.

La: What, mona, I should put something ugly like that [on my head], viado? You look like a Rastafarian man.

4 **Sheila**: Meu amor, isso é nylon.

S: Sweetheart, this is nylon.

5 **Lalesca**: Você pra mim é um negão, viado.

La: To me you're a big black man, viado.

6 **Sheila**: Mas foi com batalha que eu comprei esse nylon pra botar na minha cabeça.

S: But I earned the money to buy this nylon go put on my head [the implication being that Sheila must be attractive enough for clients to pay for sex, no matter what Lalesca says].

7 **Lalesca**: An-rã, tá. Você é um negão.

La: Uh-huh, right. You're a big black man.

8 **Sheila**: Agora a senhora sempre com esse pixaim não pode nem comprar nylon pra botar na cabeça.

S: Look at yourself with this frizzy Afro hair—you can't even buy some nylon to put on your head.

9 **Lalesca**: O quê?! Não mona, que se eu tiver de botar, eu boto um bonito, ⌈não boto um feio desse. Isso é ridículo.

La: What?! No, mona, if I had something to put in my hair I'd put in my hair I'd put in a pretty one, ⌈I wouldn't put in something ugly like yours. It's ridiculous.

10 **Sheila**: ⌊Agora comprar um nylon você não compra. Eh bicha? Eu não acho ridículo.

S: ⌊You'll never buy any nylon [the implication being either that Lalesca will never make any money on the street and/or that her hair is so ugly that it wouldn't matter if

	she bought nylon extensions, because her hair would remain ugly]. What, bicha? I don't think it's ridiculous.
11 **Lalesca**: Ah? Quem é você viadinho? Quem é você?	La: Ah? Who do you think you are, stupid little viado? Who do you think you are?
12 **Djanine**: Eh queridinhas, eh queridinhas.	D: Eh little darlings, eh little darlings.
13 **Sheila**. Ah?	S: Ah?
14 **Djanine**: Tão nervosas?	D: Are you two hyper?
15 **Leila**: Esses viadinhos.	L: These stupid little viados.

Although Keila had not been present during this interaction, when she and I were transcribing the tape on which it was recorded, she immediately pricked up her ears at the tone of this dialogue, and she pointed out to me that Lalesca was being aggressive and that the other travestis had stopped speaking for the entire duration of this segment of talk. All this meant, Keila knew without even having been there, that the interaction between Lalesca and Sheila was on the verge of developing into a fight (*briga*). It was only the intervention of Djanine and Leila that defused the situation long enough for the two travestis to withdraw from direct engagement and, in doing so, avoid flying at each other.

What is most noteworthy in this context about the impending fight between Lalesca and Sheila is the speakers' use of address forms. Lalesca uses *viado* (lines 1, 3, 5, and 11) and *mona* (lines 3 and 9) in speaking directly to Sheila. But she does not use these words in the relaxed, inclusive, in-group manner in which they are normally bandied about by travestis. Here, *viado* and *mona* are deployed aggressively, as openings or closings to direct insults. They accompany the offensive assertions that Sheila is not only a man, but a stereotypically masculine man—*um rasta* (a Rastafarian man) and *um negão* (a big black man). By linking *viado* and *mona* to exaggeratedly masculine referents, Lalesca foregrounds their gendered—as opposed to their phatic, inclusive—meanings. That is to say, she strips the words of their normal function as address forms signifying in-group membership and makes explicit the fact that *viado* and *mona* refer to males. The effect of the words, then, is to draw attention to and mock Sheila's gendered presentation of self—to publicly remind her that all the hair extensions in the world cannot disguise the fact that she will only ever be "a big black man."

Sheila counters these insults with irony at first, addressing Lalesca with exaggerated politeness as *a senhora*, "the lady," even as her comments about Lalesca's lack of hair show that she considers her to be anything but a lady. Near the end of this interaction, though, Sheila begins responding in kind, and in line 10 she issues a direct challenge to her opponent, addressing her as *bicha*. Lalesca then ups the ante, calling Sheila by the derogatory *viadinho*—stupid little viado. It is at this point, when any response from Sheila would have escalated the conflict into a fight, that Djanine enters the fray and defuses the situation, and Leila dismisses both travestis as "stupid little viados."

Running through this interaction is a series of reminders that travestis are not women, and not even particularly feminine. Although individuals may consider themselves to be attractive and womanly, other travestis tell them that they are not—they are in reality "big black men," "effeminate homosexuals," or "stupid little viados."

"Feeling like a Woman"

The most subtle and cutting form that these reminders take in travesti talk is the expression *se sentindo mulher* or *se sentindo amapô*, or simply *se sentindo*—all phrases that mean "feeling like a woman." Travestis use these expressions when speaking to or referring to other travestis. When I first heard travestis using them to talk about others, saying that such and such a travesti was "feeling like a woman," I figured it was complimentary—I assumed it meant that that travesti had reached some kind of desired plane of existence that they all strove for. But like so many of the assumptions I made during my first few months in Salvador, that one was completely wrong. Far from being laudatory, the expression *se sentindo mulher* is one of the cattiest criticisms that one travesti can level at another.

A travesti will be said by others to be *se sentindo* when she is the object of particular, special attention from a male. One of the first times I heard the expression was on the street late at night, when one travesti was talking about another who had been picked up by a man in an expensive car. "Ela deve tá se sentindo"—she ought to be feeling (like a woman), the travesti sniffed. Another time I heard the phrase was in reference to Keila, when she and I were on our way to find a taxi to take us to a party thrown by the landlady of the house on São Francisco Street. Both of us were dressed up, and Keila was wearing four-inch heels. I was holding her arm to help her pick her way around the garbage and to help prevent her from getting a heel stuck in one of the innumerable potholes that make walking along São Francisco Street a risky venture in any footwear. As we walked by a couple of travestis standing against a wall watching for customers, one of them laughed and called out to Keila, "Ah Keila tá se sentindo"—Ah, Keila is feeling like a woman. "Of course I am, sweetheart," Keila hollered back. "I'm beautiful, I have my gringo, and the whole world can go fuck itself."

I did not understand the criticism implied by the phrase *se sentindo* until Erica told me one night that other travestis were making snide comments about her because she had recently taken to walking around in public together with her new boyfriend, Renato. Those travestis, Erica complained, were accusing her (wrongly, she repeatedly emphasized) of *se sentindo mulher*. I had seen Erica and Renato out on the street together several times, walking close together side by side much like a heterosexual couple. Sometimes, while walking down São Francisco Street, Erica even linked her arm with Renato's.

Erica's public appearances with her boyfriend generated comments from other travestis because such actions contrast starkly with the way most travestis behave with their boyfriends. Most travestis rarely appear in public with their boyfriends, and certainly not on city streets during the day. Even when travestis go out with their boyfriends to private parties or to the one nightclub in Salvador that is frequented by travestis, they will often travel to and from the location in the company of other travestis, while the boyfriends make the trip in the company of other males. Although I have seen open displays of affection between travestis and boyfriends inside that nightclub, I have only rarely seen a travesti touch or hold a boyfriend outside that context (and I can count on the fingers of one hand the number of times I have seen a boyfriend reach out, in any context, to touch or hold his travesti girlfriend).

Generally speaking, whatever affection may exist between travestis and their boyfriends is something that gets displayed in private, behind closed doors. Travestis do not socialize in the company of their boyfriends, and vice versa. There are two reasons for this. The first is jealousy—on the part of both the travesti and the boyfriend. Travestis discourage their boyfriends from talking to other travestis (and they make it clear to other travestis that they do not want them talking to their boyfriends) because they fear that any conversation will provide an opportunity to arrange an erotic rendezvous. Boyfriends seem to have the same concern, and the majority of them would react strongly if they saw their travesti girlfriend socializing with another male who they had reason to suspect might be interested in becoming a boyfriend. Some boyfriends go so far as to object if travestis spend too much time in the company of other travestis, since they assume (correctly) that travestis pass on messages from other men and help one another arrange erotic liaisons with particularly attractive males.

But another reason for this lack of public display is that most boyfriends are ashamed (*têm vergonha*), as travestis put it, to be publicly known to be the boyfriend of a travesti. Boyfriends are perched precariously on the edge of two conflated but conflicting understandings of homosexuality that coexist in Brazil. The first is the idea that if two men have sex, the only one who is a homosexual is the one who was penetrated. The second, related idea is similar to—but, importantly, not identical with—dominant conceptions of sexuality that exist in contemporary North American and European contexts: that men who engage in sexual activity together must *both* be homosexual. The tension in Brazil today between these two intertwined perceptions of male same-sex sexual activity parallels the tension that George Chauncey (1994) documents as having existed in Western urban industrial culture in the early decades of this century. Those decades saw a decisive shift from the understanding that the only abnormal person in male same-sex relations was the "fairy" who allowed himself to be penetrated, to the contemporary idea that all males engaging in same-sex relations are "homosexuals," and therefore equally abnormal.

It is very plausible that, as in the New York of the 1930s and 1940s described by Chauncey, these different ideas about same-sex sexual behavior can be correlated to class, and probably even to region in contemporary Brazil: middle-class people in the southern, more urbanized and "European" parts of the country are probably more likely to see both males engaged in same-sex sexual relations as homosexuals than lower-class northerners are (Parker 1995, 1991:85–97; Whitam 1995). However, in contrast to the situation that Chauncey describes for the United States, in Brazil the linchpin of *both* ideas about male same-sex sexuality is the concept of penetration. In Brazil, those who consider that only one of the males engaged in same-sex sexual relations is homosexual do so because they think that a male is homosexual only if he enjoys being "eaten"—anally penetrated. Those who think that both males are homosexual do so *for the same reason.* The difference is that they believe that any male who has sex with another male chooses to have sex with a male, instead of with a woman, because he desires to be anally penetrated by that other male. There is a temporal component here as well—whereas many people can accept that a male may once in a while find himself in a situation where he finds it expedient to have sex with a viado (for example, to earn some money, since "viados pay"), most people assume that a male *living with* a viado does so out of desire, not expediency.

The predicament for the boyfriends of travestis is that whereas they, their travesti girlfriends, and other people in their milieu steadfastly apply the first understanding of male same-sex relations to travesti-boyfriend relationships, they know that many other people who become aware of the relationships they maintain with travestis are likely to think in terms of the second understanding, and think therefore that the boy-friends are not "men" but viados, just like their travesti girlfriends.

In a discussion about police violence against travestis, Keila told me that until fairly recently, police who arrested travestis would not allow them to leave the police station dressed in female clothing. Travestis knew this, and tended to stuff a T-shirt and a pair of Bermuda shorts or long trousers into their purse every night before they went off to work. Sometimes, however, travestis were caught short, finding themselves arrested with no male clothes and hence no way of leaving the detention cell at the police station. Usually the only person other than the travesti who has a key to the padlock on the door to her room is her boyfriend—so, Keila told me, travestis would send word to their boyfriends to find them some male clothes and bring them to the police station. Boyfriends would respond to these calls for help by sending the clothes with a travesti or a woman who was willing to go to the police station. They almost never delivered the clothes themselves, because, Keila said, they were ashamed.

The reason they were ashamed was that if they arrived with clothes to help the travesti get out of jail, the policemen would all laugh at the boyfriend and accuse him of being a viado too, like his travesti girlfriend. "It's pure prejudice," Keila explained. "They think that just because a man lives with a viado, he must be a viado too." I asked Keila why. "Because they think like this: 'You're living with a viado, so that means you want what? You don't want a woman, you want a viado, and a viado has what? A dick to penetrate you with. So you're a viado too."

The knowledge that many people are likely to misunderstand the relationship and think that a boyfriend is a viado, combined with the jealousy factor mentioned above, means that travestis and their boyfriends almost never appear in public together, even in the house where they share a room. Boyfriends slip in and out of a travesti's room with no fanfare or notice, often passing by other travestis hanging out in the doorway without even greeting them. Although the travestis living on São Francisco Street all knew immediately whenever a travesti had a new boyfriend, it sometimes took me several weeks, and the repeated silent comings and goings of a particular male, to discover that fact, because I never saw the travesti and her boyfriend appear together in any public space—not even the corridor of the house that connected all the rooms.

When a travesti's boyfriend arrives in her room, she will often leave the room to go and sit with other travestis in their rooms or in the doorway of the house. Or, if she is still in the "impassioned" stage of her relationship, she will stay inside her room with her boyfriend, often with the door closed (a signal not to enter without first knocking and asking permission—the only times a travesti closes her door when she is in her room is when she is doing a programa, when she is smoking marijuana or snorting coke, when she is getting "pumped" with silicone, when she is sleeping, or when she is with her boyfriend). Unless a boyfriend has been together with a travesti for several years (and sometimes not even then), he will not generally associate with anyone else in the house, often not even with the boyfriends of other travestis.[2]

The private nature of travesti-boyfriend relationships contrasts with the expressed desires of most travestis to have a man who, in Luciana's words, "will accept you totally, twenty-four hours a day, who will go out places with you, have you like a woman, make you feel like a woman, take you anywhere at all" (chapter 2). The irony of this desire is that in those rare instances when a travesti does manage to get together with a man who does those things and makes her "feel like a woman," she is harshly criticized by other travestis precisely for "feeling like a woman." Far from encouraging this feeling in one another, travestis actively *discourage* it, and they are swift to formulate tart comments involving the phrase *se sentindo mulher*—to remind one another, lest anybody should ever forget, that travestis are not, and can never be, women.

Males, Not Men

But if travestis are not and can never be women, does that mean that they see themselves and one another as men? The answer to that question is not immediately evident. Two specific linguistic facts, especially, would seem to indicate that travestis do overtly see themselves as men: their occasional use of the masculine pronoun *ele* (he) when talking about travestis, and their occasional use of the word *homem* (man or male) in talking about themselves and others.

In Portuguese, the word *travesti* is grammatically masculine (*o travesti*). This compels speakers talking about travestis to use masculine pronouns, articles, and adjectival endings. So newspaper articles about travestis will say things like:

Os travestis de São Paulo estão *apavorados. Eles* estão mudando o comportamento e fugindo dos locais onde, só neste ano, já morreram 16, quase *todos* com um tiro no olho.	*The travestis* of São Paulo are *panicstricken. They* are changing their behavior and fleeing from the places where, just this year, 16 have already died, almost *all* of them with a bullet in the eye.
	(*Folha de São Paulo*, 24 March 1993)

This passage uses the masculine definite article *os*, the grammatically masculine adjectival ending *-os*, and the masculine pronouns *todos* and *eles*. These grammatical concord (agreement) rules are shared by all speakers of Portuguese, including travestis. Although I have recorded a few instances of travesti speakers suddenly and inconsequentially using the neologism *uma travesti* (with the feminine indefinite article) in the midst of a conversation, travestis for the most part do not break with the grammatical conventions of their language: when they use a grammatically masculine noun, they use masculine pronouns, articles, and adjectival endings; when they use a grammatically feminine noun, they use feminine forms.

In the course of a short conversation on the type of partner that different types of males find attractive, Keila clearly demonstrated the influence that grammatical gender exerts on referential gender. Speaking first about "homosexuals"—a word that usually is a blanket term for all males who experience same-sex desire, but that Keila uses here as synonymous with what she normally would call "gays" (homosexual males who seek out other homosexual males for sex)—Keila chooses pronouns and adjectival endings in concordance with the fact that the word *homosexual* is grammatically masculine in Portuguese:

O *homossexual*, *ele* já é *intuído* para transar com homossexuais, que *ele* tem atração por homossexuais e tem atração por heterossexuais. Mas só que *ele* sabe que na consciência *dele*, que os heterossexuais vão ser avesso a transar com *ele*. *Ele* já pensa assim. Então *ele* tem que procurar transar no meio *dele*, ou seja, com *os homossexuais*.	The *homosexual* [masculine article], *he* is *tuned* [masculine adjectival ending] into having sex with other homosexuals, 'cause *he* is attracted to homosexuals and heterosexuals. But in *his* mind *he* knows that heterosexuals are not going to want to have sex with *him*. *He* thinks like that. And so *he* has to find sex in *his* own milieu, that is, with other *homosexuals*.

After this explanation of "homosexuals'" desire, Keila made a contrast with travestis. In terms of grammar, the same thing happens here—her use of the grammatically masculine *travesti* seems to compel a masculine gendered pronoun:

O *travesti* já tem uma ressalva porque o *travesti* tem uma porção de mulher dentro de cada travesti. Então *ele* já pode atrair alguns heterossexuais, embora atraía homossexuais também.	The *travesti* [masculine article] is already exempt from this because *the travesti* has a portion of femaleness in each travesti. And so *he* can attract some heterosexuals, even though [*he*] attracts homosexuals too.

A few minutes later, Keila began talking about effeminate gay men—
what she here calls *bicha fechativas*. The word *bicha* is grammatically feminine. Note which pronoun this grammatical fact seems to compel:

Eu acho que *as bichas* muito *fechati-vas, elas* também não têm atração por *outras* muito *fechativas. Elas* nor-malmente têm atração por homens.	I think that really *effeminate queens* [feminine article and adjectival ending], *they* [she-plural] aren't at-tracted to *others* [feminine adjecti-val ending] who are really *queeny* [feminine adjectival ending]. *They* [she-plural] are attracted to men.

Now in any conversation about these three types of individuals, Keila
would be unhesitant in explaining that neither "homosexuals," travestis,
or *bichas fechativas* are "men." Instead, she would say, they are all viados
(faggots) and they are all effeminate, even though many "homosexuals"
try hard to disguise this fact. The most effeminate of all these types of
viados, however, are not *bichas fechativas*—the ones Keila refers to using
the pronoun *she*. The most effeminate, and feminine, homosexuals of all
are travestis, who fully live out their effeminate natures by adopting females names, dressing in female clothing, and modifying their bodies to
give them feminine features. Despite this social reality, though, the
grammatical restraints of the Portuguese language seem to push Keila
into speaking of travestis, *when she uses the word "travesti" to talk about them*, using masculine pronouns and grammatical forms.

What this means is that when travesti speakers use the word *travesti* to
talk about travestis, they will normally use grammatically masculine articles, pronouns, and adjectival endings. In their speech to one another
and to nontravestis who live in their milieu, however, travestis in fact
only rarely use the word *travesti*. Instead, the preferred term is *bicha*,
which, being grammatically feminine, permits travesti speakers to un-
problematically refer to other travestis as "she."

Most travestis would normally use the word *travesti* only when asking
whether a certain person is a travesti (as opposed to a transformista or a
woman, for example); in a formal speech situation, such as an interview
with a journalist; or when writing about travestis. In such contexts, many
travestis seem to know that the word *bicha* is regarded as slangy and in-
appropriate: it would be like saying "queens" or "fags" instead of "gays" in
formal English linguistic contexts. There are also individual differences
and preferences here—some travestis avoid any labels at all when they
speak generally about travestis, simply using the inclusive term *a gente*,
which means "we" or "us." And a few travestis who are used to speaking
to journalists or to researchers like myself about travestis will often

generalize using the word *travesti*. Keila, for example, uses it uncommonly often, and it is not at all impossible that this particular speech pattern is an artifact of her work with me and of my continual questions about how common or how idiosyncratic she thought that particular travesti practices and ideas were among travestis in general

Even in such contexts, however, speakers like Keila invariably switch from masculine to feminine grammatical forms when they stop talking about travestis in general and begin speaking about specific individuals. This kind of grammatical and pronominal gender switching occurs continually throughout the book *A Princesa*, as the author glides from speaking generally about travestis to discussing particular, named ones. For example, in discussing Elisa, a travesti who forced others to pay for the right to stand on a particular street in Paris, Fernanda Farias de Albuquerque (Albuquerque and Janelli 1995:156) recounts:

Ela já ficava sabendo quando *um trans* [Albuquerque's word for "travesti," not used in Salvador] saía do Brasil e sabia quando *ele* chegava em Paris. Caso *ele* não aceitasse as suas condições, *ela* fazia que *ele* fosse *expulso.*	*She* already knew when *a travesti* [masculine article] left Brazil and knew when *he* arrived in Paris. If *he* didn't accept her conditions, *she* saw to it that *he* was *deported* [masculine adjectival ending].

Another example of this linguistic practice occurred when I asked Keila if self-mutilation—the practice of cutting one's arm to escape arrest and detention—was practiced by travestis before the discovery of AIDS. She told me that it was, using the word *travesti* to speak in general terms:

Não, antes da AIDS existia, e depois da AIDS existia ainda um pouco mais porque aí servia de ameaça para os policiais. Porque, se *o travesti* se auto-mutilasse, e falasse ao policial: "Eu estou com AIDS, eu vou espirrar sangue em você," o policial via ali o diabo na frente, ele não queria mais acordo, ele deixava *o travesti* ir até pro inferno se *ele* quisesse.	No, it existed before AIDS, and after AIDS it was even more common because AIDS made it even more threatening to the police. Because if *a travesti* cut [him]self and said to a cop: "I have AIDS, I'm gonna spray blood on you," the cop would see the Devil in front of him, he wouldn't want to make an arrest anymore, he would let *the travesti* get away all the way to Hell if *he* wanted to.

Immediately following this, however, Keila recalled a concrete example of a travesti who had cut herself in her company. Note the change of the word to describe the named individual and the change of pronoun:

Uma vez fomos presas em oito. E nesse meio tinha *uma bicha*, ela não tinha AIDS na época, disseram até que depois *ela* veio a ter, mas na época ela não tinha, Alcione. Estavámos todas presas . . . Os policiais pegaram a gente e levaram pra Jogos ali nos Barris. Aí a gente chegou na Jogos, *ela* fez assim: "Eu vou me cortar." Eu digo: "*Mona,* num tem nada pra se cortar, cê vai se cortar com o quê?"	One time eight of us were arrested. And among us was *a bicha* [feminine article], *she* didn't have AIDS at the time—they say that later *she* came to have it, but *she* didn't at the time, Alcione [was her name]. We were all arrested . . . The police picked us up and took us to the vice squad precinct in Barris. We got to the vice squad precinct, and *she* went like: "I'm gonna cut myself." I say, "*Mona,* you don't have anything to cut yourself with, what are you gonna cut yourself with?"

The point here is that while travestis do indeed sometimes use masculine grammatical forms to speak about travestis, this linguistic usage is tied to certain contexts, and it is a reflection of grammar—not of subjective understandings of the gender of travestis. Furthermore, unless an insult or a joke is intended, individual travestis are always spoken about using feminine pronouns and grammatical forms, and they are always addressed with feminine forms.

Context is also important in understanding how travestis use the word *homem* (plural *homens*), which can be translated as "man" or "male." Travestis employ the word in a number of senses that are always relational—that is, exactly what *homem* refers to in travesti talk always depends on who is speaking, what is being spoken about, and what is being contrasted with *homem* in that particular context.

Travestis use words like *homem* in reference to other travestis only when they want to joke with, ridicule, or insult them. Lalesca's accusations that her antagonist Sheila is a "Rastafarian man" and a "big black man" are typical examples of this kind of usage among travestis. But in cases like the argument between Lalesca and Sheila, the use of the words signifying masculinity to describe another travesti is not meant to accurately describe a travesti's subjective understanding of herself. On the contrary, words like 'big black man' are chosen—and they sting—precisely because they contrast with a travesti's sense that she is not a man at all.

When it comes to self-reference, travestis use the word *homem* only in very specific contexts. One of these sometimes occurs when travestis contrast their own way of viewing the world with women's perspectives. Whenever travestis talk about issues such as dominance and subordination, sexual appetite, and promiscuity, many of them readily explain that their opinions are the result of their having *a cabeça de homem*— a male head. This "male head" makes it difficult for them to accept the subordination, the virginal modesty, and the desire for monogamy that they attribute to women. It is the perceptive faculties of a travesti's "male head" that allow her to see past the fantasies that delude women, as Martinha expressed it, and to "face reality."

A second context in which travestis use *homem* in reference to themselves is when they talk about their genitals. It should be abundantly clear at this point that no travesti denies having male genitals (quite the opposite). The conclusion that they all readily draw from this biological fact is that those male genitals, irrevocably given to them by God, render them male. It is no coincidence that Banana's remark "I was born a man and a man I will die" (*Eu nasci homem e homem morrerei*) was uttered in the context of a discussion about sex-change operations, where she was contrasting her own genitalia with those of women and explaining the impossibility of ever changing one's sex. In contexts like this, to refer to oneself as *homem* is to contrast oneself with those people who were not born with male genitals, namely, females. In all such instances in which travestis use the word *homem*, either in reference to other travestis or in self-reference, what is being repeated and reinforced is, once again, their conviction that they are not, and will never be, women.

When it comes to their relationships with men, travestis use the word *homem* to talk about themselves in one context only—namely, when they are penetrating a client, a *vício*, or (woe to him) a boyfriend. In these instances, travestis do not say that they *are* men, but they will say—as Mabel did when I asked her how she felt when she was penetrating a client, or as Keila explained when she recounted stories of clients who called her "big, sexy brute" (chapter 4)—that they feel "like" or "as if" they were *homens*.

In other contexts, the word *homem* is used by travestis to designate males who *contrast with* travestis—males who have a different nature, a different sexuality, and different desires. *Homens* are the males who lust after a woman's *buceta*. They are the males who only ever penetrate others—males who will not turn into a woman at the "Moment of Truth." They are the males with whom travestis can become impassioned and whom they install in their rooms as their boyfriends. They are the males who are "men," the ones who can make a travesti feel *mulheríssima*—like a total woman.

Travestis thus use one word, *homem*, to mean two different things: "male" (when talking about themselves in relation to female genitals and "heads") and "man" (when talking about males who only penetrate their partners, and their relationship to travestis). They thus elaborate and position themselves within a subtle and fluid gender system (at least as far as males are concerned), a gender system in which being a male does not limit one to being a man.

There is one further context in which travestis will use the word *homem* to refer to themselves: when they want or need to "pass as a man" (*passar por homem*). In such situations, travestis will sometimes attempt to highlight their maleness in the hope that it will convince others of their "man-ness." A common context in which travestis will attempt this is when they venture out onto city streets during the day. This is an exposed, uncomfortable sensation for many travestis, because they know from weary experience that they are likely to get stared at and harassed as soon as they step beyond the few city blocks on which they are well known. Some travestis refuse to be intimidated by people on the street, and they have developed caustic tongues and aggressive demeanors that ensure that any person insulting them will receive *uma boa resposta*—a good response—in turn. But many other travestis hate having to cope with the stares and the shouts, and they avoid leaving the immediate vicinity of their rooms as much as possible during the day. If they need to go shopping or run an errand, they often pay others—usually older women or older travestis who no longer work the streets much—small sums to buy bread or deliver a message for them.

If a travesti does walk or travel somewhere during the day, she may decide to do so *vestido de homem* (dressed as a man) or *fazendo a linha homem* (appearing as a man). Dressing or appearing as a man involves removing lipstick and earrings and many of the rings and bracelets that a travesti may wear, and donning long trousers, a T-shirt, and, inevitably, a baseball cap, up into which her hair is stuffed. This outfit rarely results in travestis completely blending in with the crowd (any eye for detail might notice plucked eyebrows and distinctly unmasculine nail polish on fingers and toes, for example), but many travestis find it sufficient to ward off the kinds of open gawking that a travesti in shorts and a halter top would attract.

Once a travesti reaches a certain point in her self-transformation, however—especially once she has prominent breasts—it becomes difficult for her to dress or appear as a man. A "man" outfit on such a travesti risks attracting just as much attention as female dress, or perhaps even more. And what is worse, travestis with breasts, large bundas, and rounded features are convinced that everybody who sees them dressed in male clothing thinks that they are lesbian—a misrecognition that no travesti finds amusing in the slightest.

Despite the deep misgivings a travesti may have about being taken for a lesbian, however, there are occasions when even large-breasted travestis will take a deep breath, don a T-shirt and a baseball cap, and attempt to pass as a man. Usually those occasions involve dealings with doctors or government officials in contexts in which the travesti's identity card is required and where she will be publicly identified by her male name. The most spine-tingling experience of this nature for any travesti is crossing an international border. Travestis who have to do this on their way to Italy face one of the most difficult decisions of their lives: what will they wear? Will they go *de homem* (as a man) and risk looking like what Chica called "some common drug smuggler," or do they go *de mulher* (as a woman) and risk being humiliated or deported on the spot, as the passport-control officer tries to pair the male name in the passport with a person in lipstick and a dress? The transsexual British essayist Jan Morris described an experience before her sex-reassignment surgery when she had to pass through a similar situation in an airport as "an awful moment" (1987: 106). Chica was much more graphic, characterizing her own few minutes of waiting in the Austrian passport-control queue as a moment when her sphincter was so tight that it could cut a cord in two. That description probably resonates profoundly with the experience of every travesti who has ever found herself in the passport-control queue of a foreign country, fingering her passport and wondering stiffly if she had really made the right decision when she chose her travel wardrobe earlier that day.

Perfectly Homosexual

The extreme tension travestis experience in situations like passport-control queues arises from their perception that even when they are dressed as men, they are not really men at all. Instead of "men," what travestis feel themselves to be (they tell anyone who asks them and reaffirm continually in their speech to one another) is homosexuals—*viados*, *bichas*. The core of their subjective experience of themselves is that they are attracted to men. This attraction is cited by all travestis as the most significant motivating force in their initial understandings of themselves as "different" from other boys, and it is the force that compels their increasingly focused efforts to manage their bodies and transform them from masculine to feminine. Homosexual desire is the current that buoys up and gives meaning to travestis' bodily practices, their affective engagements, and their professional activities. Being homosexual is at the heart of the travesti project. Before anyone is a travesti, that person is first a viado. Elisabeth makes the links particularly explicit in her account of how she came to understand, at age twelve, that she was a travesti:

Eu num sabia o que era um tra/num sabia o que era um travesti, né? Eu sabia que eu dava, né, gostava de dar e que era homossexual, dava, né, então é, o povo dizia, "Ah, isso é uma vergonha," minha família falava, "Isso é uma vergonha," num sei o quê, essas co, essas coisa de família, né? Então eu fui embora de casa por causa disso. Mas que eu nunca tinha visto um travesti antes, entendeu, como eu vi a primeira vez, eu vi, muitos travestis no Recife, né, eu fiquei assim apavorada, de boca aberta quando eu vi. Eu falei, é isso aí que eu quero ser, travesti . . . Eram bonita, né? Grande, bonita . . . Então eu queria ser igual a elas, né? . . . Eu falei, "Ah, é assim que eu quero ficar." E fiquei [laughs].

I didn't know what a trav/I didn't know what a travesti was, you know? I knew that I got penetrated, right, I liked getting penetrated and I was a homosexual, I "gave," right, and so everybody said "Ah, this is shameful," my family said "This is shameful," and stuff like that, those things that families say, you know? And so I left home [and traveled to Recife] on account of that. But I had never seen a travesti before, you understand, and when I saw one for the first time, I saw lots of travestis in Recife, right, I was like shocked, my mouth fell open when I saw them. I said, this is what I want to be, a travesti . . . They were beautiful, you know? Big, beautiful . . . And I wanted to be just like them, you know? . . . I said, "Ah, that is how I want to become." And I became just like them [laughs].

Elisabeth's story succinctly weaves together the threads of sexual activity ("I got penetrated"), sexual desire ("I liked getting penetrated"), sexual orientation ("I was a homosexual"), feminine appearance ("They were beautiful, you know? Big beautiful . . .") and personal agency ("I said, 'Ah, that is how I want to become,' and I become just like them") that are common to all travesti narratives of self-discovery and that constitute the warp and woof of travesti subjectivity.

Travesti subjectivity is thus not that of a woman nor that of a man, but that of an effeminate male—a homosexual. "I'm neither a man nor a woman," a travesti named Cláudia Wonder tells a Brazilian newspaper. "I'm a bicha."[3] The Salvadorean travesti Carlete declares the same thing for another publication: "I love being a bicha," she explains (*Prática Journalística*, no. 1, 1981), enunciating and demarcating a subjectivity that all travestis in Salvador would unhesitatingly agree that they share.

But travestis are not only homosexuals. They are also, in their own opinion, Brazil's only truly "out" homosexuals. Indeed, travestis are so ostentatiously homosexual that some of them can argue with great eloquence that travestis are radical homosexuals who have more or less single-handedly created a homosexual space in an otherwise rigidly heterosexual Brazil. They note that while the majority of gay men and lesbians in Brazil are still afraid to come out in public and let people know they are homosexual, travestis, at tremendous personal cost, publicly proclaim their homosexuality through their dress and demeanor. And despite the rejection, the daily humiliation, and the continual threat of violence that that proclamation entails, travestis don't give up, they don't run away and hide.

Whenever this topic came up in conversation, Keila always enjoyed repeating, to me and to others, what a travesti named Baby had once told her. Baby was well known throughout Salvador partly because she never hesitated to walk down the city's main streets in broad daylight in high heels, a tiny midriff top, and a miniskirt. "And Baby herself said it like this," Keila would remember: "'I go out onto the street in high heels in the middle of the day. They'll all have to look at me like that, because that's the way I am. When they get tired of seeing me, they won't notice me anymore. Because I'm not going to stop walking by if they throw a rock at me, if they hit me with a stick, if they shout things at me—they'll shout and I'll keep walking by . . . sooner or later they'll get tired of noticing me.'" Keila usually continued by saying that a gay male would not react that way: "If someone shouts something at a queen (uma bicha), she'll run away. And the next time she walks by she'll walk by pretending to be hard and tough, pretending to be a man (ela vai passar, bem dura, como se fosse homem)."

This phrase, "pretending to be a man" (como se fosse homem), initially confounded me, especially when it was used by travestis in reference to me. One Sunday afternoon, for example, I was standing with Adriana and Stefani in one of Salvador's main plazas. Both travestis were wearing short skirts and tops, and Adriana, who was preparing for her evening of work, had a few large curlers pinned loosely in her hair. We were eating candy that we had just bought from a street seller when two policemen walked by. As they were passing, Adriana began to giggle. "They see you standing here with us," she said to me, "and they probably think you're a man." Both Adriana and Stefani then collapsed in laughter at the sheer outrageousness of such a profound misunderstanding. It took me, however, a long time to figure out what was so funny.

By the end of my stay in Salvador, I had finally come to realize that as a gay man, I am assumed by travestis to dar, to be penetrated by "men." I am, therefore, a viado, a bicha, just like them. However, I, and all other gay men who do not dress as women and modify their bodies to be more feminine, disguise this sameness. Unlike travestis, who openly embody their homosexuality, gay males like myself hide—we deceive, we pretend to be men, when we really are not men at all. It is in this sense that travestis can perceive themselves to be more honest, and much more radical, than "butch" (machuda) homosexuals like myself. It is also in this sense that travestis simply do not understand the discrimination that they face through Brazil at the hands of gay men, many of whom feel that travestis compromise the public image of homosexuals and give gay men a bad name.

This kind of unanimous insistence by travestis that they regard themselves as open and obvious homosexuals remains oddly unheard by journalists, scholars, and commentators who have written about travestis. Many of those analyses have misunderstood travesti subjectivity completely and claim that travestis want to be women. But even those observers who have perceived that travestis do not want to be women still have not understood what it is that travestis are doing, and why. Instead of listening when travestis explain that they are homosexuals, those writers fashion travestis into postmodern icons and claim that they reject identity altogether. The Brazilian filmmaker and essayist Arnaldo Jabor asserts that "a travesti doesn't desire identity. He wants ambiguity" (1993:27). Hélio Silva agrees (1993:125, 162), adding poetically but unhelpfully that the condition of being a travesti is a "noncondition" and that travestis don't occupy space—they occupy "not-space" (91). Neuza Maria de Oliveira argues something similar, stating that travestis "prefer not to define or classify themselves" and that they "want to be Difference" (1994:115). A full-page article on travestis in the newspaper *Diário Catarinense* declares, "A travesti doesn't want to be either a woman or a man. He wants to be ambiguous" (29 August 1993). The Rio de Janeiro street paper *Beijo da Rua* (no. 3, 1989) calls travestis "postmodern androgynes." And so on.

All these analyses miss the point.[4] Just as travestis are not striving for womanhood, neither are they rejecting identity or striving for ambiguity. What they are striving for, they readily tell anybody who will listen, is homosexuality. They desire to embody homosexuality. And they desire to do this in the most complete, beautiful, and perfect manner possible. Whereas other males who experience same-sex desire deny that desire and disguise it, travestis embrace it and luxuriate in it. They anchor their lives in it. They build their bodies around it. So while the bodies of individual travestis—with their exuberant bundas, their tight little hormone-enhanced breasts, and their readily employed penises—may strike some commentators as ambiguous or androgynous, they are completely *un*ambiguous statements as far as travestis and many of the people who see them and interact with them are concerned. Far from conveying ambiguity, those bodies convey certainty: this is a viado.

From this perspective, the main question to be answered about travestis becomes not why do travestis want to look like women, but rather: why does it make sense for homosexuals to become travestis? What is it about the understandings, representations, and definitions of sexuality and gender in Brazilian society that makes it logical and meaningful for males who desire other males to understand that desire in ways that compel them to radically modify their bodies and structure their affective and sexual relationships with those other males in the specific ways that travestis do?

Of course, not all Brazilian males who experience same-sex desire become travestis; there are other options available. A male who acknowledges homosexual desire can become what Keila earlier referred to as a *bicha fechativa*—an effeminate and limp-wristed (*desmunhecando*), but still clearly male, homosexual. Or he can become what travestis call a *bicha machuda*, which signifies a homosexual who masquerades as "butch" and who passes for—and often lives as—a heterosexual man.[5] There is even a socially acknowledged role for males who prostitute themselves as males. They are called *michês*, and although the majority of them do not consider themselves to be homosexual, some of them call themselves *gay* (Perlongher 1987:117–20, 178–82). The appearance cultivated by *michês* tends to be a stereotypically macho or a stereotypically tough gay-boyish one—appearances that serve to uphold the public impression that *michês* will restrict their behavior with their clients to the role of penetrator.

In the eyes of travestis, however, all these individuals—whether they be limp-wristed queens, straight-acting "butches," or tough, muscular *michês*—are viados, homosexuals, just like themselves. But they are viados who disguise their true nature and pretend to be something that they are not. Travestis dismiss these other homosexual subjectivities and subsume them as dishonest and arrested stages of what they see as their own fully developed and acknowledged identity. In doing so, travestis are asserting that the only true homosexuality is the one enacted and embodied by themselves. In other words, travestis see themselves as constituting not merely one incarnation of homosexual desire among many possible others. They see themselves, rather, as the Ur-incarnation, the True Embodiment, and the ultimate, desired end point of homosexual desire. Travestis consider themselves to be homosexual desire in its fullest and most perfect form. And so the question, once again, is this: what are the understandings of sexuality, gender, and bodies that allow travestis to elaborate and maintain this conviction?

The Gender of Travestis

Travesti subjectivity is a subjectivity that is made possible and desirable only because particular connections are felt to exist between a person's physical body, that person's social roles and cultural positioning, and his or her sexual activity. It is, in other words, a result, an embodiment, and an enactment of specific configurations of biological sex, gender, and sexuality that are available to travestis in the society in which they live. In order to understand and account for travesti subjectivity, therefore, it is necessary to be clear about the ways in which sex, gender, and sexuality configure, and it is necessary to trace the ways in which those configurations provide individuals with a conceptual framework that they can draw on in order to understand and organize their desires, their bodies, their affective and physical relations, and their social roles.

Throughout this book, I have argued that travestis draw on and articulate a social world populated by three distinct types of gendered individuals: *homens* (men), *mulheres* (women), and *viados* (faggots). Out of this trinity of gendered types, it would be possible to construct the argument that travestis operate within, and indeed themselves embody, a system in which there are three genders—men, women, and travestis (or homosexuals). Such an understanding of gender in Brazil would not be completely novel. Although the words *third sex* or *third gender* are not common in the language of Brazilian writers who discuss the phenomenon of travestis, those commentators who contend that travestis constitute "ambiguity" or "difference" are essentially echoing the thesis of the American literary theorist Marjorie Garber, who in her book *Vested Interests* lavishly argues that the very essence of transvestism is its refusal to be contained by binary thinking or social structures, and that it always, wherever it appears, constitutes what she calls a "third" (1992a:11). The language of "third"—in this case, specifically "third gender"—has recently also been appearing in anthropological accounts of people in various societies around the world who, at least superficially, resemble travestis, in that their social behavior and sometimes even their physical selves are marked and recognized as differing from those that typify men and women.[6]

In an academic context where ideas about "thirdness" are increasingly popular, it is interesting to note that such language appears to be absent among Salvadorean travestis. Although travestis regard themselves, as I have documented, neither as women nor as men, and continually refer to themselves as viados or bichas, the suggestion that they might constitute a third gender or third sex is not something I ever heard any of them speculate about amongst themselves.

Instead of talking about themselves as a third gender, travestis spend a lot of time situating themselves and others in relation to a very specific gendered binary. That binary, however, is a *different* binary, anchored in and arising from *different* principles than those that currently structure and give meaning to gender in places like northern Europe or North America.

The fundamental difference is that whereas the northern Euro-American gender system is based on anatomical sex, the gender system that structures travestis' perceptions and actions is based on *sexuality*. The dominant idea in northern Euro-American societies is that one is a man or a woman because of the genitals one possesses. That biological difference is understood to accrete differences in behavior, language, sexuality, perception, emotion, and so on. As scholars such as Garfinkel (1967), Hausman (1995), Kessler and McKenna (1985), Shapiro (1991), and Raymond (1979) have all argued at length, it is within such a cultural system that a *transsexual* subjectivity can arise—because here, biological males, for example, who do not feel or behave as "men" should, can make sense of that difference by reference to their genitals. They are not "men," therefore they must be "women"; and to be a "woman" means to have the genitals of a female.

While the anatomical differences between men and women are certainly not missed or ignored in Brazil, the possession of genitals appears to be fundamentally conflated with what they can be used for, and in the particular configuration of sexuality, gender, and sex that travestis draw on, the determinative criterion in the identification of males and females is not so much the genitals as it is the role those genitals perform in sexual encounters.' Here the locus of gender difference is the act of penetration—if one *only* penetrates, one is a "man"; if one gets penetrated, one is something other than a man—one is either a viado, a faggot; or a *mulher*, a woman. Tina makes the relationships and parallels between all these statuses explicit in a story about the main reason she eventually left one of her boyfriends:

1 Tina: Três anos era hom/foi homem pra mim. Foi homíssimo. Depois, eu era o homem e ele era o viado.

2 Don: Como?

3 Tina: Entendeu como é?

4 Don: Sim . . . Mas não. Como é?

5 Tina: Três anos ele foi pra mim homem, e depois dos três anos, ele foi mulher. Eu era o homem, ele era a mulher. Entendeu como é? Os três anos que eu passei com ele, a primeira vez, entendeu como é, ele

T: For three years he was a ma/he was a man for me. A total man. Then, I was the man and he was the viado.

D: What?

T: Do you see?

D: Yes . . . But no. How?

T: For three years he was a man for me, and after those three years, he became a woman. I was the man and he was the woman. Do you see? The first three years I spent with him, do you see, he penetrated me

me comia, e eu chupava ele. Eu era
a mulher dele.

6 **Don:** Sim . . .

7 **Tina:** E depois dos três anos, eu
era o homem dele. Entendeu
agora? Agora cê entendeu.

8 **Don:** Mais o que aconteceu? Que/
que/fez que ele/

9 **Tina:** Modificou?

10 **Don:** Modificou, sim.

11 **Tina:** Modificou que ele pegando.
Ele criou medo de mim perder, ia
na rua que ele viu que eu era uma
bicha viciada que queria comer
os boys. Aí ele viu que/com medo
de me perder, e perder a mor-
dormia, né?

12 **Don:** É.

13 **Tina:** Aí começou tirando/
brincando de sexo comigo. "Não
carece você gozar na rua não. Eu
bato uma punetinha pra você.
Daqui à pouco vamos fazer outra
coisa diferente." Me dá o cu/me deu
o cu, começou a me chupar, aí
pronto.

and I sucked [his penis]. I was his
woman.

D: Yeah . . .

T: And after those three years, I was
his man. Do you understand now?
Now you get it.

D: But what happened? What/what/
made him/

T: Change?

D: Yeah, change.

T: It changed with him touching my
penis. He became afraid to lose
me, I was always on the street and
he saw that I was a promiscuous
bicha who liked penetrating boys.
And so he saw that/he got afraid
he'd lose me, and lose his com-
forts, right?

D: Right.

T: And so he started pulling/playing
with other kinds of sex things. [He
told me:] "You don't have to cum
on the street [with clients and
vícios]. I can jerk you off. And later
on we can do other new things."
He gives me his ass/gave me his
ass, started to suck [my penis],
and, well, there you are.

Note how Tina explains that she was her boyfriend's woman, in that
"he penetrated me and I sucked [his penis]" (line 5). Note also how Tina
uses the words *viado* and *mulher* interchangeably (lines 1 and 5) to express
whet her boyfriend became after he started expressing an interest in her
penis and started "giving his ass" to her. This discursive conflation between being a viado and being a woman is continually assumed in all travesti talk about themselves, their boyfriends, and their clients. And those
two identities are firmly and consistently differentiated from and contrasted with the identity that lies on the other side of the penetrative
boundary—that of being a man.

The idiom (and the practice) of penetration is the axis around which
every aspect of travesti life turns. An individual's self-discovery as a travesti is signaled by attraction to males—an attraction that inexorably,
sooner or later, leads to her being anally penetrated. Her respect for (and
her definition of) her boyfriend hinges on his sexual behavior: interest

in her penis marks him as a viado and buys him a one-way ticket out of her room and out of her life. Her conviction that "there are no more men anymore" is reinforced every time a cute, muscular boyzinho gropes for her crotch. Her impatience with homosexuals who do not fully "come out" (se assumir) is fueled every time she sees someone who she knows "give ass" walk by wearing a shirt and trousers instead of a dress.

At every turn, penetration provides explanations and defines identities for travestis. It constitutes the interpretive framework that they draw on in order to be and to act, and in order to understand the being and the actions of others. And because penetration, as far as travestis are concerned, is an either/or experience (one either enjoys penetration or one doesn't—and recall that it is enough for a boyfriend to request penetration only once for him to change status in the eyes of his travesti girlfriend. From her perspective, such a request is revelatory, unveiling the boyfriend to have always been a viado. She will assume both that his request is an expression of a secret desire he has always had—and will always have—and that he will continue to actively pursue the fulfillment of that desire with other travestis, even if he does not again request penetration dentro de casa),[8] it produces two categories of people. The salient difference in such a system, however, is not between "men" and "women." It is between those who penetrate (comer, "eat") and those who get penetrated (dar, "give"), in a system where the act of being penetrated has transformative force. Those who only "eat" and never "give" in this system are culturally designated as "men"; those who "give," even if they also "eat," are classified as being something else—something that I will call "not-men," partly for want of a culturally elaborated label and partly to foreground my conviction that the gender system that makes it possible for travestis to emerge and make sense is one that is massively oriented towards, if not determined by, male subjectivity, male desire, and male pleasure, as those are culturally elaborated in Brazil. What this particular binary implies is that females and males who enjoy being penetrated belong to the same classificatory category—they are on the same side of the gendered binary. They share, in other words, a gender.

This sharing would appear to be the reason why the overwhelming majority of travestis do not self-identify as women and have no desire to have an operation to become a "woman," even though they spend their lives dramatically modifying their bodies to look more feminine. Culturally speaking, travestis, because they enjoy being penetrated, are structurally equivalent to women, even though they are not biologically identical to them. Because travestis already share a gender with women, a sex-change operation would—again, culturally speaking—give a travesti nothing that she doesn't already have. All it would do is rob her of a significant source of pleasure and income. It might also constitute a step down on the aesthetic and social ladder, as travestis like Magdala imply when they assert that travestis are more feminine and more sensual than many women, and as travestis like Martinha indicate when they say that women live sad, deluded lives.

Travestis may well be considered to be a "third," in some of the senses in which Marjorie Garber uses that term, but they are not a third that is situated outside or beyond a gendered binary. On the contrary. Indeed, one of the greatest weaknesses of all ideas about thirdness is that, far from denaturalizing or displacing dichotomous systems of sex and gender, as proponents of such ideas have claimed, there is a real danger that theories of third gender in fact radically naturalize and reinforce traditional understandings of sexual dimorphism, by suggesting that individuals who do not fit the male-female binary fall outside it and transcend it, rather than disturb it, blur it, or reconfigure it. Third-gender language leaves the traditional male-female binary intact. Instead of expanding, nuancing, and complicating understandings of masculinity and femininity, third-gender language seals those categories and locates fluidity, juxtapositions, ambiguity, and dynamics outside their borders, in the realm of the third. The concept of the third makes it hard to perceive that the "two" might not be as straightforward as we often seem to think they are. It prevents us from seeing that people like travestis might not fall outside binary gender at all. But what they might do is suggest that that binary is configured in radically different ways than we are conditioned to expect.

Perhaps the single most important and invigorating advance in recent gender theory has been the collapse of the distinction between "sex" and "gender" that had for decades been a cornerstone of feminist theory. The canonical text that precipitated this collapse is Judith Butler's *Gender Trouble*, which was published in 1990. *Gender Trouble* sharply criticized feminist understandings of gender that saw it as the cultural reading of a precultural, or prediscursive, biological sex. In a series of deft arguments, Butler demonstrated that the concept of a biological sex is itself a gendered notion, dependent on culturally generated notions of difference for its meaning and its ability to seem "natural." "And what is 'sex' anyway?" asks Butler in a key passage.

> It is natural, anatomical, chromosomal, or hormonal, and how is a feminist critic to assess the scientific discourses which purport to establish such 'facts' for us? Does sex have a history? Does each sex have a different history, or histories? Is there a history of how the duality of sex was established, a genealogy that might expose the binary options as variable construction? Are the ostensibly natural facts of sex discursively produced

by various scientific discourses in the service of other political and social interests? If the immutable character of sex is contested, perhaps this construct called 'sex' is as culturally constructed as gender, indeed, perhaps it was always already gender, with the consequence that the distinction between sex and gender turns out to be no distinction at all. (6–7)

Butler's point is not only that sex does not determine gender, but also that sex stands in no particularly privileged or even necessary relation to gender. This means that gender does not have to be about "men" and "women." It can just as probably be about "men" and "not-men"—a slight but extremely significant difference in social classification that opens up different social configurations and facilitates the production of different identities, understandings, relationships, and imaginings.

One of those imaginings is that of the ostentatiously effeminate male homosexual. Although I have been careful in this book to discuss only the ethnographic situation that I myself know best, even a brief glance through the ethnographic literature on Latin America reveals the existence, throughout this area, of males who act and think in ways very similar to the travestis of Salvador. Called *maricón, cochón, joto, marica, pajara, loca,* or any number of other names, depending on where one finds them (for a sampling, see Murray and Dynes 1987; and Dynes 1987), these males all appear to share certain behavioral characteristics, and they seem to be thought of in quite similar ways throughout Latin America, even though the majority of them do not go so far as to continually wear female clothing and modify their bodies in the ways that travestis do.[9] These effeminate males, wherever they appear, have always presented something of a conundrum for researchers, who are uncertain how to understand them. The conundrum has been generated largely because researchers have assumed that gender is a cultural reading of biological males and females and that there are, therefore, two genders—man and woman. From this perspective, they have been unable to comprehend effeminate male homosexuals, because those males do not fit into that particular binary. Individuals like travestis are clearly not women, but, culturally speaking, they are not men either. So what are they? Most analyses take the rather hedging line that they are "not quite men, not quite women" (Lancaster 1992:274); or they refer to them, in melancholy tonalities that certainly have no resonance among the travestis I know, as "failed" men (Parker 1995:244). Some scholars even go so far as to suggest in starkly censorious language that effeminate homosexuals who dress in women's clothing and modify their bodies to make them more feminine are "stealing femininity" from those to whom it properly belongs.[10]

Instead of understanding travesti social and bodily practices in terms

of failure or as a form of theft (and thereby adding another dimension—
an existential one, no less—to the stereotype of travestis as criminals),
what would happen if we asked whether there is a perspective from
which travesti actions, opinions, and subjectivities might be seen as
commonsensical, cogent, and perfectly logical? And what sorts of understandings would we gain if we argued that femininity, seen from
within the system in which travestis emerge and organize their lives,
properly belongs not just to anatomical women, but to all individuals
who enjoy penetration? This is certainly how travestis see things, which
is why they go to so much trouble (and pain) to alter their physiog-
nomies and why they express annoyance at homosexual males who
"hide" their inherent femininity under the masquerade of what travestis
consider to be male drag, thereby leaving travestis to fight their battles
and bear the weighty burden of demonstrating to the world that homosexuals do exist. There is also ample evidence that others have a similar
perspective on sexuality and gender. The doctor who gave Martinha her
first hormone injections and the pharmacist who procured for Adriana
her first boxes of birth-control pills clearly understood travesti desire in
terms of a femininity that could be improved upon and enhanced.
Women like the one who complimented Elisabeth on her elegance are
expressing something of the same sentiment. And this is not even to
mention boyfriends, or the clients of travestis, who, as Pastinha and
Magdala explained clearly, desire travestis with big, feminine bundas
and breasts and who, as I discussed in the previous chapter, often glee-
fully become "not-men" themselves when they pay a travesti to penetrate them.

If we understand masculinity and femininity not as adhering to or
arising from male and female bodies but, instead, as signs or processes
that are invoked and enacted through specific practices, then we are in a
much better position to begin to understand travesti subjectivity. If, furthermore, we listen for the underlying understandings about sex, gender,
and sexuality that make it logical and sensible for travestis to modify
their bodies, to refer to themselves and their clients as "she," and to disparage and leave their boyfriends because they have expressed an interest in the travesti's penis, then we will be able to move beyond a view of
travestis as being campy failed men (at best) or misguided gender-
snatchers (at worst). If we do all that, and engage with travesti ideas
and practices seriously—without assuming that they are engaged in
a futile or tragic attempt to slip or squeeze themselves into the
"wrong" gender—then what we might hear, in the end, is the voices of
travestis perceptively and incisively reading off and enunciating core

messages generated by their culture's arrangements of sexuality, gender, and sex.

It is important to understand that the claim I am making here is that travestis share a gender with women, not that they *are* women (or that women are travestis—even if that latter proposition might be a fruitful one to explore further). The distinction is crucial. Individual travestis will not always or necessarily share individual women's roles, goals, or social status. Just as the worldviews, self-images, social statuses, and possibilities of, say, a poor black mother, a single mulatta prostitute, and a rich white businesswoman in Brazil (to draw on stereotypical images that have a high salience throughout the country) differ dramatically, even though all those individuals share a gender, so can individual travestis be interpreted as having, in some instances and from some points of view, more social status, independence, and power than individual women—even though they all share a gender. On the other hand, in other contexts and from other perspectives they will have much less status, independence, and power than individual women.

However, inasmuch as travestis share the same gender with women, they are understood to share (and they feel themselves to share) with women a whole spectrum of tastes, perceptions, behaviors, styles, feelings, and desires. And one of the most important of those desires (for travestis, *the* most important and fundamental one) is understood and felt to be the desire to attract and be attractive for persons of the opposite gender. This desire puts pressure on individuals to attempt to approximate cultural ideals of beauty, thereby drawing them into patriarchal imperatives that guide aesthetic values and frame the direction and content of the erotic gaze. And even though attractive male bodies get quite a lot of attention and exposure in Brazil, the pressure to conform to cultural ideals of beauty there—as in most other societies—is much stronger on females than on males. In all these societies, the ones who are culturally incited to look (with all the subtexts of power and control that that action can imply) are males, and the ones who are exhorted to desire to be looked *at* are females.

In Brazil, the paragon of beauty, the body that is continually held forth, disseminated, and extolled as desirable—in the media, in popular music, during Carnival, and in the day-to-day public practices of both men and women (comments and catcalls from groups of males at women passing by; "dental floss" bikinis worn by women at the beach)—is a feminine body with smallish breasts, ample buttocks, and high, wide hips. Anyone wishing to be considered desirable to a "man" should do what she can to approximate that ideal. And this, of course, is precisely what travestis do. There is nothing confused or odd about travesti perceptions of gender; quite the opposite. They understand their desire for men in the culturally appropriate way (that is, as heterosexual desire), and they lay claim to and incorporate the ideals of beauty that their culture offers them in order to be attractive for those men—both "real men" (i.e., boyfriends, some clients and vícios) and males who publicly "pretend to be men" (clients and vícios who enjoy being penetrated).[11]

In all of this, there is one gendered, absolutely central, culturally incited feminine desire that is absent from travesti presentations or understandings of themselves—namely, the desire for motherhood. I have had nothing to say about maternal feelings or desires among travestis in this book largely because they hardly exist. Travestis do sometimes send money and presents to their younger siblings and relatives, and I know of three travestis in Salvador who have assumed the main fostering responsibilities for a child (in two cases the child is the daughter of a close relative, in the other case the daughter of a lesbian prostitute friend). But talk about children and extended interaction with children play no role in the lives of the vast majority of travestis—certainly not in the lives of the travestis I know well. Children who live in the area in which travestis reside are spoken to, teased, and sometimes even played with for brief moments (travestis will kick a ball once or twice in a game of soccer being played on the street by little boys, or they may suddenly hop in and take a turn when little girls bring out some cords and play double Dutch jump rope). But whenever children are spoken about, it is exclusively in terms of their being a burden. All travestis are acquainted with any number of stressed and haggard women who have been abandoned by the fathers of their children and who spend their days struggling to scrape together enough money to be able to feed and care for those children. Surrounded by such women, travestis see few advantages in having children—indeed, they regularly express relief that they can "give their ass" to as many men as they want and not risk getting pregnant, whereas women who "give their buceta" often end up with another mouth to feed. (This is, perhaps not surprisingly, yet another area in which travestis can readily argue that they are superior to women.)

So while it could be argued that lack of maternal desires, or of social rewards for such desires, suggests that travestis do not belong to the same gendered category as women, it is important to remember that the gendered category of "woman" is a broad and complex one, encompassing many different desires and subjectivities. Not all women desire to be mothers, or are mothers, or receive social recognition and status for being mothers. Furthermore, in a Latin country like Brazil, the gendered category "woman" is in many important respects structured along a complex and compelling binary of its own—that of Virgin Mother and Whore. From this perspective, it is possible to interpret the absence of maternal desires in the discourse of travestis as a reflex of *that* binary: travestis align themselves, exuberantly and literally, with the Whore avatar of Latin womanhood, not the Mother incarnation. But because motherhood is indisputably a crucial component of female roles and desires in Brazil (as in most other places) in that a female may not be considered to have achieved full womanhood without it, travestis—like female prostitutes?—can only ever remain incomplete, or failed, women (to use a language that *does* have, as I have documented, a certain resonance among travestis).[12]

Travestis as incomplete or failed women is a theme that also surfaces in another context: the commonplace refusal in Brazil to treat travestis in accordance with their gender. Throughout the country, people generally do not refer to travestis as "she"; and many people, travestis will be the first to tell you, seem to enjoy going out of their way to offend travestis by addressing them loudly and mockingly as "o senhor" (Sir or Mr.). As I have discussed, the fact that the word *travesti* is grammatically masculine makes it not only easy but logical to address the word's referent using masculine forms.

There are certainly many reasons why Brazilians generally mock travestis and contest individual travestis' claims to femininity by calling them *senhor*. Not least among these reasons are travestis' strong associations with homosexuality, prostitution, and AIDS—all highly stigmatized issues that tend to elicit harsh condemnation and censure from many people. Refusing to acknowledge travestis' gender is one readily available way of refusing to acknowledge their right to exist at all. It is a way of putting travestis back in their (decently gendered) place; a way of denying and defending against the possibilities that exist within the gender system for males to shift from one category to the other. But during the time I have spent in Brazil, I have also noted that the harshest scorn is reserved for unattractive travestis. Travestis like Roberta Close and some of my own acquaintances in Salvador who closely approximate cultural ideals of feminine beauty are generally not publicly insulted and mocked and addressed as men. On the contrary, such travestis are often admired and regarded with a kind of awe. One conclusion I draw from this is that the commonplace denial of travestis' gender as "not-men" may be not so much a reaction against them as gender crossers as it is a reaction against unattractiveness in people (women and other not-men) whose job it is to make themselves attractive for men. Seen in this light, some of the hostility against (unattractive) travestis becomes intelligible as a reaction against them as incomplete or failed women—not failed men, as more orthodox interpretations have argued.

It is difficult to speculate about how widespread or dominant the binary gender system consisting of "men" and "not-men" that I am postulating might be. In a society as divided and diverse as Brazil, many different and competing discourses and understandings about sexuality and gender will be available in different ways to different individuals. And because I have worked only with travestis, one contentious issue that I am ultimately unable to fully resolve here is the extent to which women (both heterosexual and lesbian) perceive their bodies, desires, and identities to be implicated in a gendered framework that is grounded in penetrative sexuality. Unfortunately, several decades of sociological, anthropological, and (especially since AIDS) public health work focusing on women has not resulted in any material that can unambiguously shed light on that issue.[13] The standard volume on the sexuality of Brazilian women, a five-hundred-page tome entitled *The Sexuality of Brazilian Women: Body and Social Class in Brazil* (Muraro 1983), contains no information about how women think about penetration, nor does it contain any analysis of what role a woman's first heterosexual intercourse and later penetration play in her subjective understandings of her body or her social roles.[14] Richard Parker's rich analysis (1991) of Brazilian sexual symbolism contains no accounts of how women subjectively experience penetration. Neither are there any published analyses, to my knowledge, that discuss sexual practices among Brazilian lesbians—particularly lower-class lesbians, who, like Salvadorean travestis, organize their affective and erotic relationships relatively unaware of, and uninfluenced by, North American trends. Lack of any material of this kind makes it difficult to actually prove or disprove my argument that the configurations of gender articulated and practiced by travestis are distillations of patterns that exist throughout Brazilian society and influence many different individuals' perceptions and practices of gender.

At the same time, though, some of the idioms used in Brazil and other Latin American societies to talk about sex do suggest that the significance that travestis attach to penetration as an engendering act is not particularly distorted or idiosyncratic. A recent article by the Brazilian sociologist Maria Betânia Ávila and the psychologist Taciana Gouveia, for example, points out that

> In our society, the idea that we become men or women almost exclusively from the moment of sexual relations is still very much alive. The expres-

sions "she became a woman" (*tornou-se mulher*) and "he turned into a man" (*virou homem*) are still common enough when one speaks of someone after their first sexual relation. . . . The boundary is still genital sex and penetration; [they constitute] the delimiting and limiting space of who is a man or a woman, of roles, and of positions. (1996:167; see also Goldstein 1994:923–24)

The existence of similar expressions in Mexico has been noted by Annick Prieur (1998, 1996, 1994a) and Marit Melhuus (forthcoming, 1996). Both authors have discussed the role that penetration plays in heterosexual relations, and both have argued that in Mexico, penetration is a creative act that has dramatic social consequences for both men and women. Melhuus contends that "[t]he cultural implications of penetration . . . are such that they have important ramifications for both identity and social position, for both women and men. For women, penetration may represent the glories of motherhood, or her fall from grace" (forthcoming; see also Parker 1991:51).

Arguments like these suggest that the pivotal role that travestis accord penetration in their understandings and practices of gender may very well be expressive of much wider cultural concerns, in much the same way that the pivotal role accorded genitals by North American transsexuals is expressive of a set of widespread, tacit understandings about gender that they make explicit, not invent. The existence throughout Latin America of similar ideas about penetration and of effeminate male homosexuals who resemble travestis also indicates that the configurations of gender that travestis elaborate and draw on may extend far beyond the city limits of Salvador. But whatever the demographic and areal extension of these configurations, it is clear that travestis did not just pull their understandings of sex, gender, and sexuality out of thin air. On the contrary, it is very possible that they have distilled and clarified a relationship between sex, sexuality, and gender that may prove to be widespread throughout much of Latin America.[15]

At the very least, it would seem that in the end, those Brazilian commentators I mentioned in the introduction to this book—the ones who look at travestis and see in them a symbol of Brazil itself—might be more accurate than they know. But rather than signaling a national penchant for deceptive appearances, or the illusion of democracy, or a dreaded crisis of virility, the real message parlayed by travestis is that Brazilian bodies, desires, and subjectivities are configured in a manner that allows and even encourages the elaboration of cultural spaces such as those inhabited by the travesti. Whether those commentators or anyone else likes it or not, travestis will continue inhabiting those spaces, luxuriating in their possibilities, fashioning their bodies to suit their desires, and attempting to survive and maybe even prosper in a society that disparages them and regularly tries to hurt and destroy them. And as the sun sets and the streetlamps begin to glimmer, travestis will continue to tuck in their penises, fluff up their hair, and sail out onto the streets—resplendent in their minimalist clothing, protected by their tiny nail scissors, and ready for another round of "battle" on the streets where they work.

Notes

INTRODUCTION

1. Others who do something similar are those Euro-American transsexuals who wish to be identified publicly *as* transsexuals (see, e.g., Bornstein 1994; Stone 1991; and Hausman 1995:195–200). And many Indian *hijras*, of course, dramatically alter their own bodies (they slice off their penis and scrotum) without claiming to be women (Nanda 1990, 1993).

2. Conrad Kottak's book *Prime Time Society* (1990:168–74) contains a short discussion about Roberta Close and her prominence as a national sex symbol.

3. All quotations are from the magazine *Nova* 1984.96 (issue unknown). Unless otherwise noted, all translations throughout this book are my own.

4. The anthropologists Hélio Silva and Cristina de Oliveira Florentino estimate that the Rio de Janeiro equivalents of daily tabloids like the British *Sun* or *Daily News* feature articles about travestis on the average at least twice a week (1996:107).

5. Hélio Silva subsequently published another book on the material that he gathered for his original study of travestis. However, as he himself states, the newer work is more of "an epilogue or a postscript" to the 1993 study than it is a new monograph (Silva 1996:9). As such, it contains little new material and seems intended primarily as a forum that allows him to extend some of the observations made in the 1993 book, and to respond to reviews of it.

6. Throughout this eight-month period, I also rented a room in an apartment in the center of town, fifteen minutes' walk from São Francisco Street. This is where I kept my tape recorders, camera, field notes, etc., and it was here where Keila Simpsom and I completed most of the transcription work. I normally arrived at the apartment about eight in the morning and stayed writing field notes until about lunchtime, when I returned to São Francisco Street to see if anybody had woken up yet. Three or four days a week, I returned to the apartment at about 3 P.M. and was joined there by Keila, who sat transcribing tapes with me until about 7 P.M.

7. The word *viado* is homophonous with *veado*, which means "deer" (apparently, *viado* originally derived from reference to that animal, which is popularly perceived to be frail and delicate). The correspondence between the words for "faggot" and "deer" gives rise to endless punning throughout Brazil. *Bicha* is the feminine form of *bicho*, a word that designates nonhuman animate things, ranging from germs and parasites to animals. Parker (1991:45–46) provides a thorough contextualization of both terms in the Brazilian sexual vocabulary.

8. Annick Prieur's concern was different, although I was too inexperienced in the ways of Latin American homosexuality to understand that at the time. She tells me that she never meant to express doubts that I, as a man, would be accepted by travestis. Her worry was that I would be under pressure to enter into a sexual relationship with a travesti: "I know that among the *jotas* I worked with it would have been a

contest to see who could bag you [*nedlegge deg*]—to see how big your penis was and if you let yourself be penetrated," she wrote me in an email message on 8 November 1997. She was concerned that my ability to do fieldwork would potentially be damaged no matter how I decided to resolve that issue.

I think I misunderstood Annick's concern because before I started working in Salvador it hadn't occurred to me that travestis might not understand that as a gay man I liked men, not men who looked like women. As I mention in the main text, this never really was a problem, and most travestis pretty much immediately defined me, when I identified myself as a gay man, as one of the girls. Once, though, when I had been in Salvador for only a few weeks, a travesti did explicitly come on to me.

This happened late at night at a club where I had been dancing with travestis. At one point, a travesti whom I had seen around but never spoken to called me over to the bar and asked me to buy her a beer. I did, and we sat and talked (or mostly she talked). Then she said something that I did not understand, and she began running her fingers through my hair and massaging my scalp. I was a bit nonplussed, but at that very early stage of my fieldwork, my main concern was to ingratiate myself with travestis and not give them any reason to think that I might find them unpleasant or repellent. Also, the scalp massage felt very nice.

When we finished the beer, my companion pulled me up onto the dance floor and put her arms around me. This is when the alarm bells started ringing. She then turned her back to me and, gyrating sensuously, she took my hands and guided them up *under* her halter top, so that I suddenly found myself grasping two tiny, hormone-filled breasts. I stiffened. I saw that the travestis with whom I had come to the club, and who knew me better, were staring at me with consternation. I began to sweat and wonder what advice the anthropological fieldwork manuals would have for this situation. After a few (very long) minutes, I somehow managed to politely disengage myself from the breasts and leave the club. I suppose the look on my face during the dance was sufficiently pained to convey a message that travestis really weren't my thing, because nobody ever mentioned the incident to me afterwards. And no travesti ever tried to seduce me again.

9. There is also a paper in English on travestis in Salvador—Cornwall 1994. As far as I can see, however, all the ethnographic data on travestis in that article are drawn from Oliveira's unpublished master's thesis—which later became her 1994 monograph—and from other published sources. Furthermore, the author is clearly more interested in (and knowledgeable about) the Afro-Brazilian religion candomblé than she is in travestis, and that interest seems to have compelled her to unquestioningly accept some highly inaccurate information about travestis, such as claims by members of the Grupo Gay da Bahia that 90 percent of the travestis in Salvador are devotees of candomblé. I discuss this in chapter 2, note 20.

10. All of the tape recordings of spontaneously occurring speech and three of the interviews were transcribed by me, together with Keila Simpsom. With two sets of headphones, we listened to the same tape, and I transcribed the speech, relying on Keila for advice and for explanations concerning background information, slang expressions, the history of speakers' relations with one another, etc. The remaining interviews (except for one that was transcribed by Magda Carvalho and another by Joceval Santana) were transcribed by Inês Alfano, a professional transcriptionist. When they were completed, all transcripts were double-checked by Keila and

myself, by going through the text as we sat together listening to the tape. In some cases, the transcript of an interview was also checked through together with the travesti who had given the interview.

Readers of Portuguese will note that I have not used standard spelling in the texts. Rather, I have attempted to preserve the flavor of the speech patterns of individual travestis. Hence, the spellings used reflect the pronunciation of different speakers.

CHAPTER ONE

1. The responses given by travestis in this questionnaire were analyzed by Luiz Mott and Marcelo Ferreira de Cerqueira. They published this material in 1997 as *Os travestis de Bahia & a AIDS: Prostituição, silicone e drogas* (The travestis of Bahia and AIDS: Prostitution, silicone, and drugs)—a title that manages, in a few words, to invoke and reinforce virtually every public fear about travestis. Whatever the intentions of the authors may have been with this report, all travestis I know who have read it find it offensive in the extreme and interpret it as a direct provocation against travestis. Readers consider the tone of the report to be insulting, and they object to the highly pejorative terms—such as *rapazes de peito* (boys with breasts)—that are used throughout the text to denote travestis.

While I am deeply respectful of much of the activist work carried out by Mott and de Cerqueira, I find it difficult to disagree with travesti readers who feel insulted by the text. The language is consistently patronizing and sensationalistic, and some of the assertions, such as the outrageous claim that "[s]ome travestis end up applying such exaggerated quantities of silicone to their buttocks that they have to dig a crater (*uma cratera*) in their mattress to accommodate their enormous backsides" (14), are hard to interpret as anything other than deliberately malicious slurs.

Because the report derives much of its authority from the authors' claims that their conclusions are based on "an extensive familiarity between the interviewers and the informants" (4), I feel obliged to note here that in fact, the vast majority of the questionnaires were *not* administered by the authors of the report (who, furthermore, were personally acquainted with almost none of the travestis interviewed) but by Keila, who was neither consulted about the analysis nor acknowledged in the report for her work in administering the questionnaires. The seventy questions were asked by a harried Keila to travestis standing impatiently in a queue in the middle of São Francisco Street, waiting to receive free condoms (they were denied condoms if they refused to answer the questionnaire). Based on answers that those travestis gave to questions such as "Do you think you are HIV positive?" (asked in full hearing of everyone on the street) and "If you could, would you change your life?" (a question unlikely to elicit a negative response from most people), Mott and de Cerqueira draw far-reaching conclusions about the lives of travestis and about how interventions to "improve" those lives might be organized

2. The only published study of which I am aware that specifically discusses the HIV antibody status of travestis is a brief article by Italian doctors who tested forty-nine Brazilian travestis who were attending (for reasons unexplained in the paper) an HIV clinic in Rome. Thirty-nine of them, or 79.6 percent, tested HIV positive (Gattari et al. 1994). In addition to this, the Brazilian daily *Folha de São Paulo* (12 October 1996) printed a short article on a study of travesti seropositivity conducted in São

Paulo by a nurse. Of 233 travestis included in that study, 51.5 percent tested HIV positive. The article gave no data concerning how the study was conducted or how the travestis involved were recruited, which makes it difficult to know how to interpret such findings in relation to the city's (or the nation's) travesti population. The two reports do, however, lend some confirmation to my own suspicions that HIV seropositivity remains high among travestis, despite widespread knowledge about HIV transmission and despite travestis' widespread use of condoms while working.

3. In her autobiography *A Princesa,* the Brazilian travesti Fernanda Farias de Albuquerque (Albuquerque and Janelli 1995:99) notes that two specific practices marked the transition when one of her regular clients became her boyfriend. The first was that he stopped paying Fernanda for sex. The second was that he stopped using condoms while penetrating her. Travestis' unwillingness to use condoms with their boyfriends and husbands has exact parallels in the literature on female prostitution in Europe and the United States (e.g., Davies and Feldman 1997; Day 1990; Faugier and Sargeant 1997; McKeganey and Barnard 1996). Prostitutes commonly seem to feel that condoms signify work, and therefore that asking a boyfriend to use a condom would be like redefining him as a client.

4. In Rio de Janeiro alone, in 1996, more than sixty bystanders were hit by stray bullets, and twenty died (*Istoé,* 13 November 1996:40–41). According to recent statistics, the homicide rate in Rio (60.74 murders per 100,000 inhabitants) is *double* that of New York (30.66 per 100,000), though lower than the rate for Washington, D.C. (77.77 per 100,000) (Soares et al. 1996).

5. And, one might add, in the lives of homosexuals generally. Citing a recent report on the situation of homosexuals around the world (Amnesty International 1997), the weekly magazine *Istoé* (which is the Brazilian equivalent of *Newsweek*) ran a cover story on how "Brazil [is] one of the countries with the most discrimination against homosexuals" (2 July 1997). Homophobia and hate crimes against gay men, lesbians, and travestis in Brazil are also documented and discussed in Mott 1996.

6. In fact, the DJC was officially dissolved by President José Sarney in September 1989, six months before Collor de Mello assumed office. That travestis associate the end of the DJC with Collor is probably a reflection of the amount of time it took to implement the decree that dissolved the vice squad.

7. On at least two occasions, *A Tarde* has published explicit calls to murder homosexuals: "Keep Salvador clean, kill a faggot every day!" (*Mantenha Salvador limpa, mate uma bicha todo dia!*) and "To kill a homosexual is not a crime, it's hunting" (*Matar veado não é crime, é caçada*). Both these exhortations were authored by the newspaper's in-house film critic, José Augusto Berbet (cited in Mott 1996:1). Berbet impressively manages to squeeze references to homosexuality into so many of the reviews he writes that one would be tempted to call him a queer analyst if his column weren't so consistently full of hate. At least once a week, and sometimes as many as three times a week, Berbet finds excuses to opine on homosexuality and homosexuals in ways that range from the gratuitous (in a review of the newly released film *The Island of Dr. Moreau* [23 October 1996], Berbet closes with: "Happily, on the island there is no deer-man [*veado-homem*], something which, unfortunately, exists in abundance in Bahia") to the tacky (his review of *A Night in Cairo* [7 October 1996] comments, "Seeing the film today, it seems comic for different reasons. Today we know that Ramon Novarro was an invert [*falso-ao-corpo*] and was killed in the faggot way—murdered

by young men he took to his apartment. *Bichas* only die of two things, AIDS and being murdered by partners who want to rob them") to the sinister: his review of a film called *Starship Troopers* (25 October 1996) draws a parallel between AIDS and a disease that apparently features in the movie. "There the disease began just like it did here on Earth, with inverts *(invertidos)* propagating it among the population. . . . In the film, the solution is to exterminate the transmitters. I guess it's too late [to do that in real life], they've already disseminated it."

8. It is interesting to note in this context that many *blocos de travestidos* have rules that explicitly prohibit openly homosexual men from joining (Félix and Nery 1993:165–66).

9. Without wishing to make too much of the parallel (given that it is drawn from a very different society), I still find it interesting to compare travestis' mistrust of one another with Roberta Perkins's description of the transsexual community in Sydney, Australia (1996:55):

> [M]any of the girls complain of bitchiness within the group. With so much low self-esteem, insecurity and superficial props, hostility that is internalised as a result of individual sufferings, when it does surface, tends to be aimed laterally at one another, rather than vertically in the direction of the real source of their oppression. Perhaps each girl sees in the others a reflection of herself and a reminder of her guilt as the reason she has been made to suffer. . . . [R]ather than a community of supportive people cooperating to offer a united front and to close ranks against oppression, what has occurred is a community of guilt-ridden, fearful and divided people, who can be scorned, laughed at and jeered at as one.

CHAPTER TWO

1. Even when same-sex activities are featured in transsexual autobiographies, it is only to make the point that sex is not what transsexualism is about. Jan Morris, for example, who informs us early on in her account of her sex change that transsexualism "is not a sexual mode or preference. It is not an act of sex at all" (1987:15), mentions public school sex with other boys principally to underscore that she was not particularly interested. "I think it a telling fact that of those first sexual experiences," she explains in characteristically lush prose, "I remember most vividly, and most voluptuously, not the clumsy embraces of Bolsover Major, not the heavy breathing of his passion or his sinuous techniques of trouser-removal, but the slightly rotted sensation of the hay beneath my body, and the smell of fermenting apples from the barn below" (30).

2. This phrase is part of a derogatory call shouted after travestis and effeminate males in northeastern Brazil. Here, effeminate males—who are all assumed to be homosexual—are called *frango*, which literally means "chicken." People shout out the following, often with one person yelling one part, and other people responding with the other part:

A: Bota a agua na fogo!   A: Put water on to boil!
B: Por quê?   B: Why?
A or C: Para pelar o frango! A or C: To skin the chicken/faggot!

3. When I was sitting on a doorstep on São Francisco Street going through the text of this chapter with Keila, she burst out laughing when we got to the word "dilated" that Mabel had chosen here. Keila clearly thought it an odd and funny choice of words, not least because Mabel mispronounces it (the standard pronunciation is "dilatei," not "delatei"), and she hollered up the street at Mabel, "Ô Mabel, a delatada!"—Oh Mabel, Miss Dilated! Mabel responded with a smile and a dismissive flick of her hair.

4. Note that one of the adjectives Keila uses here (*reprimida*) is inflected with a grammatically feminine ending and the other (*depressivo*) is grammatically masculine. Grammatical gender mixing of this nature is common in travestis' narratives about their past. Unlike transsexuals, who generally spend a great deal of time concealing their past or reconstructing it to make it correspond with their postoperative sex (Bolin 1988; Garfinkel 1967; Kessler and McKenna 1985; Shapiro 1991), travestis usually divide their past into "when I was a boy" (*quando eu era boy*) and "after I became a travesti" (*eu já virei* [or *botei*] *travesti*). They tend to use masculine articles and adjectival endings when talking about their "boy" period, and feminine grammatical forms when discussing their lives after the point at which they consider they became travestis. This gender-referencing system works smoothly as long as travestis are talking about what other people said to them or thought about them (for example, when they say that a person said something like "Boy, you're little"). But when they reflect about how they felt or what they thought as children, the system becomes unwieldy, because the ontological grounding of the discourse can never be entirely clear-cut. When Keila responds to my question about how she felt after her experience with José Silva, is she directly reporting the thoughts that passed through the head of an eleven-year-old boy (in which case she should use masculine forms), or is she reporting what she now, as an adult travesti, thinks that the boy, who in some sense knew that he would later become a travesti (especially after the experience she is talking about here), must have thought, or should have thought, at the time (in which case feminine forms might be appropriate)? The irresolvable indeterminacy of the identity of the speaking subject in this kind of discourse results in travestis often doing what Keila does here, that is, mixing gendered grammatical forms in narratives of their past.

5. This is called *fazer o chuchu* (do the *chuchu*) by travestis. A *chuchu* is an avocado-sized, light green vegetable with small protrusions that resemble whiskers.

6. This *novela* and the character Babalu are discussed in Browning 1996 and 1998.

7. Tensions in the relationship between travestis and transformistas in Salvador are similar in many ways to the antagonisms that Esther Newton's monograph *Mother Camp* (1972) documents between "street fairies" and "stage impersonators" in the United States.

8. The quotations are translations from the information and instruction leaflets that come folded in the small boxes in which Benzoginoestril and Perlutan, respectively, are purchased.

9. The price for a month's supply of hormones in late 1996 ranged from 3.40 to 5.25 reais (about the same in dollars), depending on the brand.

10. Travestis also inject silicone into many other places, such as their cheeks, arms, and forehead. Several travestis told me that travestis will put silicone anywhere, *do pé à testa*—from the bottoms of their feet to the top of their head. Keila told

mc of a travesti who went so far as to inject silicone into her knuckles, to make them look smoother. After this application, the travesti could never again straight out her fingers, Keila said. But they sure looked smooth.

11. The medication most commonly used by travestis for this purpose is called Decadronal. Decadronal is a steroid preparation for the relief of severe rheumatism and allergic or asthmatic reactions. One of its many side effects is that it stimulates the appetite, which is the reason travestis take it. And, as always, they take a lot of it. Instructions accompanying the medication advise that one 2 ml ampoule be injected every one to three weeks in the most severe cases. It is not unusual for travestis wanting to gain weight to inject several ampoules at once.

12. Despite a voluminous literature, there is still no firm consensus within the medical community about the effects of silicone on the human body. Much of the evidence does, however, seem to indicate links between silicone and severe health disorders such as connective-tissue disease and lupus. As a result of that evidence, together with a growing number of lawsuits in the United States throughout the 1980s and early 1990s and the inability of the silicone manufacturers to prove that their implants were safe, the U.S. Food and Drug Administration (FDA) in 1992 imposed a total ban on implants, except in clinical trials of breast reconstruction after cancer surgery. Those same factors also resulted, in 1994, in the largest class-action settlement in history. Silicone-implant manufacturers agreed to establish a fund of $4.25 billion (known as the Breast Implant Global Settlement) that would pay off the approximately four hundred thousand claims in the suit, the litigants' lawyers, and apparently healthy individuals with implants who became ill over the next thirty years. (The settlement collapsed a year after it was crafted, because the largest manufacturer of silicone implants, Dow Corning, declared bankruptcy).

Among the many recent summaries of the controversies over the medical evidence linking silicone to health problems are Shoaib, Patten, and Calkins 1994; Nemecek and Young 1993; Rohrich and Clark 1993; Ms. special issue, 1996; Park, Black, and Watson 1993; Yoshida et al. 1995; and Angell 1996. Medical reports on silicone injected directly into the body are rare, but see Chastre et al. 1987 for cases involving what they call "transsexual men" injecting silicone into their breasts; Bjerno et al. 1993 for a case of a male injecting what is known to be industrial silicone into his chest (an abbreviated version of this report, in English, is in Siemssen, Basse, and Bjerno 1992); and Behar et al. 1993 for a review of the medical literature on the topic.

13. I have been unable to confirm whether the sale of industrial silicone to private persons is in fact illegal under Brazilian law. The important point here is that everybody, including travestis, *believes* it to be illegal.

14. Carlinhos is also the only travesti I know who is always addressed by her male name (she uses her female name, Gabriela, only with clients, when she prostitutes herself in her spare time). Carlinhos has five liters of silicone in her lower body and two large breast implants, and there is little about her appearance that would clue a casual observer to the fact that she is male. However, the hospital where she works requires her to wear male clothing, and she wears a name tag with her male name printed on it. Everyone at work knows her as "Carlinhos Boneca" (Carlinhos Travesti), and she is so used to being addressed as "Carlinhos" that she maintains that name even outside work contexts.

15. A bombadeira who *quebra o copo* will refill a glass of silicone before the previ-

ous glassful has been used up. She then claims to have refilled the glass the agreed-upon number of times, and thus ends up with a surplus of silicone that she can sell to someone else.

16. Another famous Jô riposte was "The one who did me [i.e., the bombadeira who "did" Jô's body], the one who put her fingers on me, isn't going to do another one, sweetheart. Go cut yourself with a razor [out of envy], love. The one who did me will do no more. There will never be another Mamãe (*A que me fez, a que botou o dedo em mim não bota mais em nenhuma, querida. Se corte de gilete, meu bem. Quem me fez, não faz mais. Não vai ter uma outra Mamãe*).

17. Several travestis told me authoritatively that they had heard that Brazil's most famous transsexual, Roberta Close, had come to regret her genital surgery "because she can't orgasm like she needs to" (*porque ela não tem o gozo que ela precisa*).

18. This idea corresponds to, and possibly arises from, a widespread belief in Brazil that accumulated sexual tension in anyone "sobe para a cabeça" (rises to the head) and results in irrational behavior. Exactly *what* rises to the head seems never to be considered by people who habitually use the phrase "subiu para a cabeça" (it rose to the head) to explain other people's seemingly crazy actions or words.

19. In a lengthy magazine interview that I discovered in the archives of the Grupo Gay da Bahia without a source or date, a twenty-six-year-old travesti named Isa, from São Paulo, talked about sex-change operations in language that was similar to what I heard among travestis in Salvador. When asked by the reporter what she thought of travestis who wanted a sex-change operation, Isa responded:

> São bichas doentes, não dou mais de três anos para elas ficarem completa-mente loucas, porque não vão mais ter por onde gozar. Elas vão tirar o pênis, e as bolas fora, elas vão usar só o saco pra virar dentro e fazer a boceta. É uma pessoa castrada, que não vai mais ter prazer pra nada . . . [O] buraco . . . fede demais, porque é o saco onde o esperma é gerado, e aquilo aberto é horrível.

> They're sick bichas, I don't give them more than three years before they go completely crazy, because they don't have anywhere to ejaculate. They re-move the penis and the testicles and they just use the scrotum turned inside out to make a cunt. It's a castrated person who won't have any more pleasure at all . . . [The] hole [i.e., the constructed vagina] . . . smells terrible, because the scrotum is where the sperm is generated, and when that is opened up, it's horrible.

20. Magdala was also one of the *two* travestis in Salvador who were actively in-volved in candomblé, having been attending and assisting candomblés since age seven and having achieved the ritual rank of *abicu*. Because of her long experience and deep knowledge of candomblé, Magdala was paid by some travestis to *receber o santo*—"receive saints" (i.e., allow her body to be temporarily inhabited by minor candomblé deities, called *pombas giras* and *padilhas*, all of whom are female and the ma-jority of whom are prostitutes) and tell them how to win over men they were inter-ested in.

Ever since the American anthropologist Ruth Landes published her landmark ethnography of Bahian candomblés, *The City of Women* (1947), there has been con-siderable and often heated discussion over the preponderance and the place of homosexuality and homosexuals in candomblé (the most recent and rewarding summary of this discussion is in Birman 1995; see also Fry 1995 and Murray forthcoming for English-language summaries). Although neither Landes, Peter Fry, Patrícia Birman, Jim Wafer (1991), nor anybody else who has written about homosexual participation in candomblé *terreiros* (ritual houses) has reported active participation by travestis (the discussion is always about effeminate homosexual men, *not* travestis), there is something of a myth circulating both within Brazil and among foreign scholars concerned with Brazil that travestis are heavily involved in candomblé. This myth most recently appeared in Andrea Cornwall's 1994 paper on travestis in Salvador—a paper that, as I have already noted (see preface, n. 9), seems not to have been based on any independent fieldwork among travestis. Cornwall states that "an estimated 90% of travestis are devotees of candomblé" (111), citing the Grupo Gay da Bahia as the source of this information. I do not know how anyone from the GGB can possibly have come up with this figure. It is grossly incorrect.

One reason for the confusion may be that many of the words used in travesti argot (words like *mona*, which means "travesti," *ocó*, which means "man," and *edi*, which means "ass") are derived from Yoruba, the African language in which many candomblé chants and rituals are performed. The historical basis and symbolic resonance of those words deserve further research, as Browning 1996 has noted. However, I want to stress that the Yoruba origin of many travesti slang words is not salient to many of the travestis who use them. Furthermore, a recent short dictionary of travesti slang from Rio de Janeiro (ASTRAL 1996) contains a great many more terms of Yoruba origin than are used in Salvador (about two-thirds of the words in that sixteen-page dictionary are not used among, or in many cases even known by, Salvador's travestis). This suggests to me that those words may not even have originated in Bahia at all (as seems commonly assumed) but in other parts of the country, such as Rio de Janeiro.

In any case, because the assertion that the majority of Salvador's travestis are devotees of candomblé risks being repeated and disseminated as fact, I wish to clearly state here that the overwhelming majority of travestis in Salvador maintain *no* active involvement in candomblé *terreiros*, and they cannot be considered "devotees" of candomblé in anything but the very weakest sense of the word.

Like a great percentage of the population of Salvador, the majority of travestis do believe in the power of the candomblé saints and of the ritual candomblé *mães-* and *pais-de-santo*. They also use candomblé instrumentally—they ask people who they think might know what they ought to do to improve their luck on the street or hook a particular man as a boyfriend. Many travestis follow whatever advice is offered to them and perform whatever small rituals they are told to perform, such as pouring bottles of herbal mixtures over their bodies, lighting candles for particular candomblé saints, placing small plates of food for them on the corners of crossroads or on small altars they keep in their rooms, or ritually cleansing their rooms with incense or rock salt. But few travestis know *why* they do these things (they only know that they should do them to effect desired changes). And no travesti (not even Magdala or the other travesti in Salvador who has attained a ritual rank) regularly participates in candomblé *terreiros* (as Cornwall 1994, with no supporting evidence, states that most travestis do). Indeed, most travestis in Salvador have *never* participated in a candomblé ceremony as adults.

21. The literal translation of this phrase is "to feel oneself woman," and out of context it could be read as meaning that travestis feel themselves to *be* women. As I have argued, and will continue to argue throughout this book, travestis do not feel themselves to be women. In all contexts in which it is used by travestis, the phrase *se sentir mulher* means "to feel *like* a woman," to feel as if one were a woman [even though one isn't]." Its contrastive opposite is *ser mulher*—"to be a woman." No travesti in Salvador ever claims to *ser mulher*, except as a joke, and travestis reading or hearing about transsexuals who make such claims regard them as disturbed, the victims of a psychosis (*uma psicose*).

22. Needless to say, it is not only travestis who are made to feel like women through their relationships with men. Many biological females also find themselves confirmed and fulfilled as women through the relationships they maintain with men. A quote from one of the women interviewed in Mirian Goldenberg's study of Brazilian middle-class women who were having affairs with married men, for example, could easily have been uttered by a travesti. Speaking about her lover, this woman commented, "For the first time, I feel like a real woman, treated like a woman" (*Pela primeira vez eu me sinto realmente mulher, tratada como mulher*) (1990:39).

CHAPTER THREE

1. I use the feminine pronoun here to highlight that the literature I am discussing concerns female, not male, prostitutes. Indeed, one of the most significant differences between how male and female prostitution are treated in the literature is that whereas male prostitution is often seen as an activity (see, e.g., West 1993; McNamara 1994; and Davies and Feldman 1997), female prostitution is portrayed as an identity (see also Marlowe 1997, for other reflections on differences between the representations of female and male prostitution). Even though travestis are biologically male, both this chapter and the following one build on and draw contrasts primarily with the literature on female prostitutes. There are two reasons for this. One is the fact that travestis self-identify and live as feminine homosexuals (and hence are different from the male prostitutes discussed in the literature, the majority of whom self-identify as masculine heterosexuals). The other reason is that it is in the literature on female prostitution where one finds the strongest claims made about the partners of prostitutes and about the relationship between a prostitute's work and her own sexual pleasure.

2. This is not to suggest that researchers like Barry, Høigård, and Finstad are unsympathetic to prostitutes as individuals, even if their writing about prostitutes does lend itself to some uncomfortable analogies with the "God-loves-homosexuals-but-hates-homosexuality" rhetoric of certain right-wing Christian groups. My point is that the vocal political opposition of Barry, Høigård, and Finstad to prostitution naturally influences the way in which they understand the private relationships of prostitutes, and it results in their classifying boyfriends almost definitionally as pimps. Høigård and Finstad's typology of pimps (1986:215), for example, which ranges from "boyfriend-pimp" (*kjærestehallik*) to "sex club pimp" (*sexklubbhallik*), makes it unclear whether it is ever possible for a boyfriend of a prostitute to *not* be a pimp.

3. When Tiane met Marília, he was working sometimes as a security officer at a parking lot. Marília told him to quit his job, and he has never worked since.

Michelle's lazy boyfriend Maurílio was also told to quit his security-guard job by his former travesti girlfriend. He, too, has never worked since.

4. The unmistakable implication of "God made woman for man and man for woman"—that all homosexuality, not just lesbianism, is unnatural—is always deflected in travesti talk by observing that male homosexuality is not problematic because men have the equipment needed to give one another pleasure. As Tina once put it in an interview with me:

Entendeu como é? Que Deus fez a mulher pro homem e o homem pra mulher. Como ai tem a mulher sa/a mulher sapatão e o homemsexual [sic], entendeu como é? . . . Mas o homemsexual tudo bem—um tem o negócio pra botar no outro, né? E a mulher? Fica aquela nojeira. Uma esfregando a buceta na outra, acho uma decepção.

You understand how it is? God made woman for man and man for woman. And there's like les/lesbians and homosexuals, you know? . . . But homosexuals, there's no problem—one has the thing to stick into the other, you know? But women? They can just make gross suds. One rubbing against the cunt of the other, I think it's a fraud.

Travesti understandings of and opinions about lesbianism are discussed in detail in Kulick 1998.

5. A recent monograph on female prostitutes in Rio de Janeiro claims that the stereotypical violent pimp who forces unwilling individuals into prostitution is, at least in the area in which the researcher worked, almost "extinct" (Moraes 1995: 149–56). See, however, Leite 1992 for an account of how men who do earn their living as stereotypical pimps operate in Rio.

6. This kind of reasoning is echoed in how some Brazilian women talk about their relationships to men. A woman interviewed by Mirian Goldenberg remarked, "I think men were made to be waited on by women. I love waiting on my men" (1990:48). Another woman talked about her lover in the following language: "It gives me pleasure (Me dá prazer) to do things for him, and I swear that he likes it. I want to do things that he likes because I am investing in the relationship. I like to cook for him, make him breakfast, lunch. It's different when you do things for pleasure and when you do them because you have to—because society tells you to do them. He doesn't demand anything from me" (39).

7. Viado should be understood here in its broad sense of "homosexual," not just as "travesti." It would seem that the system Edilson refers to is widespread in Brazil. Teresa Adada Sell's 1987 book Identidade Homossexual e Normas Sociais (Homosexual identity and social norms) is a series of interviews with homosexual men living in Florianópolis, capital of the southern state of Santa Catarina, at the opposite end of the country from Salvador. Many of the interviewees mention that macho men often expect to be (and usually are) paid if they have sex with a viado (35, 51–52, 155). Economic remuneration to macho men from effeminate homosexuals has also been reported in Ecuador (Streicker 1993), Mexico (Prieur 1996a), and Honduras (Fernandez 1996).

8. The sources of this information are sometimes rather unexpected. On São Francisco Street there lived a young boy of about eight whom several travestis

enjoyed teasing whenever he walked by, calling him "gostoso" (sexy) and telling him to come to them so they could kiss him. He was always upset by these attentions (which was precisely why travestis enjoyed showering them on him) and shouted back that he "didn't like viados." Once when he was walking down the street with his mother, a travesti called out to him that he was a "tesão" (i.e., he was turning them on). He complained to his mother that the viados always teased him and that he didn't like viados. The boy's mother, who sold drugs in the area and knew all the travestis on the street well, stopped in the middle of the street and answered him loudly, to the delight of the travestis standing in the doorway: "But you have to like viados. Because you like to eat and sleep, don't you? And I'm not gonna support you for the rest of your life" (*Você tem que gostar de viado mesmo. Que você gosta muito de comer e dormir, e eu não vou lhe sustentar pelo resto da sua vida*).

9. Two travestis living together as a couple are talked about as a *lesbian* couple, and one of the words used to describe the kind of sex they are publicly imagined as having is *roça-roça* (rub-rub)—the same word used to describe lesbian sex. See also Fry 1995:204.

10. See Murray 1995b:59 for similar statements in Latin American and Mediterranean societies that being anally penetrated can easily lead to an addictive, unquenchable desire for more.

11. At least some boyfriends are aware of this. When we were talking about whether he would ever allow a travesti to penetrate him, Edilson told me that "one likes travestis, right? And so we want to make that person happy, too, make them feel pleasure. But at the same time, we hold ourselves back (*a gente se segura*) because if we do that [i.e., "give" to a travesti], that person [the travesti] is gonna discriminate against us, think that we're viados too (*vai discriminar a gente, achar que a gente é viado também*). And then we'll be seen in a bad light by them (*já fica mal visto por elas mesmo*)." And here Edilson began quoting abuse that he had heard many travestis hurl at boyfriends they were in the process of leaving: "Ah, who do you think you are? You gave me your ass! I penetrated your ass, you sucked my dick! You think you're so great, but the other day you were on top of my dick! Giving all night long!" (*Ah quem é você? Você me deu o cu! Comi seu cu, cê chupou minha pica! Porque você é muito bom, mas um dia desse cê tava na minha pica! Deu toda noite!*).

12. In an interesting choice of words, Edilson explained that this was a sign that travestis wanted to be "more than women" (*elas quer ser mais do que uma mulher*). By this, he meant that whereas a woman would accept (or would be forced to accept) the infidelities and social life of her man, travestis don't. I think that Edilson here comes intriguingly (and for him probably dangerously) close to articulating my own argument that boyfriends are feminized in their relationships with travestis.

13. Stephen Murray has pointed out to me that this argument equates sexual pleasure with ejaculation and that it seems to disallow the possibility that travestis might derive great pleasure from being anally penetrated, whether they actually ejaculate or not. However, my discussion of sexual pleasure here is based on how travestis talk about sex, not on my own personal assessment about what constitutes good sex. Although individual travestis undoubtedly derive erotic pleasure from being penetrated, even when they don't ejaculate, whenever travestis talk among themselves about great sex, that talk usually focuses on how they *penetrated* their sexual

partner, and it unfailingly includes detailed descriptions of how many times they themselves ejaculated.

CHAPTER FOUR

1. I am aware of the discussions among North American, Australian, and European prostitutes concerning the political implications of words such as *prostitute, harlot, whore, sex worker,* etc. (Bell 1995; Nagle 1997). My own use of the terms *prostitute* and *prostitution* throughout this book is not intended as a covert contribution to any of those debates. My choice of those terms has been guided solely by, and is meant to reflect, travestis' habitual use of the words *prostituta* and *prostituição.*

2. Rua da Ajuda literally means "Street of Help," and Os Aflitos means "The Afflicted" or "The Heartsick." I have never heard a travesti develop any of the possibilities for humor and irony that these names would seem to offer them.

3. This sometimes happens even in other places. Djanine told me that once she was doing a programa on a backstreet in which a man was penetrating her. She was holding onto the wall with her skirt and panties down around her ankles. As soon as the client ejaculated, he pulled out his penis and, without any word or warning, took off running down the street as fast as he could. "What was I supposed to do," Djanine laughed, "with my panties there around my ankles? I was fucked, girl" (*me fudi, mulé*) Both literally and figuratively.

4. Travestis guard against bad checks by noting down, on the back of the check, the client's license plate number, identity card number, and any telephone numbers and addresses they find in his wallet or address book. They leave the client with a promise that if the bank does not honor the check, he can expect to see them again soon—with his name on their lips and in a very bad mood—on the doorstep of his workplace or his residence.

5. Scandals are discussed in relation to resistance theory in Kulick 1996.

6. Foreign tourists from places like Germany, Israel, Argentina, and the United States do visit Salvador, especially in the season leading up to Carnival in January and February, but it is exceedingly rare for any of them to solicit the services of travestis. And although travestis sometimes muse about the possibility of snagging a gringo who has a lot of money on him, they are not especially keen to do programas with tourists, mostly because they feel inhibited about robbing them. Travestis know that the great majority of Brazilian men they rob never go to the police out of fear that the circumstances of the robbery might leak out to family and friends. Most tourists, however, don't have that problem—their family and business associates are thousands of miles away and unlikely to get wind of an event that occurred in Salvador. Travestis also know that the local policemen regard crimes against tourists as more serious than crimes against the local population, and they fear that robbing a tourist might have consequences much too grave to justify the risk.

7. When I discussed this part of the chapter with Keila, she suggested a fourth reason why travestis say that the majority of their clients want to be penetrated, even though this assertion is not empirically substantiated. "Even if we don't penetrate them," she told me, "80, 87 percent of them grab for our dick. You'll be sucking them and their penis will be soft, they'll reach down and feel that our dick is hard, and right

away, theirs gets hard. What's that? That's desire for a dick (*É tesão por pica*)." Because travestis equate "desire for a dick" with the desire to be penetrated, they assume that such clients really desire to be penetrated, even if they do not make that desire explicit.

8. The spellings in the Italian segments of the Portuguese transcript reflect the speakers' pronunciation of the words. Where Italian appears in the right-hand column, standard spelling is used.

9. The salience of a house for travestis seems to be an instance of a very widespread Brazilian ambition. Brazilians want to own, and many do own, their own houses. In his discussion of Brazilian society and economy, Ronald Schneider remarks that "Brazilians have a marked propensity to own their residences. In 1987 some 20.6 million Brazilian families were owners, and only 6.7 million rented. . . . A great number of lower-income Brazilian families live in substandard homes but at least own them" (1996 : 173; see also Sarti 1996 : 41–50, and the references cited there).

That travestis place such a high priority on buying a house for their mother is surely a reflection of a number of interrelated factors, including the importance of mothers and the elaborate links between mothers and houses in Brazilian culture (Aragão 1983, Da Matta 1991b), a wish on the part of the travesti to prove to her family that she has made something of herself, and the fact that mothers often do not reject their sons who become travestis in the same definitive way as fathers and other family members frequently do. It is important to note, however, that the desire to see one's mother own her own house is not by any means something that only travestis experience or act on. A telling indication of the more widespread salience of the dream of providing one's mother with a house occurred in a popular television *novela* called *Salsa e Merengue* that aired on the Globo network during 1996–97. Early on in the *novela*, one of the main characters unexpectedly received a check for a large sum of money from his father (whom he had never known about and who, it was later revealed, was a Brazilian mafia boss living in Miami). The first thing the character did with the money was pay off his mother's mortgage so that the house in which she and everyone else lived officially passed into her ownership.

10. Brazil is a country where industrialization has been accompanied by increased concentration of wealth and where the disparity between rich and poor is among the greatest in the world. There are conflicting statistics, but some idea of this disparity can be gleaned from figures quoted in the Brazilian press at the beginning of the 1990s. There it was claimed that 70 percent of the working population earned $250 a month or less, and the poorest 50 percent of Brazilians share only 2.5 percent of the country's national income (cited in Simpson 1993 : 8). Schneider estimates that the richest 10 percent of the population earns nearly 50 percent of the country's income. The poorest 10 percent, on the other hand, earns less than 1 percent. Official statistics put over 20 percent of the population (32 million people) below the poverty line. And in the northeastern region of the country, where Salvador is located and from where the majority of travestis who live in Salvador have come, 54 percent of the population earns *less* than one minimum salary (which in 1996 was the equivalent of $112) a month (Schneider 1996 : 172, 174).

11. Studies that do mention that some prostitutes sometimes derive pleasure from sex with clients include Savitz and Rosen 1988; Moraes 1995 : 173–74;

McLeod 1982:39–40; Järvinen 1993; Scrambler 1996:115; Nelson 1987; and Leite 1992:18, 57, 76, 169. See also the interviews included in Bell 1995 and the papers in Nagle 1997.

12. The reference here is to a belief widely held in many parts of Brazil that excessive admiration or praise will draw the Big Eye—negative energy of some sort—to the object of admiration and that it will dry it up. To deflect the Eye, compliments on hair, complexion, or body parts like Xuxa's bunda are often followed by the formulaic phrase *Benza Deus*, "God bless it."

13. Somewhat unusually, Keila refers to the young man with the masculine pronoun *he* (normally, the feminine *she* would be used of a male who desired penetration). One reason for Keila's choice of pronoun may be that she wishes to foreground the fact that this male was stereotypically masculine in his appearance (the two earrings are somewhat ambiguous, but many young men who reside and hang out in the areas where travestis live and work wear big earrings, or several earrings, to signify hipness and toughness. And that this particular young man looks stereotypically masculine is something I saw myself, when Keila later pointed him out to me on the street). Despite her use of the masculine pronoun here, though, in later conversations about his same man, Keila openly dismissed the possibility that she would ever want him as a boyfriend, even though she had so thoroughly enjoyed their encounter in the hotel room. The reason for this disinterest in him as a boyfriend, she explained, was that the young man's willingness to be penetrated meant that "she's a viado."

CHAPTER FIVE

1 This comment is very similar to one made by Vanessa, a travesti interviewed by the magazine *Manchete* (16 March 1996). Vanessa remarks that female prostitutes "look like a bunch of domestic servants. Men say that they don't even turn them on; that women let themselves go at home, that they are sloppy *(desleixada)*. Men like to see pretty women. Travestis don't have that problem. We're always at our best."

2. These factors made it extremely difficult for me to develop any kind of social relations with the boyfriends of travestis. The only boyfriend I came to know and talk to regularly was Edilson, the man who became Keila's ex-boyfriend during my fieldwork in Salvador. Edilson and I maintained friendly relations even after his breakup with Keila, and he agreed to be interviewed by me shortly before he finally moved out of the house on São Francisco Street. Parts of that interview are discussed in chapter 3.

3. This quote is from an article found in the GGB archives entitled "Cláudia Wonder: Não sou homem, nem mulher. Sou bicha," by Márcia Denser. It has no date or source.

4. They also may work to reinforce ideas that are harmful to travestis. To the extent that the homosexual component of travesti identity is elided or denied, travestis risk being marginalized and scapegoated by gay activists and others who work to improve the conditions for homosexuals in society. This risk was recently illustrated with brutal clarity in comments made by the mayor of Rio de Janeiro, Luis Paulo Conde, in an interview with the monthly gay magazine *Sui Generis* (no. 23, 1997). In an otherwise generally affirmative and sympathetic interview about homosexuality, the mayor suddenly announced that he found travestis "offensive" (*O que agride é o*

travesti). The reason? "A travesti doesn't admit to being gay. He dresses in women's clothes to be accepted by society. When he puts on the clothes, it's to be accepted by society. Since society doesn't accept homosexuality, he creates a woman so that he will be accepted."

One can, of course, wonder what might be the basis for the mayor's intriguing conviction that Brazilians are more accepting of men in dresses than of homosexuals. But no matter where that idea has its origin, the mayor's eruption of prejudice displays a profound misunderstanding of travesti subjectivity. It also contributes to the formation of a climate in which travestis are conceptually and politically regarded as different from homosexuals and hence not subject to any of the rights or protection that legislators like the mayor might eventually be willing to grant gay men and lesbians.

5. Most of the males to whom travestis refer using this appellation would reject it as offensive. Most clients called by this name probably do not consider themselves to be homosexual at all. And even self-acknowledged homosexual males referred to by travestis as *bichas machudas* usually do not use that label in self-reference. Instead, they tend to call themselves *homossexual* or *gay*.

6. See, for example, Nanda 1993 on *hijras* in India, Roscoe 1993 on "two-spirit" people among native North Americans, and Herdt 1993 for a general theoretical statement on third gender.

7. In a recent article on the socialization of masculinity in Brazil, Roberto Da Matta (1997a : 48) notes something similar. "More important than having a masculine apparatus," he explains, "[is] knowing how to use it and who to use it with (*saber relacionar-se*)."

8. The same is true, needless to say, for clients. Any client requesting penetration is known by the travesti to be a viado, not a man, no matter how many wives or children he may have.

9. See Almaguer 1991; Carrier 1995; Fry 1986, 1995; Guttman 1996; Lancaster 1992; Leiner 1994; Mirandé 1997; Parker 1991; Prieur 1998, 1994a; Streicker 1993; Trevisan 1986; and articles in Murray 1987, 1995a.

10. "Stealing Femininity" was originally announced (in Prieur 1996a : 105) as the title of Annick Prieur's English-language monograph (1998) on effeminate Mexican homosexuals. The title of the monograph was changed for some reason before the book went to press, but it was retained in a paper summarizing some of the main arguments made in the book (Prieur 1996b), and as the title of one of the chapters in the monograph. All of Prieur's published writings on Mexican *jotas* (1998, 1996a, 1994a, 1994b) are exceptionally compassionate and original, so I want to stress that when I draw attention to the phrase "stealing femininity" and call it "starkly censorious," I am referring to the way in which those words draw on and invoke imagery that I think many people would interpret as negative and condemnatory. I am in no way suggesting that Prieur herself condemns the people she writes about. On the contrary, any reader of her work cannot help but be deeply impressed by its sensitivity and thoroughness.

The recurrence of "stealing femininity" in rubrics summarizing Prieur's work belies an attachment to the phrase that is somewhat puzzling, since she nowhere explicitly argues that this is what *jotas* do. Nevertheless, I highlight the phrase because I think it is a useful one for drawing attention to interpretive differences between

Prieur's treatment of transgenderism and my own (and I do this because her recent monograph is the only other English-language book-length treatment of transgenderism in a Latin American society).

The idea that the *jotas* with whom Prieur worked might be "stealing femininity" can only arise from within an analytical framework that views femininity as somehow owned, or properly possessed, by women. And this, it seems to me, is essentially what Prieur argues. Despite its attention to context, detail, and the perspectives of her friends and informants in Mexico City, Prieur's analysis displays a firm unwillingness to accept transgendered practices as much more than pretense. The words "game," "play," and "pretense" all figure prominently in her writing. Her conclusion about the relationships between *jotas* and their boyfriends, for example, is that "[o]ne partner pretends to not be a man; the other partner pretends to not be homosexual" (1998:252). This is an interpretation that can only make sense if Prieur believes that she somehow possesses the truth about what *jotas* and their boyfriends "really" are.

The same difficulty arises in her final conclusions about the transgendered project pursued by the *jotas*. In Prieur's interpretation, their project is and must remain futile, because *jotas* do not possess female biology. "Biological sex is also a social reality," she asserts in the final pages of her book, thereby sidestepping the whole generation of feminist work, cited by Prieur herself, that has argued that biological sex, in fact, has *no* social reality of its own—it is always interpreted through cultural schema and in the context of social relationships. But seeing biological sex as objectively real allows Prieur (1998:274) to conclude that "[g]ender is a question of discourses, of signs, of presentations and representations, of gestures, speech, garments and clothes, but it is also a question of naked bodies. And when two persons with the same male sexual organs are naked, the construction of one of the partners as a not-homosexual man and of the other as a not-male person is difficult to upkeep."

If Brazilian travestis taught me one lesson during my work with them, it was that this kind of commonsense view of the relationship between gender and "naked bodies" is something that needs intense critical examination. Even leaving aside the problematic assumption here that there is some kind of clear-cut, objective way of "being naked" together with another person that necessarily draws vivid attention to sexual organs (Bernard Boursicot and Shi Peipu, whose twenty-year-long relationship inspired the play *M Butterfly*, would presumably be among those who might disagree; Garber 1992b), one might wonder about the analytical (or subjective) perspective that sees "naked bodies" as the final arbiter of gender. One might also ask in whose opinion, and in what senses, exactly, are the "male sexual organs" possessed by *jotas* and their boyfriends "the same"? Readers of Prieur's monograph might want to contemplate her account in light of questions like those, even as they might productively use Prieur's arguments to critically reflect upon the analysis of travestis that I present in this book.

11. Judith Shapiro makes a similar point about Euro-American transsexuals. "To those who might be tempted to diagnose the transsexual's focus on the genitals as obsessive or fetishistic," she explains, "the response is that transsexuals are, in fact, simply conforming to their culture's criteria for gender assignment" (1991:260, reference omitted). If one changes "transsexual" here to "travesti" and replaces "genitals" with "penetration," this passage succinctly summarizes my own argument about travestis and gender in Brazil.

12. One might also note here that female prostitutes, who cross (and therefore blur and challenge) the all-important boundary dividing the Latin American "house" from the "street," are sometimes thought of in *masculine* terms. Joel Streicker, for example, writing about Colombia, has observed that "[s]exually assertive women are seen as less feminine and more masculine. . . . The respectable [people in the neighborhood in which Streicker worked] called attention and disparage these women's 'masculine' pursuit of sex by referring to them as *callejeras* (street-women) or women who operate in the pre-eminent male space. This is often a euphemism for whores" (1993:367). See also Richard Parker's discussion of the *puta* in Brazil (1991:51–52).

13. Lack of this kind of data is not unique to Brazil. As Marit Melhuus and Kristi Anne Stølen point out in a recent essay, gender research throughout Latin America has been so thoroughly dominated by what they call "an economic bias" (1996:13–14) that cultural representations and the ways in which those representations are subjectively experienced and enacted have received little attention until very recently.

14. The book does contain repeated assertions that the sexuality of women "appears to be less centered on the genitals than that of men" (Muraro 1983:326; see also 320, 328–29), but it is not at all clear what the basis of those assertions might be. None of the questions to which the one hundred women in the study (or the forty-four men, who were asked the same questions) responded were specifically about penetration or any other sexual act, and as far as I am able to tell, the author's conclusions about the supposedly "diffuse" (320, 328) sexuality of women are grounded in a combination of a Freudian view of sexual development (319–20) and the facts that (*a*) the men interviewed were clearer and more emphatic than women in their answers to the question "Do you have sexual relations? Do you cum?" (see, e.g., the author's comments on p. 127); and (*b*) women displayed a greater concern about the consequences of sexuality than men did—unsurprisingly, they worried more that sexual relations could result in pregnancy (328–29). In any case, regardless of whether or not Brazilian women generally experience sexuality more "diffusely" than men, the question remains of what role penetration plays in their subjective experience of themselves and others as gendered individuals.

15. One brief paper even discusses travestis in Spain (Haller 1992). The fact that the European countries most receptive, as it were, to travesti prostitution are Mediterranean countries like France and Italy also implies that the gender configurations I postulate in this book may have some validity outside Latin America, and may be an inflection of some particularly Mediterranean constellation of bodies, sexualities, and gendered subjectivities (see also Lancaster 1988:121; and the articles by Stephen Murray in Murray 1995a, in which he consistently discusses Latin American male homosexualities as part of a complex of "Mediterranean-influenced cultures" [1995b:57]).

References

Albuquerque, Fernanda Farias de and Maurizio Janelli. 1995. *A Princesa: Depoimentos de um travesti brasileiro a um líder das Brigadas Vermelhas*. Rio de Janeiro. Nova Fronteira.

Almaguer, Tomás. 1991. Chicano men: A cartography of homosexual identity and behavior. *Differences* 3:75–100.

Amnesty International. 1997. *Breaking the silence: Human rights violations based on sexual orientation*. London: Amnesty International, United Kingdom.

Angell, Marcia. 1996. Evaluating the health risks of breast implants: The interplay of medical science, the law, and public opinion. *The New England Journal of Medicine* 334 (23):1513–18.

Aragão, Luiz Tarlei de. 1983. Em nome da mãe: Posição estrutural e disposições sociais que envolvem a categoria mãe na civilização mediterrânea e na sociedade brasileira. *Perspectivas Antropológicas da Mulher* 3:109–45.

ASTRAL (Associação de Travestis e Liberados). 1996. *Diálogo de bonecas*. Rio de Janeiro: ASTRAL.

Ávila, Maria Betânia, and Taciana Gouveia. 1996. Notas sobre direitos reprodutivos e direitos sexuais. In *Sexualidades brasileiras*, edited by Richard Parker and Regina Maria Barbosa. Rio de Janeiro: Relume Dumará.

Bacelar, Jeferson Alfonso. 1982. *A família da prostituta*. São Paulo: Ática.

Barry, Kathleen. 1995. *The prostitution of sexuality*. New York: New York University Press.

———. 1979. *Female sexual slavery*. Englewood Cliffs, N.J.: Prentice-Hall.

Behar, Ted A., E. Everett Anderson, William J. Barwick, and James L. Mohler. 1993. Sclerosing lipogranulomatosis: A case report of scrotal injection of automobile transmission fluid and literature review of subcutaneous injection of oils. *Plastic and Reconstructive Surgery* 91 (2): 352–61.

Bell, Shannon. 1995. *Whore carnival*. Brooklyn, N.Y.: Automedia.

Birman, Patrícia. 1995. *Fazer estilo criando gêneros: Possessão e diferenças de gênero em terreiros de umbanda e candomblé no Rio de Janeiro*. Rio de Janeiro: Relume Dumará.

Bjerno, Thomas, Peter N. Basse, Peter A. Siemssen, and Thomas Møller. 1993. Injektion af højviskøse væsker: Akut eller sen excision? *Ugeskrift før Læger* 155 (24): 1876–78.

Bolin, Anne. 1988. *In search of Eve: Transsexual rites of passage*. South Hadley, Mass.: Bergin and Garvey.

Bornstein, Kate. 1994. *Gender outlaw: On men, women, and the rest of us*. New York and London: Routledge.

Browning, Barbara. 1998. *Infectious rhythm: African diasporic culture and epidemiology*. New York and London: Routledge.

———. 1996. The closed body. *Women & Performance: A Journal of Feminist Theory* 8(2): 1–18.

Butler, Judith. 1993. *Bodies that matter: On the discursive limits of "sex."* New York and London: Routledge.

———. 1990. *Gender trouble: Feminism and the subversion of identity.* New York and London: Routledge.

Carrier, Joseph. 1995. *De los otros: Intimacy and homosexuality among Mexican men.* New York: Columbia University Press.

CEI/CONDER (Centro de Estatística e Informacões/Companhia de Desenvolvimento da Região Metropolitana de Salvador). 1994. *Informações básicas dos municípios Baianos, região metropolitana de Salvador.* Salvador: CEI/CONDER.

Cerqueira, Nelson, ed. 1994. *Pelourinho, historic center of Salvador, Bahia: The restored grandeur.* 2d ed. Salvador: Fundação Cultural do Estado da Bahia.

Chastre, Jean, Patrick Brun, Paul Soler, Françoise Basset, Jean Louis Trouillet, Jean Yves Fagon, Claude Gibert, and Allan J. Hance. 1987. Acute and latent pneumonitis after subcutaneous injections of silicone in transsexual men. *American Review of Respiratory Disease* 135 (1): 236–40.

Chauncey, George. 1994. *Gay New York: Gender, urban culture, and the making of the gay male world, 1890–1940.* New York: Basic Books.

Cornwall, Andrea. 1994. Gendered identities and gender ambiguity among travestis in Salvador, Brazil. In *Dislocating masculinity: Comparative ethnographies,* edited by Andrea Cornwall and Nancy Lindisfarne. London: Routledge.

Da Matta, Roberto. 1997a. Tem pente aí? Reflexões sobre a identidade masculina. In *Homens,* edited by Dario Caldas. São Paulo: Editora SENAC.

———. 1997b [1984]. *O que faz o brasil, Brasil?* Rio de Janeiro: Editora Rocco.

———. 1991a. *Carnival, rogues, and heroes: An interpretation of the Brazilian dilemma.* Notre Dame, Ind.: University of Notre Dame Press.

———. 1991b. *A casa e a rua: Espaço, cidadania, mulher e morte no Brasil.* Rio de Janeiro: Editora Guanabara Koogan.

———. 1984. On carnival, informality, and magic: A point of view from Brazil. In *Text, play, and story: The construction and reconstruction of self and society,* edited by Edward M. Bruner. Washington, D.C.: American Ethnological Society.

Davies, Peter, and Rayah Feldman. 1997. Prostitute men now. In *Rethinking prostitution: Purchasing sex in the 1990s,* edited by Graham Scambler and Annette Scambler. London: Routledge.

Davis, K. 1961. Prostitution. In *Contemporary social problems,* edited by R. K. Marton and R. A. Nisbet. New York: Harcourt, Brace and World.

Day, Sophie. 1990. Prostitute women and the ideology of work in London. In *Culture and AIDS,* edited by Douglas A. Feldman. New York: Praeger.

Dynes, Wayne. 1987. Portugayese. In *Male homosexuality in Central and Southern America,* edited by Stephen O. Murray. San Francisco: Instituto Obregón.

Espinheira, Carlos G. D'Andrea. 1971. *Comunidade do Maciel.* Salvador: FPACBA.

Faugier, Jean, and Marey Sargeant. 1997. Boyfriends, 'pimps,' and clients. In *Rethinking prostitution: Purchasing sex in the 1990s,* edited by Graham Scambler and Annette Scambler. London: Routledge.

Félix, Anísio, and Moacir Nery. 1993. *Bahia, Carnaval.* Salvador: Published by authors.

Fernandez, Manuel. 1996. Charging for sex: Commoditization of desire and the representations of gender and sexuality in urban Honduras. Paper presented at the ninety eighth annual American Anthropological Association Meeting, San Francisco.

Finstad, Liv, and Cecilie Høigård. 1993. Norway. In *Prostitution: An international handbook on trends, problems, and policies*, edited by Nanette J. Davis. Westport, Conn., and London: Greenwood Press.

FPACBA (Fundação do Patrimônio Artístico e Cultural da Bahia). 1969. *Levamento sócio-econômico do Pelourinho*. Salvador: FPACBA.

Fry, Peter. 1995. Male homosexuality and Afro-Brazilian possession cults. In *Latin American male homosexualities*, edited by Stephen O. Murray. Albuquerque: University of New Mexico Press.

———. 1986. Male homosexuality and spirit possession in Brazil. In *The many faces of homosexuality: Anthropological approaches to homosexual behavior*, edited by Evelyn Blackwood. New York: Harrington Park Press.

Garber, Marjorie. 1992a. *Vested interests: Cross-dressing and cultural anxiety*. New York: Routledge, Chapman and Hall.

———. 1992b. The occidental tourist: *M. Butterfly* and the scandal of transvestism. In *Nationalisms and sexualities*, edited by Andrew Parker, Mary Russo, Doris Sommer, and Patricia Yaeger. New York and London: Routledge.

Garfinkel, Harold. 1967. *Studies in ethnomethodology*. Englewood Cliffs, N.J.: Prentice-Hall.

Gaspar, Maria Dulce. 1985. *Garotas de programa: Prostituição em Copacabana e identidade social*. Rio de Janeiro: Jorge Zahar.

Gattari, P., D. Speziale, R. Grillo, P. Cattani, M. Zaccarelli, L. Spizzichino, and C. Valenzi. 1994. Syphilis serology among transvestite prostitutes attending an HIV unit in Rome, Italy. *European Journal of Epidemiology* 10: 683–86.

Goldenberg, Mirian. 1990. *A outra: Um estudo antropológico sobre a identidade da amante do homem casado*. Rio de Janeiro: Editora Revan.

Goldstein, Donna M. 1994. AIDS and women in Brazil: The emerging problem. *Social Science Medicine* 39 (7): 919–29.

Guttman, Matthew C. 1996. *The meanings of macho: Being a man in Mexico City*. Berkeley and Los Angeles: University of California Press.

Haller, Deiter. 1992. Homosexuality in Seville. *Society of Lesbian and Gay Newsletter* 14 (3): 27–35.

Hausman, Bernice L. 1995. *Changing sex: Transsexualism, technology, and the idea of gender*. Durham, N.C., and London: Duke University Press.

Henley, Nancy M., Michelle Miller, and Jo Anne Beazely. 1995. Syntax, semantics, and sexual violence: Agency and the passive voice. *Journal of Language and Social Psychology* 14 (1–2): 60–84.

Herdt, Gilbert. 1993. Introduction: Third sexes and third genders. In *Third sex, third gender: Beyond sexual dimorphism in culture and history*, edited by Gilbert Herdt. New York: Zone.

Høigård, Cecilie, and Liv Finstad. 1986. *Bakgater: Om prostitusjon, penger og kjærlighet*. Oslo: Pax.

IBGE (Instituto Brasileiro de Geografia e Estatística). 1982. *Anuário estatístico do Brasil*. Rio de Janeiro: IBGE.

IPAC (Instituto do Patrimônio Artística e Cultural da Bahia). 1995. *Bahia: Centro Histórico de Salvador: Programa de recuperação.* Salvador: Corrupio.

Jabor, Arnaldo. 1993. *Os canibais estão na sala de jantar.* São Paulo: Siciliano.

Järvinen, Margaretha. 1993. Prostitution in Helsinki: A disappearing social problem? *Journal of the History of Sexuality* 3 (4): 608–30.

Jeffreys, Sheila. 1996. Heterosexuality and the desire for gender. In *Theorising heterosexuality,* edited by Diane Richardson. Buckingham, Eng., and Philadelphia: Open University Press.

Kessler, Suzanne J., and Wendy McKenna. 1985 [1978]. *Gender: An ethnomethodological approach.* Chicago: University of Chicago Press.

Kottak, Conrad Phillip. 1990. *Prime time society: An anthropological analysis of television and culture.* Belmont, Calif.: Wadsworth.

Kulick, Don. 1998. Fe/male trouble: The unsettling place of lesbians in the self-images of Brazilian transgendered prostitutes. *Sexualities* 1 (3): 301–14.

———. 1996. Causing a commotion: Scandal as resistance among Brazilian travesti prostitutes. *Anthropology Today* 12 (6): 3–7.

———. 1992. *Language shift and cultural reproduction: Socialization, self, and syncretism in a Papua New Guinean village.* New York: Cambridge University Press.

Lancaster, Roger N. 1992. *Life is hard: Machismo, danger, and the intimacy of power in Nicaragua.* Berkeley and Los Angeles: University of California Press.

———. 1988. Subject honor and object shame: The construction of male homosexuality and stigma in Nicaragua. *Ethnology* 27 (2): 111–25.

Landes, Ruth. 1994 [1947]. *The city of women.* Albuquerque: University of New Mexico Press.

Laqueur, Thomas. 1990. *Making sex: Body and gender from the Greeks to Freud.* Cambridge, Mass.: Harvard University Press.

de Lauretis, Teresa. 1987. *Technologies of gender: Essays on theory, film, and fiction.* Bloomington: Indiana University Press.

Leiner, Marvin. 1994. *Sexual politics in Cuba: Machismo, homosexuality, and AIDS.* Boulder, Colo.: Westview Press.

Leite, Gabriela Silva. 1992. *Eu, mulher da vida.* Rio de Janeiro: Rosa dos Tempos.

Linger, Daniel Touro. 1992. *Dangerous encounters: Meanings of violence in a Brazilian city.* Stanford, Calif.: Stanford University Press.

Marlowe, Julian. 1997. It's different for boys. In *Whores and other feminists,* edited by Jill Nagle. London and New York: Routledge.

McCallum, Cecilia. 1996. Resisting Brazil: Perspectives on local nationalisms in Salvador da Bahia. *Ethnos* 61 (3–4): 207–29.

McKeganey, Neil, and Marina Barnard. 1996. *Sex work on the streets: Prostitutes and their clients.* Buckingham, Eng., and Philadelphia: Open University Press.

McLeod, Eileen. 1982. *Women working: Prostitution now.* London and Canberra: Croon Helm.

McNamara, Robert P. 1994. *The Times Square hustler: Male prostitution in New York City.* Westport, Conn., and London: Praeger.

Melhuus, Marit. Forthcoming. The power of penetration/the value of virginity: Male and female in Mexican heterosexual and homosexual relations. *Ethnos.*

———. 1996. Power, value, and the ambiguous meanings of gender. In *Machos, mistresses, madonnas: Contesting the power of Latin American gender imagery,* edited by Marit Melhuus and Kristi Anne Stølen. London and New York: Verso.

Melhuus, Marit, and Kristi Anne Stølen. 1996. Introduction. in *Machos, mistresses, madonnas: Contesting the power of Latin American gender imagery,* edited by Marit Melhuus and Kristi Anne Stølen. London and New York: Verso.

Mirandé, Alfredo. 1997. *Hombres y machos: Masculinity and Latino culture.* Boulder, Colo.: Westview Press.

Moraes, Aparecida Fonesca. 1995. *Mulheres da Vila: Prostituição, identidade social e movimento associativo.* Petrópolis, Rio de Janeiro: Vozes.

Morris, Jan. 1987 [1974]. *Conundrum.* Middlesex, Eng.: Penguin Books.

Mott, Luiz. 1996. *Epidemic of hate: Violations of the human rights of gay men, lesbians, and transvestites in Brazil.* San Francisco: Calif.: Grupo Gay da Bahia and the International Gay and Lesbian Human Rights Commission.

Mott, Luiz, and Aroldo Assunção. 1987. Gilete na carne: Etnografia das automutilações dos travestis da Bahia. *Revista do Instituto de Medicina Social de São Paulo* 4 (1): 41–57.

Mott, Luiz, and Marcelo Ferreira de Cerqueira. 1997. *Os travestis da Bahia & a AIDS: Prostituição, silicone e drogas.* Salvador: Grupo Gay da Bahia.

Ms. 1996. Beauty and the breast: Silicone implants. March/April, 45–63.

Muraro, Rose Marie. 1983. *Sexualidade da mulher brasileira: Corpo e classe social no Brasil.* Petrópolis, Rio de Janeiro: Vozes.

Murray, Stephen O. Forthcoming. *Homosexualities.* Chicago: University of Chicago Press.

———, ed. 1995a. *Latin American male homosexualities.* Albuquerque: University of New Mexico Press.

———. 1995b. Machismo, male homosexuality, and Latino culture. In *Latin American male homosexualities,* edited by Stephen O. Murray. Albuquerque: University of New Mexico Press.

———, ed. 1987. *Male homosexuality in Central and South America.* San Francisco: Instituto Obregón.

Murray, Stephen O., and Wayne Dynes. 1987. Hispanic homosexuals: Spanish lexicon. In *Male homosexuality in Central and South America,* edited by Stephen O. Murray. San Francisco: Instituto Obregón.

Nagle, Jill, ed. 1997. *Whores and other feminists.* London and New York: Routledge.

Nanda, Serena. 1993. Hijras: An alternative sex and gender role in India. In *Third sex, third gender: Beyond sexual dimorphism in culture and history,* edited by Gilbert Herdt. New York: Zone.

———. 1990. *Neither man nor woman: The hijras of India.* Belmont, Calif.: Wadsworth.

Nelson, Nici. 1987. 'Selling her kiosk': Kikuyu notions of sexuality and sex for sale in Mathare Valley, Kenya. In *The cultural construction of sexuality,* edited by Pat Caplan. London: Tavistock.

Nemecek, Jane A., and V. Leroy Young. 1993. How safe are silicone breast implants? *Southern Medical Journal* 86 (8): 932–44.

Newton, Esther. 1972. *Mother camp: Female impersonators in America.* Chicago: University of Chicago Press.

O'Connell Davidson, Julia. 1996. Prostitution and the contours of control. In *Sexual cultures: Communities, values, and intimacy,* edited by Jeffrey Weeks and Janet Holland. New York: St. Martin's Press.

Oliveira, Neuza Maria de. 1994. *Damas de paus: O jogo aberto dos travestis no espelho da mulher.* Salvador: Universidade Federal da Bahia.

Park, A. J., R. J. Black, and A. C. H. Watson. 1993. Silicone gel breast implants, breast cancer, and connective tissue disorders. *British Journal of Surgery* 80 (9): 1097–99.

Parker, Richard G. 1995. Changing Brazilian constructions of homosexuality. In *Latin American male homosexualities,* edited by Stephen O. Murray. Albuquerque: University of New Mexico Press.

———. 1991. *Bodies, pleasures, and passions: Sexual culture in contemporary Brazil.* Boston: Beacon Press.

Pateman, Carole. 1988. *The sexual contract.* Cambridge: Polity Press.

Perkins, Roberta. 1996. The 'drag queen scene': Transsexuals in Kings Cross. In *Blending genders: Social aspects of cross-dressing and sex-changing,* edited by Richard Ekins and Dave King. London and New York: Routledge.

Perlongher, Nestor. 1987. *O negócio do michê: prostituição viril em São Paulo.* São Paulo: Brasiliense.

Pheterson, Gail. 1996. *The prostitution prism.* Amsterdam: Amsterdam University Press.

———, ed. 1989. *A vindication of the rights of whores.* Seattle: The Seal Press.

Prieur, Annick. 1998. *Mema's house, Mexico City: On transvestites, queens, and machos.* Chicago: University of Chicago Press.

———. 1996a. Domination and desire: Male homosexuality and the construction of masculinity in Mexico. In *Machos, mistresses, madonnas: Contesting the power of Latin American gender imagery,* edited by Marit Melhuus and Kristi Anne Stølen. London and New York: Verso.

———. 1996b. Stealing femininity: On bodily and symbolic constructions among homosexual men in Mexico. Paper presented at the ninety-eighth annual American Anthropological Association Meeting, San Francisco.

———. 1994a. *Iscensetteleser av kjønn: Transvestitter og machomenn i Mexico by.* Oslo: Pax.

———. 1994b. 'I am my own special creation': Mexican homosexual transvestites' construction of femininity. *Young:* 2 (3): 3–17.

Raymond, Janice. 1979. *The transsexual empire.* London: The Women's Press.

Rohrich, Rod J., and Clifford P. Clark. 1993. Controversy over the silicone gel breast implant: Current status and clinical implications. *Texas Medicine* 89 (9): 52–58.

Roscoe, Will. 1993. How to become a berdache: Towards a unified analysis of gender diversity. In *Third sex, third gender: Beyond sexual dimorphism in culture and history,* edited by Gilbert Herdt. New York: Zone.

Sarti, Cynthia Andersen. 1996. *A família como espelho: Um estudo sobre a moral dos pobres.* Campinas, São Paulo: Editora Autores Associados.

———. 1995. Morality and transgression among Brazilian poor families: Ambiguities. In *The Brazilian puzzle,* edited by David J. Hess and Roberto A. Damatta. New York: Columbia University Press.

Savitz, Leonard, and Lawrence Rosen. 1988. The sexuality of prostitutes: Sexual enjoyment reported by "streetwalkers." *The Journal of Sex Research* 24: 200–208.

Scambler, Graham. 1996. Conspicuous and inconspicuous sex work: The neglect of the ordinary and the mundane. In *Rethinking prostitution: Purchasing sex in the 1990s,* edited by Graham Scambler and Annette Scambler. London: Routledge.

Scheper-Hughes, Nancy. 1992. *Death without weeping: The violence of everyday life in Brazil.* Berkeley and Los Angeles. University of California Press

Schneider, Ronald M. 1996. *Brazil: Culture and politics in a new industrial powerhouse.* Boulder, Colo.: Westview Press.

Sell, Teresa Adada. 1987. *Identidade homossexual e normas sociais: Histórias de vida.* Florianópolis: Editora da Universidade Federal de Santa Catarina.

Shapiro, Judith 1991. Transsexualism: Reflections on the persistence of gender and the mutability of sex. In *Body guards: The cultural politics of gender ambiguity,* edited by Julia Epstein and Kristina Straub. New York and London: Routledge.

Shoaib, Britta Ostermeyer, Bernard M. Patten, and Dick S. Calkins. 1994. Adjuvant breast disease: An evaluation of one hundred symptomatic women with breast implants or silicone fluid injections. *The Keio Journal of Medicine* 43 (2): 70–87.

Siemssen, Peter, P. N. Basse, and T. Bjerno. 1992. Injection of commercially available silicone in body sculpturing. *Plastic and Reconstructive Surgery* 89 (6): 1185.

Silva, Hélio R. S. 1996. *Certas cariocas· Travestis e vida de rua no Rio de Janeiro.* Rio de Janeiro: Relume Dumará.

———. 1993. *Travesti: A invenção do feminino.* Rio de Janeiro: Relume Dumará.

Silva, Hélio R. S., and Cristina de Oliveira Florentino. 1996. A sociedade dos travestis: Espelhos, papéis e interpretações. In *Sexualidades brasileiras,* edited by Richard Parker and Regina Maria Barbosa. Rio de Janeiro: Relume Dumará.

Simmel, Georg. [1907] 1990. *The philosophy of money.* Edited by David Frisby and translated by Tom Bottomore and David Frisby. London and New York: Routledge.

Simpson, Amelia. 1993. *Xuxa· The megamarketing of gender, race, and modernity.* Philadelphia: Temple University Press.

Soares, Luiz Eduardo, João Trajano Sento Sé, José Augusto de Souza Rodrigues, and Leandro Piquet Carneiro. 1996. Criminalidade urbana e violência: O Rio de Janeiro no contexto internacional. In *Violência e política no Rio de Janeiro,* edited by Luiz Eduardo Soares. Rio de Janeiro: Relume Dumará.

Sonia, interviewed by Gail Pheterson. 1989. "Despite everything, we are men." In *A vindication of the rights of whores,* edited by Gail Pheterson. Seattle: The Seal Press.

Stone, Sandy. 1991. The *Empire* strikes back: A posttranssexual manifesto. In *Body guards: The cultural politics of gender ambiguity,* edited by Julia Epstein and Kristina Straub. New York and London: Routledge.

Streicker, Joel. 1993. Sexuality, power, and social order in Cartagena, Colombia. *Ethnology* 32 (4): 359–74.

Trevisan, João Silvério. 1986. *Perverts in paradise.* London. Gay Men's Press.

Veras, Renato P., and Maria Isabel C. Alves. 1995. A população idosa no Brasil: Considerações acera do uso de indicadores de saúde. In *Os muitos brasis: Saúde e população na década de 80,* edited by Maria Cecília S. Minayo. São Paulo and Rio de Janeiro: Huicitec-Abrasco.

Wafer, Jim. 1991. *The taste of blood. Spirit possession in Brazilian candomblé.* Philadelphia: University of Pennsylvania Press.

West, Donald J., in association with Buz de Villiers. 1993. *Male prostitution.* London: Duckworth.

Whitam, Frederick L. 1995. Os entendidos: Gay life in São Paulo in the late 1970s.

In *Latin American male homosexualities*, edited by Stephen O. Murray. Albuquerque: University of New Mexico Press.

Winice, C., and P. Kinsie. 1971. *The lively commerce*. Chicago: Quadrangle Books.

Yoshida, Steven H., Shanna Swan, Suzanne S. Teuber, and M. Eric Gershwin. 1995. Silicone breast implants: Immunotoxic and epidemiologic issues. *Life Sciences* 56 (16): 1299–1310.

Index